Homelessness Is a
Housing Problem

T0385678

The publisher and the University of California Press Foundation gratefully acknowledge the generous support of the Anne G. Lipow Endowment Fund in Social Justice and Human Rights.

Homelessness Is a Housing Problem

*How Structural Factors
Explain U.S. Patterns*

Gregg Colburn
and
Clayton Page Aldern

UNIVERSITY OF CALIFORNIA PRESS

University of California Press
Oakland, California

© 2022 by Gregg Colburn and Clayton Aldern

Library of Congress Cataloging-in-Publication Data

Names: Colburn, Gregg, 1972- author. | Aldern, Clayton
    Page, 1990- author.
Title: Homelessness is a housing problem : how structural
    factors explain U.S. patterns / Gregg Colburn and
    Clayton Page Aldern.
Description: Oakland, California : University of California
    Press, [2022] | Includes bibliographical references and
    index.
Identifiers: LCCN 2021037026 (print) | LCCN 2021037027
    (ebook) | ISBN 9780520383760 (cloth) | ISBN 9780520383784
    (paperback) | ISBN 9780520383791 (epub)
Subjects: LCSH: Homelessness—United States. |
    Metropolitan areas—Housing—Social aspects—United
    States. | Homelessness—Government policy—United
    States. | Homeless persons—Substance use—United
    States.
Classification: LCC HV4505 .C656 2022 (print) |
    LCC HV4505 (ebook) | DDC 362.5/920973—dc23
LC record available at https://lccn.loc.gov/2021037026
LC ebook record available at https://lccn.loc.gov/2021037027

31 30 29 28 27 26 25 24 23 22
10 9 8 7 6 5 4 3 2 1

To anyone who lives without stable housing—
and to the policy makers, organizers, advocates,
researchers, practitioners, and those with lived
experience working to end homelessness

CONTENTS

PART III. CONCLUSION

6. Typology
147

7. Response
166

FIGURES AND TABLES

FIGURES

TABLES

ACKNOWLEDGMENTS

The motivation for this book stemmed from Gregg's observation that the roots of the homelessness crisis in many cities in the United States were being misdiagnosed, often to frustrating and harmful ends. A public focus on mental health and drugs—certainly, important risk factors for homelessness—dominates narratives in our home in the Puget Sound region, thereby narrowing the policy conversation. In discussions with stakeholders throughout the region, it became apparent that an intense focus on behavioral health might be masking a more important root cause of this crisis: housing market conditions.

Gregg shared the early vision for this book in 2019 with colleagues throughout the Seattle region. One such conversation proved to be particularly valuable and changed the course of this book project. Rogers Weed, then board chair of Building Changes (a nonprofit focused on homelessness), introduced the two authors of this book. After a number of productive and engaging conversations, Clayton and Gregg decided to collaborate on this project. The two of us collaborated on the analysis,

Gregg wrote the majority of the manuscript, and Clay applied his expertise in data visualization to the images found in this book. In a sure sign of a productive partnership, this final product is far better than any that would have resulted from a solitary effort.

Gregg is grateful to the many people who provided insight, wisdom, and support throughout this process. At the University of Washington, a wonderful community of scholars, including Arthur Acolin, Scott Allard, Kyle Crowder, Rachel Fyall, Rebecca Walter, and Thaïsa Way have supported my professional development and have provided valuable feedback at various stages of the writing process. In addition, scholars from around the country including Thomas Byrne, Brian McCabe, and Beth Shinn also provided feedback and guidance. Numerous members of the Seattle community served as sounding boards throughout the writing process; a special thank-you to Kollin Min who was a key supporter of this project. Finally, Gregg is also thankful for his wife, Jen, and children Grace and Grant for their patience and support. Much of this book was written as we quarantined together during the COVID-19 pandemic. I love you all and am grateful for the joy and laughter you bring to my life.

Clayton extends his deep gratitude to the advocates and researchers with and without the lived experience of homelessness who have worked to help him and others understand the structural roots of the crisis. To Jeff Rodgers, Tess Colby, Aras Jizan, Marc Dones, Anne Marie Edmunds, Valeri Knight, Sarah Appling, Claire Aylward Guilmette, Deborah L'Amoureux, Gerrit Nyland, Caroline Belleci, Geoff Campion, Vishesh Jain, Aman Sanghera, Annie Pennucci, Matt Lemon, Pear Moraras, Abby Schachter, Stephanie Roe, Jesse Jorstad, and Stephanie

Patterson—thank you for your insight into (and leadership in) this space, and thanks for all you continue to teach us. Thanks to Jason Schumacher and Neal Myrick at the Tableau Foundation for your deep investments in data visualization and data literacy in homelessness policy and housing stability—and for letting Clay use your software for exploratory analysis and figure drafting. To Sara Curran, Tim Thomas, and Thaïsa Way at the University of Washington for the critical support via the Center for Studies in Demography and Ecology: Thank you. Gratitude to Whitney Henry-Lester for the late-night chats to these ends and to Lowell Wyse for the late-night chats to other ends. A near-impossible degree of gratitude to Anneka Olson, whose patience knows no bounds: Thank you for your keen editing brain, critical perspective, and warm presence. Henry the Cat and Maple the Cat also offered pivotal moral support.

The final chapter of this book incorporates the ideas of researchers, practitioners, and policy makers from around the country. We are grateful to those who shared their research and opinions about the strategies needed to end homelessness: Whitney Airgood-Obrycki, Thomas Byrne, Tess Colby, Dennis Culhane, Mary Cunningham, Conor Dougherty, Mark Ellerbrook, Katie Hong, Aras Jizan, Jill Khadduri, Margot Kushel, Kollin Min, Stephen Norman, Beth Shinn, and Dilip Wagle.

Finally, we thank Naomi Schneider, Summer Farah, and the rest of the University of California Press team for supporting this book project.

PART I

Crisis

CHAPTER ONE

Baseline

Homelessness occupies a prominent place in American political life. Although less than one-fifth of 1 percent of the U.S.
population experiences homelessness on a given night in the
country, the issue receives considerable attention from policy
makers and the general public. This spotlight is striking given
the scale of the homelessness crisis when compared to other
prominent social problems. That fifth-of-a-percent figure trans-
lates to about five hundred sixty-eight thousand people. To be
sure, this number should feel large and unacceptable. But on an
absolute basis, for example, homelessness pales in comparison
to the nation's poverty crisis: Over thirty-four million Americans were living below the federal poverty line in 2019. Meanwhile, abundant evidence highlights the political preoccupation
with homelessness. In 2020, a poll in Washington State revealed
that voters ranked homelessness as the top priority for the state
legislature—far above other common public concerns like
transportation, the economy, the environment, and health care.[1]
We observe a similar focus at the national level. As depicted in

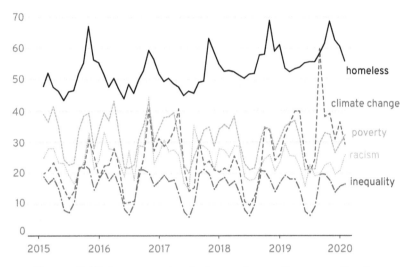

Figure 1. Public interest over time for five search terms. Data source: Google Trends

Figure 1, from January 2015 to January 2020, more people in the United States searched for the term *homeless* via Google than for *inequality, racism, poverty,* and *climate change.*[2]

How might we explain this seemingly disproportionate interest in the issue of homelessness? Two potential explanations come immediately to mind. First, maybe this interest isn't as disproportionate as it might initially appear. That is, maybe the numbers are wrong. Among astute observers, it is well understood that official point-in-time census estimates of homelessness underestimate the true size of the population experiencing homelessness on any given night.[3] For example, the federal definition excludes many precariously housed individuals and families who might be living with a friend or temporarily living in a motel room. The more expansive definition of homelessness used by the U.S. Department of Education suggests a population of 1.35 million homeless students *without* counting their parents.[4] Furthermore, across greater spans of time—say, lifetimes— roughly 5 percent of the population experiences homelessness at least once.[5] In light of these figures, it is more accurate to consider homelessness as a problem that affects millions, rather than hundreds of thousands. But even the larger figure highlights the fact that only a small fraction of people living in poverty actually lose their housing.

More fundamentally, though, a second explanation for the intense interest in the topic may stem from the simple incongruity of a half million people living in shelters and on the street in the wealthiest country in the world. Reactions to this apparent paradox are diverse. For some, homelessness is a moral and political outrage indicting the capitalist system on which U.S. society is based; for others, homelessness is a scourge ruining the nation's largest and most dynamic cities. Other observers reside somewhere in the middle of this spectrum. What is uncontroversial is that homelessness elicits strong and emotional responses from all corners of society. From the perspective of the public, the intense focus on homelessness requires—and demands—an explanation. There is a strong desire to understand the causes of homelessness and where to assign blame. This book is in part concerned with the question of blame.

In January 2020, just weeks before the outbreak of the coronavirus pandemic in the United States, a long-simmering debate about the origins of and responsibility for the homelessness crisis erupted in public. Members of the federal government, including President Trump, argued vocally that the high rates of homelessness in many U.S. cities were a function of the local failings of Democratic leadership and policies. Referencing Democratic House Speaker Nancy Pelosi, the president said,

"She ought to go home and take care of her District, where the homeless is all over the place, and the tents and the filth and the garbage is eroding right into the Pacific Ocean and into their beaches."[6] In response to this finger-pointing, state and local policy makers—most notably California's governor, Gavin Newsom, a Democrat—argued that a lack of federal assistance had starved local communities of sorely needed resources, and housing instability and homelessness had flourished in turn.

Certainly, some of this political jostling is a product of the polarized nature of U.S. politics in the 2020s. From voting rights to climate change—issues that would appear at face value to be resoundingly nonpartisan but which often provoke party-line votes—policy responses to (and public perception of) the issues of our time are characterized by tribalism. Tailored media narratives and the so-called filter bubbles of social media add fuel to the flame of confirmation bias. It's harder than it should be to find fact-checked information, and it's even harder to internalize narratives that run counter to our beliefs. In this respect, homelessness is no different: It tends to provoke hyper-partisan diagnoses and prescriptions. And as with most cases of hyper-partisanship, neither argument above—Trump's nor Newsom's—sufficiently explains the state of homelessness in the country. If inadequate federal support alone accounts for the crisis, why does the rate of homelessness vary so substantially across cities? Presumably, all cities would be equally starved of resources if federal retrenchment were the cause. Yet while some cities have seen rates of homelessness rise over the last ten years, many others have seen rates fall. And if Democratic mayors and governors are the problem, how can we account for the many cities and states with both Democratic leadership and policies and relatively low rates of homelessness? Unsurprisingly, the polarized plotlines are too simple, but they draw attention to essential questions about the nature and causes of the homelessness crisis.

As Ezra Klein writes in his recent book *Why We're Polarized,* one of the other phenomena driving polarization in the country is a grafting of our political identities onto national (as opposed to local) politics.[7] National politics, by definition, require a flattening of local variation—and in our de facto two-party system, with this flattening often comes a false dichotomization of many complex issues. This complicates the effort to respond to local issues that vary by geography—homelessness among them. In the United States, one of the most pressing and vexing questions about homelessness concerns the substantial *variation* in per capita rates of homelessness in cities across the country. Seattle and San Francisco, for example, have roughly four to five times the per capita homeless population of Chicago.[8] The stark differences between seemingly vibrant and healthy cities invite us (and many others) to ask: Why is homelessness so bad in cities like Seattle and San Francisco? Is this a failure of individuals, politicians, markets, or other structural forces? An understanding of variation might help us unlock the drivers of this crisis.

Many of us have, for good reason, struggled to identify a credible explanation for this variation. Accounts of and references to homelessness on television, online, in newspapers, and in scholarly sources offer a long list of potential causes of the issue; among them addiction, mental illness, poverty, domestic violence, eviction, high housing costs, racial discrimination, unemployment, and many others. Reports based on interviews with people experiencing homelessness highlight a wide range of potential causes, as well. A recent report from Seattle/King County for example, noted the following self-reported causes of homelessness among respondents to the annual point-in-time homelessness census: job loss (24 percent of respondents), alcohol or drug use (16 percent), eviction (15 percent), divorce or separation (9 percent), rent increase (8 percent), argument with family or friend (7 percent), incarceration (6 percent), and family/domestic violence (6 percent).[9] Confronted with the question of why some cities have far greater per capita rates of homelessness than others, a reasonable, logical reaction might be to assume that higher levels of homelessness stem from higher incidences of these self-reported causal factors in these cities. In this book, we examine this logic.

While perusing any list of potential causes of homelessness, one can generally break the ostensible explanations down into two overarching categories. Some causes are individual in nature, and some are structural. The bifurcation is consistent with decades of research on poverty and homelessness. On one side of the debate are those who argue that poverty and homelessness are the result of individual factors, that vulnerabilities related to housing instability are fueled by illness, mental condition, laziness, or poor decision-making, including—for these observers—excessive drug and alcohol use. And in the central downtowns of cities like Los Angeles, San Francisco, or Seattle, thousands of unsheltered people experiencing homelessness may indeed be suffering from a substance use disorder, mentally ill, and/or unemployed. Following this logic, it is the disproportionate presence of people with these vulnerabilities in certain cities that explains the substantial variation in per capita homelessness rates around the country. Whether born in or attracted to these cities, *people* comprise the homelessness crisis, and so homelessness is an individual problem. (It is not uncommon for some to argue that homelessness is exclusively an individual choice.) On the other side of the debate are those who argue that larger, structural forces, such as market conditions, housing costs, racism, discrimination, and inequality, causally explain the prevalence of homelessness. Under the structural explanation, homelessness is a consequence of broader and deeper societal factors driving people at the margins of society out of their housing.

Perhaps there is a middle road. The individual explanation is alluring—it's individual people who lose their housing, after all. Surely there must be systematic factors at play, though; otherwise, how could we possibly account for the dramatically different rates of homelessness around the country? Even if you were entirely convinced of the individual explanation, you would have to acknowledge that some kind of systemic variation— some combination of environmental, political, economic, and demographic trends—characterizes different places. In 2019, less than 1 in 1,000 residents were unhoused in Alabama and Mississippi, while California and Oregon had over five times that rate. Why? Existing research provides a helpful roadmap to navigate the seemingly complex and, at times, contradictory evidence about the causal drivers of homelessness. Homelessness researcher Brendan O'Flaherty, for example, suggests that to generate causal explanations of homelessness, one must consider the interaction between individual characteristics and the context in which that person resides. Either explanation alone is insufficient to explain or predict individual homelessness. By extension, he argues that people who lose their housing are effectively the wrong people in the wrong place.[10] This frame helps to provide a vantage point from which to consider the central question of this book: What explains the substantial regional variation in per capita homelessness rates in the United States?

To cut to the chase, the answer is on the cover of this book: *Homelessness Is a Housing Problem*. Regional variation in rates of homelessness can be explained by the costs and availability of housing. Housing market conditions explain why Seattle has four times the per capita homelessness of Cincinnati. Housing market conditions explain why high-poverty cities like Detroit and Cleveland have low rates of homelessness. Housing market conditions also explain why some growing cities, like Charlotte, North Carolina, are not characterized by the levels of homelessness that coastal boomtowns like Boston, Seattle, Portland, and San Francisco are. Variation in rates of homelessness is not driven by more of "those people" residing in one city than another. People with a variety of health and economic vulnerabilities live in every city and county in our sample; the difference is the local context in which they live. High rental costs and low vacancy rates create a challenging market for many residents in a city, and those challenges are compounded for people with low incomes and/or physical or mental health concerns.

．　　．　　．

According to estimates from the U.S. Department of Housing and Urban Development (HUD), at least 567,715 people experienced homelessness on a single night in 2019.[11] But this aggregate figure masks significant geographic variation in the distribution of per capita homelessness across the country. The metropolitan areas of New York, Los Angeles, Washington, D.C., San Francisco, Seattle, and Boston alone account for over 29 percent of the homeless population in the country, despite being home to only about 7 percent of the general population. Regardless of one's view of the problem—and the political lens through which one considers homelessness—it is reasonable to wonder what it is about these cities that produces (or, according to some, attracts) such large and disproportionate populations of people experiencing homelessness. To explore this phenomenon, we shift the unit of analysis away from the individual and turn our attention to the metropolitan area. From this perspective, we are not interested in predicting whether a given person will experience homelessness or why someone lost their housing in the past; we are interested in understanding why, for example, the crisis is so much more extreme in Boston than in Cleveland. This analytic pivot does not preclude individual explanations for homelessness; instead, it clarifies the object in which we are interested: the city-to-city variation itself.

Understanding this variance is critical to formulating an appropriate policy response. In cities with substantial unhoused populations, it is common for rival political factions to blame one another for the crisis—a microcosm of the Trump–Newsom sparring cited above—and for the issue to devolve into a political hot potato. Often caught in the middle of this dispute are municipal leaders who are tasked with "solving" the problem (with resources that many consider to be inadequate). Societal cleavages emerge in which compassionate responses to homelessness—those that stress social service provision and respect for the dignity and rights of people experiencing homelessness—are criticized by community members who advocate a tougher response to the crisis. Proponents of the latter approach argue that overly permissive local policies have incubated an underlying problem, all while individual desperation facilitates property crime, threatens public health, and abets a deterioration of a city's overall quality of life. The severity and polarization of homelessness is evident in public polling that identifies the problem as the highest-ranked public concern. In the 2020 State of Washington poll of eligible voters mentioned earlier, 31 percent of voters ranked homelessness as Washington's top issue: an increase of ten percentage points over 2019.[12]

Accordingly, it is worth considering the relationship between perceptions of homelessness and its reality, not least because personal experience and anecdote play formidable roles in shaping opinions and perceptions about the issue. For housed city dwellers in Seattle, San Francisco, and Los Angeles, seeing and interacting with people experiencing homelessness is a daily occurrence. Tents dot the urban landscape; large encampments move (either voluntarily or forcibly) from neighborhood to neighborhood. There is a profound chasm in human experience in these cities, between new million-dollar condos and the tents and tarps that the unhoused use to protect themselves from the elements. And while large unsheltered populations in many coastal cities raise legitimate concerns about public safety and health—for the housed and unhoused alike—these visible reminders do not accurately reflect the homelessness problem as a whole. In most cities, the majority of people experiencing homelessness are not visible to the general population, because most people without housing sleep in shelters or other supportive housing facilities. On any given night in this country, the chronically unsheltered constitute only about one-tenth of the population experiencing homelessness. Yet the visibility—the literal conspicuousness— of the chronic, unsheltered population in many cities helps to cement a belief that people experiencing homelessness are mentally ill and/or addicted to a substance, as these conditions are disproportionately represented in the unsheltered population. Accordingly, the narrative about homelessness is often dominated by a focus on drugs and mental health, which may obscure other (often structural) explanations for the crisis.

In this book, we make an important distinction when considering the causal drivers of homelessness. First, we note *precipitating events* that can lead to a bout of homelessness. For example, in the survey of people experiencing homelessness in Seattle/King County, self-reported "primary reasons" for homelessness include divorce, domestic violence, and arguments with family or friends.[13] As they are identified in interviews with people then-without housing, we can indeed consider these events to have produced a spell of homelessness. But we can't consider each reason a *root cause* of a given housing crisis. If divorce is a cause of homelessness, for example, why don't far more people lose their housing after leaving a spouse? A key point to which we return in this book is that *under certain conditions*, a range of precipitating events (like divorce) can result in homelessness—but these events ought not be considered root causes of housing instability and loss. Underlying vulnerabilities matter.

Consider the following vignette about musical chairs, often deployed by homelessness researchers, to think through causality and homelessness. We use this example to highlight the difference between a precipitating event and a root cause:

> Ten friends decide to play a game of musical chairs and arrange ten chairs in a circle. A leader begins the game by turning on the music, and everyone begins to walk in a circle inside the chairs. The leader removes one chair, stops the music, and the ten friends scramble to find a spot to sit—leaving one person without a chair. The loser, Mike, was on crutches after spraining his ankle. Given his condition, he was unable to move quickly to find a chair during the scramble that ensued.

In other words, when housing is scarce, vulnerabilities and barriers to housing are magnified. Limited financial resources, mental illness, addiction, or interpersonal strife, under a specific set of circumstances, could each precipitate a bout of homelessness—just as a sprained ankle might prevent one from finding a chair in musical chairs. But the fundamental question remains: Would we say that Mike's ankle injury *caused* him to lose the game? Under the specific conditions of the game (say, nine chairs and ten people), Mike's impairment prevented him from finding a chair. But under different conditions—ten chairs and ten people—Mike would have easily found one. One could argue, and we will in this book, that the fundamental *cause* of Mike's chairlessness—was a lack of chairs, not his ankle injury. The rules of the game meant that someone had to lose.

Over the course of this book, we illustrate that personal vulnerabilities may explain *who* becomes homeless within a given community under a specific set of circumstances—but that, in aggregate, these vulnerabilities do not adequately explain regional variation in homelessness. This finding suggests that broader structural explanations of homelessness—especially those that shape housing markets—may have more explanatory power than the precipitating events frequently cited in local surveys as the "primary causes" of homelessness. Policy responses ought to be tailored accordingly. This foundation guides this project as a whole. Our central argument—that the prevalence of homelessness is driven by structural forces—is not unique in its own right. Much research has identified a causal link between housing-market conditions and homelessness. But there is little evidence that these findings have altered and shaped public perceptions about the nature of the crisis; hence our desire to package a comprehensive analysis in a single volume.

Social science research frequently relies on complex statistical methods and expansive data sources to relay a credible causal narrative about social phenomena for the subset of readers who are trained in these methods and have access to this content (usually via university journal subscriptions). For people outside of the academy, access to this information may be limited, both with respect to the specialized nature of academic social science and the expensive paywalls of academic journals. Understanding, then, is more frequently shaped by media narratives, experience, and anecdote. Cognitive dissonance is real, too. New findings from the academy may challenge deeply held ideology, and evidence doesn't always make a difference. Accordingly, in this book, we seek to present our research by means of intuitive appeals to first principles. We use geographic variation in rates of homelessness as the foundation from which to test a wide range of potential explanations for the crisis, using an accessible analytical methodology appropriate for a broad audience. In this manner, we address many of the common narratives about homelessness in a single work with relatively simple statistical methods. Basic causal reasoning allows us to dismiss several common explanations for higher rates of homelessness: If there is no fixed statistical evidence of a positive relationship between a potential cause and our outcome of interest (i.e., rates of urban homelessness), we have to conclude it does not bear on variation in this outcome in any straightforward manner. For example, if poverty rates are low in cities with high rates of homelessness, it is impossible to attribute regional variation in homelessness to differences in the relative presence of low-income households. Applied to all potential explanations in this book, this structure provides the basis from which we ultimately attribute varying rates of homelessness to the structure of housing markets—a finding corroborated by other research leveraging different data sources and methods.

HOMELESSNESS COUNTS AND TRENDS

To study variation in rates of homelessness, we shift the unit of analysis from individuals experiencing homelessness to metropolitan areas. This is a book about cities, not individual people. We seek to explain why certain geographic locations produce (or otherwise report) disproportionately high rates of homelessness. Because homelessness is largely an urban phenomenon, we focus our attention on the largest urban areas in the United States.

The first step in understanding variation in rates of homelessness is to understand the manners in which communities measure homelessness and deliver programming. In 1987, the U.S. Congress passed the McKinney-Vento Homeless Assistance Act, which created the contemporary administrative machinery behind the federal response to homelessness. A critical component of McKinney-Vento was the stipulation that federal money was to be distributed directly to jurisdictions to fund local service delivery. To facilitate the flow of funds from the federal government to local communities, HUD required states and municipalities to self-organize into units of geographic aggregation called Continuums of Care (CoC). Today, CoCs are the main administrative entities that manage homelessness programming, allocate federal funding to local service providers, and conduct the Congressionally mandated one-night census of homelessness. Virtually every locality in the country is covered by a CoC, but the construction and distribution of CoCs varies from state to state.[14] Most urban areas are covered by a single CoC, while smaller cities and rural areas might bundle together in a CoC that covers a large geographic area.

Ohio, for example, is divided into nine different CoCs (see Figure 2). Eight of the CoCs cover the most populous counties

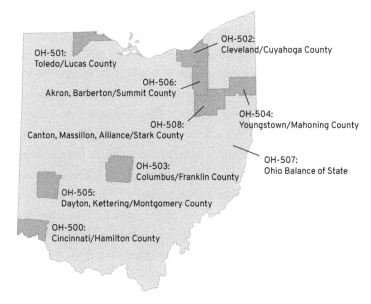

Figure 2. Ohio Continuum of Care map. The state is home to nine HUD
CoCs: eight counties and the balance of state. Data source: HUD

in the state, including Cuyahoga County (Cleveland), Lucas
County (Toledo), Franklin County (Columbus), and Hamilton
County (Cincinnati). The largest CoC (in a geographic sense) is
OH-507, which encompasses the entire balance of the state that
is not covered by one of the other eight county-based CoCs. As
CoCs administer their own one-night count of people experi-
encing homelessness—often conducted the last week of January
and known as the Point-In-Time (PIT) count—the estimated
unhoused population in Ohio, in the eyes of HUD, is the sum of
Ohio's nine distinct CoC counts.

Relationships between CoC boundaries and other state and
local boundaries can be messy. If we are interested in measuring
homelessness in Cleveland, for example, the only geographic

unit available for analysis is the Cuyahoga County CoC, which includes both the city of Cleveland and its surrounding suburbs. Therefore, for those interested exclusively in the urban homelessness, Cleveland's homelessness rates as estimated by the Cuyahoga County CoC will be imprecise. Homelessness tends to be less prevalent in the suburbs.[15] Therefore, the rate of homelessness in county CoCs is, on average, lower than it is for CoCs that cover a single city. For example, the rate of homelessness in Cook County, Illinois (including the city of Chicago) in 2019 was 1.20 per 1,000 population. In the city of Chicago alone, the per capita rate was 1.96. Because major metropolitan areas correspond to a mix of city- and county-based CoCs, in this book we compare county-based CoCs to other county-based CoCs and city-based CoCs to other city-based CoCs.

To create our study sample, we began with a list of the thirty-five largest Metropolitan Statistical Areas (MSAs) in the United States. MSAs are geographic units of at least fifty thousand people that cover a major urban center plus its surrounding areas. For each MSA on the list, we identified the primary CoC in that MSA. We then excluded six MSAs because the primary CoC in question covered too large a geographic area. (For example, the CoC that includes Houston, Texas, encompasses five different counties— and won't be useful for understanding homelessness in the Houston metropolitan area alone.) Five other MSAs were excluded using similar criteria, including Riverside, California; Denver, Colorado; Orlando, Florida; Pittsburgh, Pennsylvania; and Kansas City, Missouri. After these exclusions, our sample covers twenty-nine of the thirty-five largest MSAs in the county. We ultimately include thirty CoCs, however, because of the unique case of Cook County, Illinois—which is divided into two CoCs, one for the city of Chicago, and one for the remainder of Cook County. Chicago is the only city in our sample with this structure. Accordingly, we include the Chicago CoC in the list of city-based CoCs, but we also separately aggregate the two CoCs to get a picture of homelessness for Cook County as a whole. We include Cook County in our list of county CoCs as well, leaving a final sample of nineteen county-based CoCs and eleven city-based CoCs. In 2019, the collection of thirty CoCs in our sample accounted for roughly 45 percent of all homelessness in the United States. We compare these regions every year from 2007 to 2019.

Returning to the regional differences that motivated this book, the following graphs offer a visual explanation of the variation in per capita rates of U.S. homelessness in the country over this time period.[16] Figures 3 and 4 show the per capita rates of homelessness in the city and county CoCs in 2007 and 2019—the beginning and ending years for our sample period.

As the figures illustrate, variation in rates of homelessness is not a new phenomenon: The 2007 figures show similarly wide-ranging dynamics as those from 2019. In our sample, we see single-night rates of homelessness anywhere between about 1 and 10 unhoused people per 1,000 population. The second key takeaway from these figures is that, generally speaking, high per capita locations in 2007 also saw high rates in 2019. Washington, D.C., New York City, Boston, San Francisco, King County (Seattle), Multnomah County (Portland), Los Angeles County, and Santa Clara County (San Jose) have persistently seen the highest rates of per capita homelessness over the thirteen years covered in this book. We are interested in what differentiates these cities from others. To the extent that policy choices, macroeconomic trends, or local cultural factors may drive variation in rates of homelessness, we want to know what differentiates Multnomah County, Oregon, from Maricopa County, Arizona.

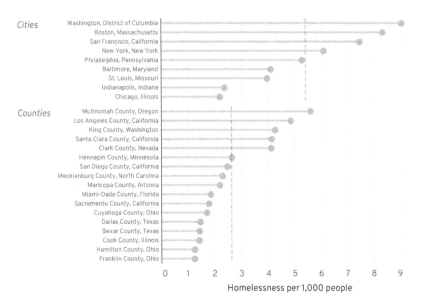

Figure 3. Per capita rates of homelessness in select U.S. regions, 2007. Dashed lines indicate city and country averages of per capita PIT counts. Data source: HUD

Throughout this book, to supplement our analyses of per capita homelessness in cities and counties, on occasion, we also deploy a simple indexing approach that allows us to compare city and county CoCs directly. To create an indexed value of homelessness intensity, we divide each measurement of city per capita homelessness by the largest observed city rate across the years in our sample (2007–2019), divide each measurement of county per capita homelessness by the largest observed county rate, and then combine the transformed values into a single measure. Doing so allows us to get a sense of how the severity of a given city's or county's homelessness crisis evolves over time, relative to other cities and counties. The indexing approach is

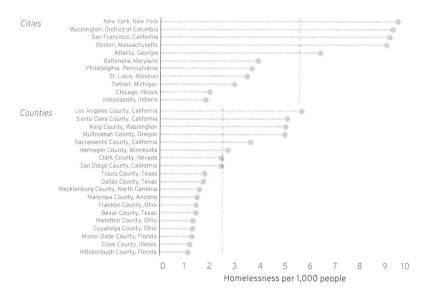

Figure 4. Per capita rates of homelessness in select U.S. regions, 2019. Dashed lines indicate city and country averages of per capita PIT counts. Data source: HUD

a kind of ranking function. It's not superior to our bifurcated approach to presenting city and county rates; it complements it.

Using indexed values, Figure 5 below provides a comparison of the relative ranks of indexed rates of homelessness in each CoC in 2007 compared to 2019. (The CoCs with observations excluded in 2007 are removed from the analysis.) We observe some modest movement in the rank ordering of cities, but generally speaking, regions with high per capita homelessness in 2019 also had high rates a decade earlier.

Over the course of the book, we also make use of some core concepts from statistics to illustrate key points. The first of these is the *median*, a summary statistic that indicates the midpoint in a distribution of values. The median may differ meaningfully from

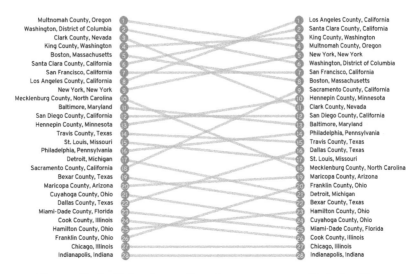

Figure 5. Rank of indexed rates of homelessness, 2010 v. 2019. Vertical position indicates rank of indexed per capita PIT counts for select U.S. regions. Data source: HUD

the average or *mean* of this distribution. Accordingly, we can understand the median as helping us understand the shape of a distribution in a manner that is less sensitive to large outliers— which drag up or down the mean. To further understand the shape of these distributions, we also measure a quantity known as the *variance*. The variance of a distribution measures how dispersed a set of values are around their mean. Mathematically, variance corresponds to the squared *standard deviation* of a distribution, a similar measure assessing dispersion. Small values for standard deviations and variance correspond to narrow distributions, while large values correspond to wide distributions. In this book, we use the word *variation* to mean "differences between measurements," while we use *variance* to indicate the mathematical quantity just described. Generally, the book attempts to account for variation between regions by examining simple statistical models and evaluating the degree to which they explain the variance of the distributions in question.

Consider an example in which we analyze the relationship between age and height among children aged eighteen and under. The vertical axis on our chart measures height and the horizontal axis measures age. We can quantify this relationship using a scatterplot of dots, in which each dot represents one person and illustrates their height and age. After placing all dots in our data set on the scatterplot, we can assess what kind of relationship exists between the variables and how much of the variation in height can be explained by age. Because children become taller as they age, we might expect to see an upward sloping cloud of dots, but we probably wouldn't expect all the dots to fall along a perfectly straight line. Instead, we'd observe some variation. Some people are short, some are tall, some grow early, and some grow later. We can use statistics to measure the amount of variation in one variable (height) that's captured by variation in the other (age).

To do so, in several graphics throughout the book, we deploy a statistic known as the coefficient of determination, which for unfortunate mathematical reasons goes by the abbreviation R^2. This quantity (pronounced "R-squared") offers an estimate of the amount of variance that we might consider to be captured— that is, explained—by a line drawn through the scatterplot of points. In particular, we'll draw a line through the points that minimizes the total vertical distance between all the points on the plot and the line itself. That exercise represents a *linear regression*—a statement about one variable in terms of another, as characterized by that best-fit line. (The formula for calculating R^2 subtracts the proportion of variance *unexplained* by this best-fit line from the number 1—leaving the proportion of *explained* variance.) R^2 tends to vary between 0 and 1, with values closer to 1 indicating a greater proportion of explained variance. There's no hard rule governing which values of R^2 imply small or large amounts of explained variance, but generally we might say that values of R^2 below 0.1 indicate very little explanation, while values above 0.3 indicate much stronger explanatory relationships. That is, it's important to note that R^2 doesn't tell us everything about these relationships. For example, on its own, it won't help us separate correlation from causality, it won't tell us if we're missing any important variables in our statistical model, and it won't tell us if we have enough data to draw solid conclusions. Nonetheless, it's a useful indicator of the coupling between two variables. Returning to our example of the relationship between age and height, it is likely that the R^2 would be high—age is a strong predictor of height among children—but it wouldn't be 1.0. There still exists plenty of variation in height among children that cannot be explained by age.

While the story about homelessness in major metropolitan areas has been generally consistent since 2007, some critical trends have emerged—see Figure 6. First, at a national level, overall levels of homelessness have fallen over this period—and this trend is apparent in the thirty CoCs in our sample.[17] While overall homelessness has fallen, the variance between different cities' rates of homelessness has increased. In practice, that means that while falling at a national level, homelessness has become increasingly concentrated in a few cities over this time period. Given the uneven progress toward reducing levels of homelessness, the task of understanding the drivers of regional variation is cast in an important light. If people and cities experience homelessness at increasingly different rates, it's worth asking why.

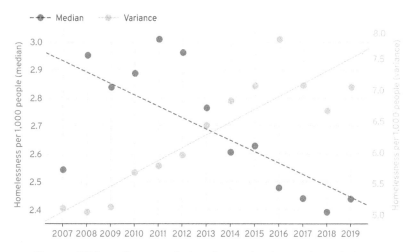

Figure 6. While median per capita homelessness has decreased over the last decade, its variance has increased. Dashed lines indicate linear regressions of year and median per capita PIT counts (and their variance) between 2007 and 2019 for a sample of U.S. regions. Data source: HUD

Over the course of writing this book, two major social events occurred with direct implications for understanding the issue of homelessness in the country. First, in March 2020, as the COVID-19 outbreak swept across the United States and residents went into lockdown, businesses and schools closed in the most immediate cessation of economic and social activity on record. The virus represented a particular concern for the most vulnerable in society, including elders, those with underlying health conditions, and people without permanent housing. Accordingly, many jurisdictions took extraordinary steps to protect the health of people experiencing homelessness—and limit community spread of the virus—by moving portions of their homeless population to hotels and motels.

In summer and autumn 2020, I (Gregg) partnered with colleagues from King County and the University of Washington to evaluate the region's COVID-19 homelessness response. In the early days of the pandemic, the City of Seattle, King County, and their partner agencies moved over seven hundred people from congregate shelter settings into hotel rooms throughout the county—with the primary aim of adhering to public health guidelines and keeping a highly susceptible population safe. Our research—which included an analysis of quantitative data on infection rates, housing stability, exits to permanent housing, and 911 dispatch calls; as well as qualitative data from interviews with shelter residents who moved to hotels and agency staff— showed that the intervention wasn't just successful at limiting the spread of COVID-19, but also in producing other benefits on various measures of well-being, including improved health, better sleep, feelings of safety and security, less interpersonal conflict, and greater and more optimistic focus on the future (including education, employment, and permanent housing).[18] These results, in part, prompted King County Executive Dow Constantine to propose an additional sales tax to fund the purchase of hotels as supplementary housing for people experiencing homelessness.[19] In other words, in the Puget Sound region, out of crisis has come a major public investment in housing solutions for people experiencing homelessness.

The economic consequences of COVID-19 have also increased the risks of falling into homelessness for many precariously housed people around the country. Early estimates suggest that tens of millions of households could lose their housing as they struggle to make monthly rental payments due to loss of income.[20] In the early months of the crisis, many states and local jurisdictions enacted eviction moratoria to prevent people from losing their housing due to an inability to pay. In September 2020, the Centers for Disease Control and Prevention (CDC) announced a national eviction moratorium, leveraging its broad authority to control the spread of the pandemic. As these eviction restrictions lapse, however, housing researchers and advocates offer dire predictions of a sharp rise in homelessness, since even under the CDC rules, renters are expected to pay any rent deferred under the moratorium.[21] Beyond the obvious public health consequences of COVID-19, this crisis highlighted the natural interconnectedness of larger, structural forces and the dynamics of homelessness.

In the midst of the country's early grappling with the novel coronavirus, the May 2020 killing of George Floyd in Minneapolis at the hands of the police ignited global protests of police violence and racial inequality. In the United States, these protests brought structural and systemic racism to the forefront of public and political discourse—and created the newest opportunity for substantive movement toward dismantling structural racism in the country. Racism is central to discussions that aim to reveal the causes and consequences of homelessness. Given their representation in the general U.S. population, Black, Native, and Hispanic/Latino individuals and families are disproportionately represented in the homeless population.[22] While Black people, for example, make up about 13 percent of the U.S. population, HUD reported to Congress in 2019 that almost 40 percent of the population experiencing homelessness was Black.[23] This fact alone ought to be unsurprising: A knot of conspicuous, racialized structural disadvantages—in housing, banking and lending practices, education, health care, employment, and policing and incarceration—readily amplify homelessness risk.

What's essential in these two extraordinarily salient crises —the coronavirus pandemic and the latest reckoning with structural and systemic racism—is the manner in which they highlight whom we're talking about when we talk about homelessness risk. To the extent that this is a book about regional variation in homelessness, it is also a book about deck-stacking. Place is where it happens. If we want to understand the factors that cause people to lose their housing, we need to understand why and how those forces vary from city to city. For many, the pandemic and the Black Lives Matter movement have driven home the interconnectedness of U.S. society, not least because the health of one's neighbor is directly related to the health of oneself. But just as racism is not a monolith, homelessness is multifaceted, and households' experiences with housing vary with identity and geography. Here, we argue that an effective policy response to homelessness will only come from acknowledging and responding to these differences.

APPROACH

This book is split into three brief sections. We conclude the first section in the next chapter, in which we lay out the current state of knowledge about homelessness in the country. We provide an overview of existing academic social-science research on the topic and offer descriptive statistics about homelessness. The purpose of the second chapter is to place the reader in a position to engage critically with the specific causal arguments presented in the second section of the book.

In part 2, we consider the various potential explanations for the substantial variation in per capita homeless populations around the country. In chapter 3, we analyze a range of individual and household vulnerabilities and attributes and ask whether these common narratives explain regional variation. These data and analyses provide compelling evidence that the answer to that question, most simply, is no. The homelessness crisis in coastal cities cannot be explained by disproportionate levels of drug use, mental illness, or poverty. In chapter 4, we then consider local culture and context, analyzing how variations in weather, local political climate, the mobility of low-income households, and the generosity of local welfare provision may influence rates of homelessness. Similarly, we find that these common explanations do not account for observed regional variation. Finally, we consider a third category of potential explanations: housing market conditions. In chapter 5, we consider housing costs, housing cost burdens, and housing availability as candidate explanations for intercity variation. In this analysis, two explanations emerge as credible factors: absolute rent levels and rental market vacancy rates. We argue that after eliminating a wide range of potential explanations for the variation in question, the descriptive and correlative findings in chapter 5 together offer the most compelling explanation of regional variation in rates of homelessness.

In part 3 of the book, we synthesize our findings in two policy-oriented chapters. In chapter 6, we propose a typology of cities to explain why certain cities—certain types of cities—experience elevated rates of homelessness; while other cities, relatively speaking, do not. Combining our data with principles from the field of urban economics, we construct a framework that, importantly, helps us understand why high-growth boomtowns don't always see significant rates of homelessness. Charlotte, for example, has grown as fast as San Francisco and Seattle, but because of a relatively robust housing supply response, the city has not faced the housing shortages that plague many coastal cities. The typology also demonstrates how population declines help to explain why a large, vibrant city like Chicago has relatively low rates of homelessness: A falling population in Chicago has created higher rental market vacancy rates and lower prices, which produces a more accommodating housing market (relatively speaking) for vulnerable households.

In chapter 7, we conclude by presenting a broad proposal to end homelessness in the United States. Ultimately, in the long run, the prescription is simple: Policymakers must increase the number of affordable housing units and provide subsidies and rental assistance to households to ensure they can access housing. In the short run, competing demands and a lack of resources makes decision-making more challenging. Local jurisdictions must balance the needs for a more robust crisis response (i.e., greater emergency shelter capacity) with the desire to increase the supply of affordable housing. In reality, cities must devote resources to both of these responses.

To create a sustainable, robust response to homelessness, we argue that three interrelated steps are required. First, public perception of homelessness must change. As long as we continue to frame homelessness as an individual problem, we will struggle to make the structural investments needed to end it. Second, this crisis requires far greater resources from all levels of government. Existing investments, while substantial, are insufficient given the scale of the problem. Last, we encourage a broader systems approach to addressing homelessness. Focusing on three stages of the system—inflow, crisis response, and outflow—are necessary to move people out of homelessness and into stable, permanent housing. A lack of focus on any one of these stages will produce a system out of balance—and high levels of homelessness will persist.

Finally, a word on the motivation for this book. Both Gregg and Clayton are engaged in the study of and response to homelessness in the Puget Sound region. As one of the areas of the country most affected by this crisis, understanding what drives homelessness in our region is a topic of great civic importance. In the years leading up to writing this book, we have been amazed that—despite our community wrestling with homelessness for many years—there is a lack of general understanding about the nature and causes of homelessness. Numerous narratives compete for the public's attention and, as a result, there is no consensus about the root causes of this crisis. Without a common understanding, it is impossible for elected leaders and the community at large to marshal the resources needed to end homelessness in our community. Much of the money spent on homelessness today constitutes a *response* to the crisis rather than an *alternative* to it. In the concluding chapter we share our vision—informed by thought leaders from around the country— for community-wide approaches that are required to prevent and limit homelessness. According to the United States Interagency Council on Homelessness, "An end to homelessness means that every community will have a comprehensive response in place that ensures homelessness is prevented wherever possible, or if it can't be prevented, it is a rare, brief, and one-time experience."[24] Fair enough. But without wrapping our head around the root of the crisis—its beginning—it'll be difficult to find its end.

CHAPTER TWO

Evidence

Between 2009 and 2019, something almost previously unthinkable occurred: Veteran homelessness in the United States fell by nearly half—a decline of about thirty-six thousand people who were without housing on any given night.[1] The progress was unambiguously good news, not least because it occurred in the wake of the financial crisis. Indeed, statistics on veteran homelessness would soon become a rallying cry for housing advocates and many urban policymakers: With enough money and attention, the injustice of a former soldier sleeping outside might be relegated to the pages of history books. But to the uninitiated observer, this policy success might also be puzzling. As the journalist J. B. Wogan wrote, most people experiencing homelessness are not veterans, and "in many of the nation's large cities, homelessness among the general population appears to be getting worse. . . . Right now, it's hard to say whether success in lowering homelessness will be limited to veterans, or whether this will be the first step in a longer campaign to fight homelessness among the rest of the population."[2] How had the country become so good at housing veterans and their families? And what about those who haven't served in the armed forces?

Certainly, the social standing of military veterans helps explain the political (and financial) commitments that were necessary to achieve this progress—few politicians disagree with the notion that a nation should support the people who risked their lives defending it—but a pressing question remains as to whether similar commitments can and will be applied more broadly, rather than toward a targeted few. Even in the case of veterans, the job remains unfinished. Policymakers mobilized the bureaucratic machinery of several federal agencies (including the Department of Veterans Affairs) to find and fund the necessary housing and institutional pipelines required to meet the needs of unhoused veterans—and still, half the military veteran population experiencing homelessness remains unhoused. To imagine replicating (and maybe doubling) this effort for all populations experiencing homelessness is perhaps a daunting task. But there is an organizing principle here: one of context-specific, systemic effort.

In this book, we argue that if we understand homelessness as a housing problem, we can also understand it as solvable. And as a scholarly and policy community, we already have the evidence that it is. By no stretch of the imagination are housed veterans the only success story homelessness policymakers and service-delivery organizations have to offer. As Beth Shinn and Jill Khadduri argue in their recent book, *In the Midst of Plenty, Homelessness and What to Do About It*, the necessary resources exist to end homelessness—the constraints are political will and commitment.[3] In other words, that homelessness still persists in the United States should not be taken as evidence that investments and programs designed to address the crisis have failed. Instead, we can only understand existing policies and programs as inadequate. The persistence of the problem of homelessness reflects these deficiencies.

In this chapter, we describe how we and other researchers have reached this conclusion. In particular, we review the existing body of academic and public research to answer five questions that will help frame the analysis found in the rest of the book:

1. What is the current landscape of homelessness in the United States?
2. How has homelessness changed over time?
3. How do we explain homelessness?
4. What are the consequences of homelessness?
5. How do we stop and prevent homelessness?

We confront these questions in turn.

WHAT IS THE CURRENT LANDSCAPE OF HOMELESSNESS IN THE UNITED STATES?

Unlike previous eras characterized by high rates of homelessness in the country, today's crisis comes at a time of unparalleled wealth and prosperity. During the Great Depression, homeless encampments dotted the landscape of many U.S. cities—a tragic but conceivable outcome. As the unemployment rate in the 1930s soared to 25 percent and economic activity ground to a halt, many could no longer afford their housing, and homelessness became all too common. Today, though, U.S. cities look very different than they did during the Depression. Homelessness looks different, too. People regularly establish encampments in the shadows of glistening office towers that house the employees of modern corporate titans in technology and finance. This incongruity is a source of confusion for many observers.

One of the first researchers to help explain this ostensible paradox was Brendan O'Flaherty, who confronted it head-on—arguing in 1996 that "income inequality is behind the increased homelessness in North America."[4] O'Flaherty offered an economic explanation for the relationship: namely, that as people with comparatively lower incomes were squeezed out of higher-quality housing, they pushed prices up at the lower end of the housing market, ultimately forcing those with the lowest incomes into homelessness. Whatever the explanation—and much of this book is devoted to testing hypotheses like these—trying to understand homelessness without placing it in the broader context of the housing market is a fool's errand. Here, we'll often think about the housing market as many economists do: that is, as a system in which *housing services* are dynamically allocated to households based on their *preferences* and *ability to pay*. Through this lens, key issues that immediately come into focus include the stock of housing, the price of housing, and the resources of households.

Each year, a nonprofit advocacy organization called the National Low Income Housing Coalition (NLIHC) publishes a report entitled *The Gap: A Shortage of Affordable Homes*. Based on 2018 data, the most recent version of this report found that for every one hundred households with extremely low incomes, there exist only thirty-six affordable and available homes.[5] This shortage of housing units presents a clear and present threat to the health and viability of this large block of households. A quarter of all renters in the United States have extremely low incomes. Despite significant variation across the country, no state offers adequate housing for households with extremely low incomes: West Virginia is the only state with sixty affordable and available homes for every one hundred households who need them. According to the NLIHC, the West Coast has the most pronounced shortages of affordable housing; Oregon, California, Nevada, and Arizona all have fewer than thirty units for every one hundred households in need.

To begin to understand how these dynamics map onto the phenomenon of homelessness, it is instructive—by way of example—to provide an overview of the housing market in one metropolitan area. Consider Hennepin County, Minnesota, where Minneapolis is located. Based on five-year estimates from the American Community Survey (ACS), Hennepin County was home to 1,235,279 people in 2018. Using data from the ACS, HUD's Picture of Subsidized Households, and the National Housing Preservation Database, we estimate that there are about 530,000 housing units in Hennepin County, which we can in turn break down into three categories: unsubsidized (owned), unsubsidized (rented), and subsidized (rented). As in many regions of the country, owner-occupancy is the dominant form of housing tenure: Over 62 percent of housing units are owned. The remaining 38 percent of housing units are rented, and the vast majority are units that renters access via the private market. Less than 7 percent of all housing units are subsidized through federal programs like the Housing Choice Voucher Program, public housing, place-based Section 8, or Low-Income Housing Tax Credits.[6]

Given consistent population growth, the overall demand for housing in Hennepin County is strong. The region's housing market is also tight: Rental market vacancy rates—that is, the percentage of units available for rent at any given point in time—have hovered at or below 4 percent since 2012. The

combination of these market dynamics and general lack of subsidized housing options presents a serious housing challenge for
low-income households in Hennepin County. In practice, that
means many households are scrambling to meet their housing
needs. In 2018, just over 10 percent of people in Hennepin County
were living in households with incomes below the federal poverty line. (For comparison, that's a bit lower than the nationwide rate of 13 percent). That year, the poverty line in 2018 was
$12,140 for an individual household and $25,100 for a household
of four. The number of households living under this definition
of poverty far exceeded the quantity of subsidized housing units
in Hennepin County that year. Because only 6.6 percent of units
are subsidized, thousands of households living in poverty were
left with no choice but to procure unsubsidized housing in the
private market.

Like most markets for goods and services, the market for
housing consists of a wide range of options that differ in terms
of quality and price. But the existence of lower-priced housing options does not necessarily imply an adequate supply of
affordable housing for all households that need it. In Hennepin County, the twenty-fifth percentile contract rent was $814/
month in 2018. If we assume that an affordable rent is that which
stays below, say, 30 percent of household income, this theoretical rental unit at the twenty-fifth percentile—including an additional $93 for utility payments each month—would only be
affordable to households earning at least $35,760 per year: much
higher than the poverty threshold for a family of four.[7] Data from
the NLIHC corroborates these statistics.[8] In Minnesota, there
are only forty-one affordable and available rental homes per one
hundred extremely low-income renter households. The remaining fifty-nine households are in an exceedingly difficult position

where, in order to keep a roof over their heads, they must devote a significant percentage of their limited income each month to rent—leaving little money for other household necessities.

For households unable to secure one of the five hundred thirty thousand housing units in Hennepin County, there are two additional options. First, a household can "double-up" with another household until they can secure their own housing. The other alternative is to turn to a county-run homelessness response system that provides temporary shelter or some form of permanent housing to those in need. Hennepin County is one of a limited number of jurisdictions in the country with a "right to shelter" policy, which guarantees shelter to any person or family who needs it. Accordingly, the county has a system in place that allows shelter capacity to expand and contract based on the present need for shelter services. Despite this right to shelter, Hennepin County still reported an unsheltered homeless count of 404 people in 2018 during its one-night census. Another 2,609 (87%) were sleeping in emergency shelters or transitional housing facilities. The homelessness response system in Hennepin County includes both emergency shelters and various forms of permanent housing for households in need, including permanent supportive housing and rapid rehousing.[9] The sum of these two populations—the unsheltered and sheltered homeless, in the parlance of HUD—suggests an estimated 3,013 people were without permanent housing in Hennepin County in 2018. On the same night as this point-in-time (PIT) count in Hennepin County, another 8,545 people were living in some form of permanent housing supported by the county's homelessness response system. Whether via short-term rental assistance or long-term subsidized units, the county had funded and operated programs that had *ended* program participants' homelessness crisis in the eyes of HUD. Accordingly, these people were not included in the annual homelessness census, despite currently receiving some form of housing subsidy only available to people who had previously experienced homelessness. This delineation—between unsheltered homelessness, temporary housing (sheltered homelessness), and permanent housing—reflects the federal definition of what constitutes homelessness and what doesn't. The point is: At least 3,000 people in Hennepin County needed a more permanent place to sleep on the night of the census.

This brief sketch of the housing system in Hennepin County highlights two critical points about the country as a whole. First, the supply of subsidized housing in the United States is limited by the relatively modest resources the federal government provides for housing assistance. An expansion of these benefits would provide needed support to low-income households in metropolitan areas around the country. Second, permanent housing programs within the homelessness response system are critical tools for moving people out of homelessness. In Hennepin County, of the 11,558 people who reside outside the bounds of the conventional housing market, roughly 74 percent reside in such permanent housing programs, almost 23 percent rely on emergency shelters and transitional housing facilities, and the remaining 3.5 percent are without shelter. If you accept the federal definition of homelessness—that is, as the state of sleeping outside (or other places not meant for habitation), in an emergency shelter, or in a transitional housing facility—then, by definition, greater investments in subsidized housing and the system of permanent housing programs could provide the housing that is needed to eliminate homelessness in many metropolitan areas in the country. Given the scope of the housing system in

Hennepin County—over five hundred thirty thousand housing units—a relatively modest increase in permanent housing (even on the scale of, say, three thousand units) shouldn't represent an insurmountable task.

But not every county is Hennepin. As most popular perceptions of homelessness are driven by the state of the issue in large coastal cities, we now turn our attention to the nation's two largest cities: New York and Los Angeles. According to the 2019 PIT count, New York City is home to the largest unhoused population in the country.[10] The composition of homelessness differs meaningfully in New York from other regions of the country: In New York, of the 78,604 people experiencing homelessness on a single night in 2019, nearly 92 percent were housed in emergency shelters while only 4.6 percent were unsheltered. (Compare this unsheltered rate to Hennepin County's 13 percent). This distribution differs meaningfully from Los Angeles County, where a far greater proportion of the homeless population is also unsheltered. The difference between New York City and Los Angeles can partially be explained by policy: New York City has a right-to-shelter law like Hennepin County, and, as a result, the city has built a comprehensive shelter system that far exceeds the shelter capacity provided by any other city in the country.

A review of the Housing Inventory Count, a report published annually by HUD for each Continuum of Care in the country, breaks down this housing support system. In 2019, New York City had 111,605 year-round beds for families and individuals in need. Included in that bed count were 75,245 emergency shelter beds and 33,203 associated with the types of permanent housing programs outlined in the previous section. (Recall that people living in the latter are not included in the federal definition of homelessness.) This substantial commitment to housing, combined with the right-to-shelter policy, helps to explain the relatively low rate of unsheltered homelessness in New York City.

From the perspective of the homelessness response system, Los Angeles looks very different. Of the 56,257 people experiencing homelessness—according to the 2019 PIT count—more than 75 percent live outside the emergency shelter system and are classified as unsheltered. Just under 11,000 people sleep in shelters in Los Angeles. Like New York, L.A. has a robust supply of beds associated with permanent housing programs (28,887). These permanent units are a critical tool used to keep people out of homelessness. The main takeaway from this comparison is that New York has a significant problem with homelessness that it currently addresses with a robust emergency shelter system. Additional investments in affordable housing and permanent housing within the homeless response system could help to limit the number of individuals and families that end up staying in one of the city's many homeless shelters. Los Angeles confronts a very different reality. L.A. could follow New York and greatly expand its emergency shelter capacity in the hopes of dramatically reducing its population of unsheltered people. But creating additional shelter capacity doesn't end homelessness: It recharacterizes it. People sleeping in shelters are still homeless—per the federal definition. A pressing question for cities like Los Angeles is whether to invest scarce resources to expand shelter capacity—in order to limit the number of people sleeping on the streets—or to apply those resources toward the development of more permanent forms of housing designed to end homelessness. This conundrum is at the heart of a housing policy challenge for other West Coast cities with high rates of unsheltered homelessness, including San Francisco, Portland, and Seattle.

Nationally, about five hundred sixty-eight thousand people experienced homelessness on a single night in 2019. Of those people, 63 percent were sheltered, either in emergency shelters or transitional housing facilities, and 37 percent were unsheltered— sleeping in tents, cars, abandoned buildings, parks, and other places not intended for human habitation. Just as the variety of homelessness experienced by Americans is not uniform, the identities and demographics of people without permanent housing vary considerably. For example, about 30 percent of the people experiencing homelessness are members of families, while the remaining 70 percent are in single-member households. Despite perceptions to the contrary, homelessness isn't just a condition experienced by mature adults: About 27 percent of people experiencing homelessness are twenty-four years old and younger. The vast majority of these young people are sheltered, but almost twenty-seven thousand are without shelter on a given night.

As with countless other injustices in the United States, homelessness is far from evenly distributed across races and ethnicities. Most notably, Black people are disproportionately represented in the homeless population: While Black people account for only 13 percent of the U.S. population, 40 percent of all people experiencing homelessness on any given night are Black. This racial disproportionality must undergird any analysis of homelessness in the country. Decades of overt and structural racism—in lending practices and employment opportunities, eviction rates and over-policing, from Jim Crow to the present day—have made it far too easy to lose your housing if you live in the United States and you're Black. Indigenous people, too, are at least three times more likely to experience homelessness in the United States than what one would expect given their proportion of the general population. And as researchers at the Center for Social Innovation noted recently, "Poverty alone does not explain the inequity. The proportion of Black and American Indian and Alaska Native individuals experiencing homelessness exceeds their proportion of those living in deep poverty."[11] While pathways into homelessness are knotty and imbued with all the complexities of individual experience, reasons for such disproportionately racialized rates of homelessness are readily available—and intuitive, given the country's broad oppression (and subsequent exclusion) of specific groups. Writing broadly, Shinn and Khadduri highlight four forms of social exclusion that provide a link between race and homelessness: lower incomes, less wealth accumulation, housing discrimination, and disproportionate rates of incarceration.[12] Each manifestation of exclusion acts to destabilize one's housing environment and can increase the likelihood of losing one's housing altogether. We return to race as a potential explanation for *regional variation* in the next chapter.

As race illustrates, homelessness is experienced differently by different people. And while this is a book about cities, it's worth understanding some of these experiences. A common tool used by researchers and analysts to understand homelessness is to identify three different categories of homelessness based on length of time spent without housing. Kuhn and Culhane, for example, used cluster analysis of homelessness spells to define a typology of homelessness with three categories: transitional, episodic, and chronic.[13] Those who are transitionally homeless lose their housing and interact with a homelessness response system (say, an emergency shelter) for brief periods of time. Episodic homelessness involves frequent entries into and exits from homelessness. People experiencing chronic homelessness remain unhoused for long periods of time—up to a year or longer.[14] A typology of homelessness matters because housing programs—and people's responses to these programs—depend on a variety of one's experiences with homelessness. For example, people who are chronically homeless often have more significant barriers to housing stability, including deep poverty, physical or mental health conditions, and substance-use issues, and by extension, will often need more than a little rent support to remain housed. Those who are transitionally homeless or homeless for the first-time might just need shelter, cash assistance, or employment support as they get back on their feet.

But these classifications of homelessness are important for another reason: When researchers analyze the annual one-night homelessness census, that cross-sectional view may not provide an accurate picture of this phenomenon. Consider the following hypothetical example in which there are two varieties of homelessness: chronic (longer than one year) and short-term (one month). Suppose a city conducts a PIT count in January—a cross-sectional estimate of the size of the homeless population—and finds ten people who are currently without housing: nine people experiencing short-term homelessness and one person experiencing chronic homelessness. This count would suggest that, on any given night, 10 percent of the city's homeless population is chronically homeless. But suppose this same city were to conduct a homeless census every month of the year. In February, for example, again the city surveys its unhoused population, and again the total count is ten. In this case, while the same chronically homeless person is included in this list of ten people, nine people the city hadn't seen the previous month are now experiencing short-term homelessness. Perhaps the people who were temporarily homeless in January had found housing and were no longer included in the count. In any case, based on the February count, 10 percent of the city's unhoused population is chronically homeless. But an analysis of both months together yields a very different conclusion: If we consider everyone who experienced homelessness in January and February—a period prevalence measure as opposed to a cross-sectional estimate—there are eighteen temporarily homeless people and one person who is chronically homeless. In other words, PIT estimates of the homeless population exaggerate the proportion of the population experiencing chronic homelessness. As the authors of one of the first studies to characterize the prevalence of homelessness over longer periods of time wrote, "Because these studies [covering shorter periods of time] overrepresent chronic, long-term homeless people, they distort our image of who becomes homeless and mistakenly overemphasize the importance of personal deficits as causes of homelessness."[15]

Regardless of the method jurisdictions use to measure rates of homelessness, they're also faced with the central challenge of finding, identifying, and counting a hard-to-reach, often invisible population. Many researchers have highlighted the myriad difficulties facing CoCs as they attempt to measure the severity of homelessness.[16] The National Homeless Law Center (formerly the National Law Center on Homelessness and Poverty, a Washington, D.C., non-profit), for example, has voiced multiple concerns with HUD's point-in-time counts. These points of objection include inconsistent methodology and definitions deployed by HUD over time, the undercount of unsheltered people—who are often more difficult to survey—and the fact that only certain types of housing instability meet the federal definition of homelessness.[17] (For example, people staying with friends or family in doubled-up living situations after losing their own housing are excluded from official homelessness statistics.) Researchers have used a variety of tools to test the validity and accuracy of the point-in-time count, and their results suggest that this approach meaningfully undercounts the population. Validation approaches range from planting research participants on the street to see if they'll be surveyed as part of a given jurisdiction's point-in-time count to statistical methods that estimate the degree of undercounting.[18] Kim Hopper and colleagues found that 29 percent of their plants were not discovered in the homelessness count, suggesting a material undercount of the total population experiencing homelessness.[19] Chris Glynn and Emily Fox leveraged statistical approaches to estimate the true population of people experiencing homelessness in the twenty-five largest cities in the country. Their findings suggest pervasive undercounting, with the estimated undercount far greater in cities with high rates of unsheltered homelessness (including Los Angeles, San Francisco, and Seattle). In New York, where the vast majority of people experiencing homelessness reside in shelters, the researchers' estimated actual 2016 count was about 4 percent higher than the HUD PIT estimates. In Los Angeles, the difference was almost 27 percent.[20] These caveats underly the many analyses that use these data to understand homelessness in the United States, including our own.

HOW HAS HOMELESSNESS CHANGED OVER TIME?

The modern era of homelessness began in the late 1970s and gained national attention during the recession of the early 1980s. As awareness of homelessness grew among policymakers and the general population, many imagined the phenomenon was a consequence of the economic downturn of the late 1970s and would evaporate once the economy rebounded.[21] Consistent with this perception, early efforts to address homelessness were managed by the Federal Emergency Management Agency (FEMA)—as if the crisis were temporary; akin to a flood or earthquake.

In light of a plainly growing problem, the federal government also sought to develop a greater understanding of the severity and scope of homelessness around the country. HUD conducted the first national PIT count in 1983–84, which revealed a national estimate of two hundred fifty thousand to three hundred fifty thousand people experiencing homelessness.[22] Subsequent research by Richard Freeman and Brian Hall estimated a national homeless population of two hundred seventy-nine thousand in 1983 and a range of three hundred forty-three thousand to three hundred sixty-three thousand in 1985.[23] As Freeman and Hall wrote, "Economic recovery will not solve the problem of homelessness, and . . . in the absence of changes in the housing market or in the economic position of the very poor, the U.S. will continue to be plagued with a problem of homelessness for the foreseeable future." The increase from 1983 to 1985 was particularly troubling to policymakers, because it came during a time of economic expansion. Given this evidence, scholars suggested that the kneejerk argument—that is, that an improving economy would ameliorate homelessness—was far from accurate.[24] By the close of the decade, those tasked with measuring the population of people experiencing homelessness agreed that the unhoused population in the country was in the range of two hundred thirty thousand to six hundred thousand. They also agreed the crisis was no earthquake. If nothing was done, homelessness would become a permanent fixture of American society.[25] In 1987, Freeman and Hall explained the problem of homelessness with echoes of today's crisis:

While we are loath to generalize from a single area, the pattern of rapidly rising land values, rents, and housing market problems for the poor in Massachusetts raises the possibility that future economic progress, including full employment of the type enjoyed in Massachusetts, may exacerbate rather than alleviate the housing problems of the poor. One can easily devise a scenario in which economic growth raises demand for land, inducing landlords to develop higher-quality properties, pricing out of the market those whose incomes do not rise with the rate of growth.[26]

We are now living in the researchers' "foreseeable future." The point-in-time estimates of homelessness from the 1980s suggested that between 0.11 percent and 0.25 percent of the U.S. population was homeless on any given night. It should not be lost on readers that these rates are very similar to that implied by the 2019 point-in-time count (0.17 percent). In 2007, HUD issued its first Annual Homeless Assessment Report to Congress based on data from 2005. In this study, an aggregation of CoCs' PIT counts, HUD estimated that 754,147 people had experienced homelessness on a single night in 2005—a number that, on a per capita basis, had not risen from a prior measure in 1996.[27] This count suggested that roughly one-quarter of one percent of the general population experienced homelessness at a single time—the high-water mark for post-1980 PIT estimates of homelessness in the country. By 2019, the rate had fallen to 0.17 percent. In sum, over the last forty years, between 0.11 percent and 0.25 percent of the general population has experienced homelessness, based on point-in-time counts.

Given the challenges of PIT estimates of homelessness outlined above, many researchers have argued for the use of longitudinal analyses to estimate the prevalence of homelessness—that is, the rate of people who experience homelessness *over* a given period of time, whether, say, a year or the lifetime of a person. Following the earlier work of Bruce Link and colleagues, more recent research suggests a lifetime homelessness prevalence between 4.2 and 6.2 percent.[28] These estimates would suggest that HUD's estimate of five hundred sixty-eight thousand people experiencing homelessness is a gross mischaracterization of the issue. Many multiples of that number lose their housing during their lifetime, and—given the well-documented negative consequences of homelessness—large swaths of the U.S. population face significant barriers as they attempt to recover from a spell of homelessness.

HOW DO WE EXPLAIN HOMELESSNESS?

Abundant research and analysis support a wide range of potential causes and drivers of homelessness. As consumers of this information and data, it can be difficult to navigate this complex, and, at times, contradictory body of evidence. One important way to sift through and organize research on homelessness is to differentiate by unit of analysis. Some studies focus on the individual; others focus on geographic units (like cities, counties, or metropolitan areas). As Brendan O'Flaherty noted, "Studies that take as their unit of observation homelessness rates in different cities have generally found that housing market conditions have large effects. . . . By contrast, studies that take individuals as their unit of observation find weak effects for housing market conditions of the cities where the individuals find themselves, and strong effects for personal characteristics. The two types of studies seem to support contrasting policy advice: city-level studies say reduce rents and increase vacancies, individual-level studies say work on pathology and poverty."[29]

O'Flaherty resolves this conflict by arguing that to understand homelessness, one needs to consider the interaction (in a statistical sense) between structural factors (like housing market dynamics) and individual factors (like job loss, mental illness, and addiction).[30] In this book, we argue that each set of factors is useful in its own right—depending on the question at hand. The distinction is hardly controversial. Studies concerning individual explanations of homelessness help to predict who, in a given city, will become homeless; and studies with cities as their unit of analysis help to explain why some regions see higher rates of homelessness than others. Because the latter question is the focus of this book, we'll devote more narrative energy to summarizing the state of this type of analysis, but in this section, we also offer an overview of the individually based research on homelessness.

Individual Attributes

The vast majority of CEOs in the United States are men. Given the present state of corporate leadership and its recent history, one can't help but concede that *maleness* increases the likelihood of becoming a CEO. And yet most of us understand the relationship between corporate leadership and gender to be a function of structural explanations that keep women out of leadership roles—among them sexism, unbalanced childcare responsibilities and parental leave policies, underpayment, and gatekeeping processes. Would we say that gender *causes* the apparent disproportionate representation of men in the C-Suite? Of course not. Gender interacts with other societal forces to produce a disparate outcome.

Are people with incomes below the federal poverty line more likely to experience homelessness than people with higher incomes? The answer is, unequivocally, yes. Are people with severe mental illness at higher risk for homelessness? Most certainly, yes. Are Black people disproportionately represented in the homeless population? For all the reasons briefly outlined previously in this chapter, we know this to be true. And while disaggregating the population experiencing homelessness is an essential focus of homelessness research, demographic attributes are never inherently causal drivers of the problem at hand. We can think about individual attributes and their relationship to homelessness in two distinct manners. First, there are individual *vulnerabilities* (including poverty, mental illness, addiction, and domestic violence) that may increase the risk or likelihood of experiencing homelessness for any given person. Second, there are individual *attributes*—such as race and sexual orientation—that may increase the risk of homelessness when they interact with structural barriers like racism and other forms of discrimination and oppression. In the next chapter, we address the relationship between these factors and our object of interest: regional variation in homelessness.

A wide range of individual vulnerabilities and attributes are associated with higher rates of homelessness, including being male,[31] unmarried,[32] having low income,[33] being older,[34] being non-white[35] and identifying as LGBTQ—especially among youth.[36] In many of these cases, these personal attributes collide with societal discrimination or other forms of social exclusion to increase the likelihood that people with these characteristics experience homelessness. Interpersonal relationships (or the lack thereof) can also contribute to housing instability. Homelessness risk is greater for people with limited support from a community, low self-esteem, and a lack of belonging.[37] Researchers have also noted that people experiencing homelessness have fewer familial ties and tend to live farther away from relatives than those who are housed.[38] Fertig and Reingold found that low levels of family support increase the risk of future homelessness.[39] In a confirmation of the psychological research underscoring the importance of social ties and connections, Corinth and Rossi-de Vries found, all else being equal, that strong social ties (especially among family) help to mitigate the risk of homelessness in adulthood.[40]

In addition to personal attributes and relationships, there are a variety of individual vulnerabilities that also increase the risk of homelessness, including suffering from depression,[41] experiencing mental illness or other psychiatric disorders,[42] use or abuse of drugs and alcohol,[43] and having a criminal record or history of incarceration.[44] Researchers have found that many of these individual risk factors also increase the length of homelessness spells.[45]

Arguably, the most common public and media narratives surrounding homelessness concerns addiction, mental illness, and behavioral health care—particularly among the chronic, unsheltered population. The use of illicit drugs, unhealthy levels of alcohol consumption, and severe mental health conditions are more heavily represented in the chronically homeless population than in the general public.[46] Several studies suggest that between 25 and 40 percent of the individual (i.e., non-family) homeless population has a substance use disorder and about a quarter of the single adult population experiences some form of mental illness.[47] By extension, researchers suggest that the odds or likelihood of someone experiencing homelessness increases with the presence of these conditions.[48]

While these rates are high, it is important to note they apply only to the subpopulation of people experiencing homelessness in single-person households—roughly 70 percent of the total population. The remaining 30 percent are members of multi-person households, and data suggests that substance use disorders, in particular, are much lower within this subpopulation of people experiencing homelessness—11 percent (alcohol) and 13 percent (drugs)—according to a recent study of people staying in family shelters.[49] Serious mental illness and substance use disorders are also prevalent in the general population. According to the 2019 National Survey on Drug Use and Health, 20.4 million people (twelve years or older) had a substance use disorder—over 7.4 percent of that population—and 5.2 percent of all adults (eighteen years and older) had a serious mental illness. Certainly, these conditions are disproportionately represented in the population of people experiencing homelessness, but two central points are worth making: First, a majority of people experiencing homelessness *don't* have these conditions; and second, the vast majority of people with these conditions never lose their housing.

A related narrative of homelessness emphasizes the lack of institutional care available to people with serious mental illness. By this logic, the de-institutionalization movement that began in the 1950s and accelerated in the 1960s and '70s is to blame for the rise of homelessness in the country.[50] Proponents of this argument suggest that the closure of institutional settings for people with serious mental illness pushed this cohort of people onto the street. More recent research, however, has questioned this explanation—not least because large reductions in institutional care preceded the rise of homelessness by more than a decade.[51] More plausibly, these researchers argue, the modern rise in homelessness stems from a growing lack of affordable housing. These rising costs exact a significant toll on households with a range of vulnerabilities, including poverty, addiction, and mental illness.

One challenge in explaining homelessness with individual factors is that the presence of various conditions may not provide a causal explanation for homelessness. Indeed, ample evidence suggests that substance abuse is not only a cause of homelessness, but also a consequence.[52] Given that causal arrows point in both directions, the disproportionate presence of mental illness and substance use in the homeless population makes further sense. Researchers also highlight the well-characterized psychological concept of negative duration dependence. Also known as "scarring," the phenomenon suggests that the longer a person experiences a condition like homelessness, the harder it is to exit that state. For people without housing, scarring can occur through declining mental and physical health, a reduction or gap in skills or work history, or alteration of one's physical appearance—all of which make securing housing and employment more challenging.[53] People experiencing homelessness suffer from poor sleep and sleep deprivation,[54] they experience physical and sexual abuse at higher rates than the general population,[55] and they are lonelier and more separated from important social networks.[56] These forms of hardship and trauma emphasize how adverse events may lower one's mental health and emotional well-being.[57] In other words, the drug use and mental illness that observers frequently blame for homelessness may instead represent a natural bodily response to the harsh and often traumatic conditions that people experiencing homelessness face on a daily basis.

Structural Factors

As noted above, individual attributes often interact with structural forces to produce homelessness. Age, gender, and race, in isolation, offer limited explanations for homelessness—until they interact with forces of systemic and systematic discrimination (policies and people) that limit access to education, health care, employment, and housing. These same forces incarcerate and evict people of color at disproportionate rates. One consequence of these structural forces is disproportionality in the population of people who experience homelessness. Prominent homelessness scholar Martha Burt summarized this relationship: "Most demographic factors quickly disappear as proximate causes [of homelessness] when other factors representing personal vulnerabilities are available for examination. The *underlying* causes of homelessness, the structural conditions of housing and labor markets that turn vulnerabilities into loss of housing, do not lie within individuals at all and are thus difficult to include in analyses based on individual data."[58]

Research on such structural factors confronts these causal pathways head-on. Studies on recessions in the 1990s and early 2000s, for example, noted (perhaps unsurprisingly) that homelessness increases during times of economic hardship—although the effect of the Great Recession of 2007–09 on homelessness was less pronounced than that of earlier crises.[59] Researchers have highlighted that the risk of homelessness increases with poverty,[60] foreclosures,[61] and high housing costs.[62] Some have emphasized the effects of regional weather as a potential structural driver of homelessness, with higher temperatures associated with higher rates of homelessness.[63] Recent research suggests, however, that the relationship between weather and homelessness is more complicated.[64] As much of this book deals with structure, we save our discussion of the mechanics of these interactions for later chapters.

A subset of the literature uses inter-community data on U.S. homelessness to generate causal explanations. Our book follows this tradition, in that we leverage communities (cities or counties) as our unit of analysis.[65] And while most of these studies use the hundreds of CoCs in the country to compare rates of homelessness across the country, examine various time periods, and deploy a wide range of statistical tools, one observation arises again and again: the importance of housing conditions on rates of homelessness. In virtually all studies that analyze intercommunity variation in homelessness rates, measures of rent costs have been identified as significant predictors of homelessness.[66]

One of the challenges of comparing these studies is that their authors draw data from different time periods, specify different analytic models, and break down their data in different manners: urban versus rural CoCs, families versus single-person households, and sheltered versus unsheltered. In aggregate, it's difficult to arrive at a perfectly consistent message about the drivers of homelessness. Beyond the clear message about housing costs, researchers have found that myriad other variables predict higher regional rates of homelessness, including the presence of more single-person households,[67] low rental market vacancy rates,[68] a higher percentage of renter households,[69] higher property values,[70] lower household income or higher poverty,[71] higher rates of home ownership,[72] a greater presence of households that recently moved,[73] as well as regional demographic attributes like higher percentages of baby boomers or greater proportions of Hispanic households.[74]

In an important study of all CoCs in the country (including urban, suburban, and rural areas), Maria Hanratty used two different statistical models to explain the drivers of homelessness and develop a causal argument. First, she used regression to explain regional variation and found rental costs and poverty rates to be important predictors of regional rates of homelessness. In a second model specification, to identify changes over time within a given community, she controlled for the presence of unobserved, regionally specific factors (i.e., fixed effects) and found that rental costs were the primary causal explanation for changes in rates of homelessness. Hanratty also identified different effects based on policy variation: Poverty had a stronger causal influence in locations with right-to-shelter policies.[75]

Structural factors may not exert the same effect in all locations. For example, Glynn and Fox suggest that the relationship between rental costs and homelessness is strongest in New York City, Los Angeles, Washington, D.C., and Seattle—some of the cities with the largest per capita rates of homelessness in the country.[76] Glynn and colleagues characterized inflection points in the rent-homelessness relationship. Homelessness begins to accelerate more rapidly in places where median rent as a percentage of median household income exceeds 32 percent. The inflection point finding parallels the conventional definition of what it means to be burdened by housing costs: the point at which housing costs consume 30 percent of income.[77] Given this literature, there is little doubt that housing market factors—notably, rent levels—play an important role in driving homelessness, even if these effects may vary based on geographic context.[78]

Bad Luck

Writing for Vox, the author Veronica Harnish notes: "There are so many ways to get down on your luck, or become homeless, and so few means to escape. Economic inequality and a system built to perpetuate it is the problem—homelessness is the result for people without a safety net."[79] At the time she penned the essay in question, Harnish had been homeless three times. She had jobs, mostly government contract work. But she didn't have a lot of savings, and upon losing a job, she couldn't afford the rent and was usually left sleeping in her car. It wasn't that she wasn't trying: It was just that the deck was stacked against her. Even her employer, the public sector, didn't quite have what she needed. "Impoverished, working single women without children do not get top priority on long waitlists for subsidized housing, rapid rehousing, or other government services or benefits," she writes.[80]

The final category of explanations for homelessness that arises in academic and popular narratives is that of bad luck. Given the dichotomy outlined above—between structural and individual factors—we might consider luck as another individual-level factor that can increase the risk of homelessness. Examples of negative luck include job loss, injury or illness, breakdown of a car, breakdown of personal relationships, and many other factors that can lead to eviction or foreclosure.[81] Certainly, not all bad luck produces a spell of homelessness. Some households hold other assets or resources that protect them from an incident of bad luck cascading into a severe personal crisis. Some people, like Harnish, don't have a backup. Marah Curtis and colleagues, for example, studied a health shock—the birth of a child with a severe health condition—to understand how unexpected life events impact the risk of experiencing homelessness. In a finding consistent with many theories of homelessness, Curtis found "the shock substantially increases the likelihood of family homelessness, particularly in cities with high housing costs. The findings are consistent with the economic theory of homelessness, which posits that homelessness results from a conjunction of adverse circumstances in which housing markets and individual characteristics collide."[82] In this book, we are interested in these collisions.

WHAT ARE THE CONSEQUENCES OF HOMELESSNESS?

Research demonstrates that even short spells of homelessness can be damaging to the people who experience it, especially children. Other consequences of urban homelessness exist at the community level: some quantifiable—such as public spending on emergency health and public safety, as well as lost tourism revenue—and others less tangible, including the sadness, discomfort, shame, or anger that people with housing may feel in the face of people without it.

For adults, the consequences of homelessness are dire. People who experience homelessness die at earlier ages,[83] contract infectious diseases at higher rates,[84] are hospitalized at earlier ages and make more trips to the emergency room,[85] are more likely to be victims of physical and sexual assault,[86] and misuse substances at higher rates.[87] Researchers have also demonstrated that the risks and stress associated with homelessness contribute to higher rates of mental illness among the chronically homeless population.[88]

The life-long consequences of homelessness in childhood are particularly troubling given the long-lasting, negative effects. Research on child and youth homelessness reports a range of negative outcomes, including developmental delays for young children,[89] high levels of anxiety,[90] poor health outcomes,[91] inadequate preventive medical care,[92] higher levels of emotional and behavior problems,[93] and academic underachievement and delays.[94] Homeless youth are also disproportionately exposed to abuse of all types, including sexual trauma.[95]

For researchers, journalists, and members of the general public alike, it is easy and convenient to pathologize homelessness: highlighting the mental and physical causes and consequences of this condition that are most conspicuous and quantifiable. But the observed and more readily measurable effects of homelessness fail to capture the harmful emotional consequences, as well. Homeless adults report much higher rates of loneliness than do adults who are housed.[96] Children who experience homelessness are much more likely to persistently feel unsafe than children with housing.[97] Naomi Thulien and colleagues conducted a qualitative study of formerly homeless youth in Toronto about their experiences attempting to effectively integrate back into (housed) society. The summary of their findings underscores the significant emotional toll of experiences with homelessness: "Unaffordable housing, limited education, inadequate employment opportunities, poverty-level income, and limited social capital made it remarkably challenging for the young people to move forward. As the study progressed, the participants' ability to formulate long-range plans were impeded as they were forced to focus on day-to-day existence. Over time, living in a perpetual state of poverty led to feelings of 'outsiderness,' viewing life as a game of chance, and isolation."[98]

Numerous studies have estimated the annual community costs of homelessness, but these estimates vary considerably. Most frequently, cost studies are based on the service histories of people experiencing homelessness. Examples of increases in public service use related to homelessness include upticks in emergency room visits, police and fire departments responding to homelessness-related calls, public health expenditures, and the direct costs associated with operating a municipal homelessness response system. In a literature review on the costs and benefits of the Housing First approach—a collection of policies that aim to eliminate barriers to housing programs for people experiencing homelessness—Ly and Latimer highlighted studies from the United States and Canada that show annual costs of homelessness between $30,000 and $100,000 per person.[99] All the studies were conducted between 2000 and 2015. A study using data from Australia reported people experiencing homelessness used an average of $48,000 of government services over the course of a year.[100] The study included costs associated with "police, prison, probation, parole, courts, emergency department, hospital-admitted patients, ambulance, mental health, and homelessness services data."[101]

The benefit of cost studies is that they help to benchmark the significant public expenditures associated with homelessness, highlight alternatives to this spending, and draw our attention to the manners in which the public sector is (intentionally or otherwise) responding to the crisis at hand. According to homelessness researcher Dennis Culhane, "An important benefit of the analyses of homelessness services utilization and costs is that this research can demonstrate that people who experience homelessness do not just use shelters, but are often the clients, sometimes the well-known clients, of these larger and more intensively funded service systems."[102]

In addition to the obvious system-wide costs attributed to homelessness, other ancillary costs are frequently ignored—and these costs may be borne by people who do not experience homelessness. These costs don't need to be financial in nature. (Consider feelings of guilt or fear in the presence of people experiencing homelessness.) Many housed urban dwellers have concerns—whether humanitarian or spiteful—related to issues of cleanliness and safety frequently associated with unsheltered homelessness. In short, homelessness exacts a considerable toll on society, and those tangible and intangible costs cannot be ignored. Frustrations or fears related to homelessness have prompted cities to respond aggressively to police or control the unhoused in an effort to mitigate these costs.

Critical sociologists, urbanists, and geographers have written extensively about exclusionary efforts that cities have undertaken to hide and/or punish the poor. The motivation for these punitive approaches is often financial: The homeless, and other people living on the margins of society, are bad for business. According to geographer Geoffrey DeVerteuil, to attract capital and the middle class, "cities must create positive images for themselves, especially with regards to the all-important tourism and convention industry. With less room to maneuver, cities are increasingly obliged to 'hide' the growing gap between rich and poor in order to remain competitive, leading to a mandatory punitive response to visible urban problems." DeVerteuil goes on to quote the geographer Gordon MacLeod: "The continuous renaissance of the entrepreneurial city [is] tightly 'disciplined' through a range of architectural forms and institutional practices so that the enhancement of a city's image is not compromised by the visible presence of ... very marginalized groups."[103] If you've ever seen concrete spikes lining the perimeter of a building, you know what MacLeod is getting at.

We see echoes of the financial logic in press accounts about the negative impact of homelessness on local commerce. Writers frequently highlight the link between unsheltered homelessness and either real or perceived reductions in commerce and tourism.[104] Reports suggest that tourism and conference business have suffered in certain cities due to concerns over homeless encampments, public safety, and a general lack of cleanliness. Oracle Corporation's "Open World" conference moved to Las Vegas from San Francisco over concerns associated with hotel costs and "poor street conditions."[105] Newspapers have chronicled the frustrations of tourists who have confronted the unsheltered homelessness crisis in West Coast cities. Take Glen Commins, a tourist from Tennessee, who recently participated in an interview with the Seattle ABC affiliate, KOMO News, in front of the iconic Ivar's waterfront seafood restaurant. "This is your touristy spot, you know, and it looks dirty," he said. "It makes the city look dirty and this is a cool city."[106] For people like Commins—and maybe businesses like Ivar's—these costs are real. While difficult to calculate, the myriad costs associated with the homelessness crisis are borne by a wide variety of a city's people.

HOW DO WE STOP OR PREVENT HOMELESSNESS?

In an echo of the literature that examines the causes of homelessness, studies focused on ending or preventing homelessness can also be divided by unit of observation. While some researchers focus on the effectiveness of specific interventions—programs designed to prevent or end homelessness—for specific types of people, others seek to understand how various treatments affect the rate of homelessness within a particular region.

While we can understand the causes of homelessness at the individual or family level as a somewhat complex interaction between individual factors, structural drivers, and misfortune, understanding responses to homelessness is a more straightforward task. In study after study, the most effective treatment for homelessness is housing. In some cases, this housing comes in the form of rental assistance; in others, it might be a subsidized housing unit with supportive services. In all cases, the housing unit in question is the difference between a homelessness crisis and the time and space needed to get back on one's feet. The evidence is also clear that attempting to resolve one's serious mental illness or substance use conditions in isolation fails to resolve one's homelessness crisis, because safe and stable housing is essential to a healthy and productive life. Treatment of individual pathologies will not end homelessness.[107] Providing housing as a human right, not as a good or service available only to those who can afford it, is the key. In a May 2020 editorial in the *New York Times*, Benyamin Appelbaum wrote, "The federal government could render homelessness rare, brief and nonrecurring. The cure for homelessness is housing."[108]

In their book *In the Midst of Plenty: Homelessness and What to Do About It*, Marybeth Shinn and Jill Khadduri devote significant attention to efforts to end and prevent homelessness at the individual or family level. Given the evidence base, they suggest different housing interventions for different sub-populations of people experiencing homelessness. For families, Shinn and Khadduri argue long-term rental subsidies are the most effective policy. Primary support for this argument comes from the Family Options study.[109] This study was a federal trial in which long-term housing vouchers (mostly Housing Choice Vouchers) were provided to families living in shelter. Families who were able to use the rental support to lease a unit were far less likely than other groups—who received short-term rental subsidies and transitional housing—to return to shelter.

For single adults experiencing homelessness, the task is more difficult. While many families are likely to end a bout of homelessness with housing support, many homeless individuals— especially those who are chronically homeless—may require housing *and* other supportive services. A central debate in homelessness policy over the past two decades has pivoted on the question of which of these needs ought to be met first. Here, the best research appears to suggest that the most promising

intervention for individuals experiencing chronic homelessness is the provision of housing itself under a supportive housing model (including via the Housing First approach), in which
support services are voluntary as opposed to mandated.[110] In
contrast, researchers have found the treatment-first model—
in which serious mental illness or substance use disorders are
treated prior to housing program participation—to be less effective than public and nonprofit programs that provide housing
without any requirement for treatment.[111] Ultimately, most contemporary scholars and policy analysts have concluded that
permanent housing programs with voluntary support services
offer the most effective intervention for single adults experiencing homelessness.[112]

A second thread of research considers whether investments
to end or prevent homelessness alter rates of homelessness at
a regional level. But because housing interventions are rarely
conducted in a manner that lends itself to analysis via the sci-
entific method—there is no randomized control trial of, say,
doubling homelessness service-delivery-budgets—determin-
ing the true comparative efficacy of these programs and investments is more difficult. Homelessness occurs within a dynamic
housing and support system in which housing availability and
rents evolve over time—as do the services and supports available to households. In many instances, the best that researchers
can do is observe a change in one or more of these factors and
assess whether there's a corresponding effect on the outcomes
of interest: rates of homelessness in a given region. Numerous
studies, for example, have sought to characterize the relationship
between funding (typically federal funding) for a public-sector
homelessness response and homelessness. The underlying question of this type of research is a fair one: Do federal investments

in homelessness reduce homelessness? As cited above, existing literature illustrates that a range of programs reduce homelessness at an individual level, so the question here is whether we can observe these effects at a community level.

Given the research conducted over the last decade, the relationship between federal investments in homelessness and rates of homelessness is frustratingly mixed. A common theme in this literature—whether stated or unstated—is the issue of moral hazard. Some argue that additional investments in shelter and permanent supportive housing (PSH) may create incentives for people experiencing homelessness to use these services at higher rates and for longer periods of time.[113] The first studies to use HUD PIT counts to estimate the relationship between federal funding for homelessness and rates of homelessness found modest, negative relationships between the two factors—that is, more spending, less homelessness.[114] Byrne and colleagues (2014) documented a modest effect of investments in permanent supportive housing on the size of the chronically homeless population, and Moulton (2013) saw this population shrink with more federal spending on homelessness in a given region. In another study of the effect of PSH investments, Igor Popov found a modest reduction in total homelessness from additional PSH investments.[115] More recent studies have examined subpopulations of people experiencing homelessness and reported varying effects of federal spending. Popov, for example, reported that federal homelessness investments reduce the individual unsheltered count—as many unsheltered individuals move into shelter—while greater total investments increase family homelessness in a given region, as additional housing and shelter capacity may draw families from other regions or from other precariously housed situations toward the sites of investment.

In an echo of the findings from Popov, David Lucas suggested that greater federal investments in homelessness increase rates of sheltered homelessness: Federal funding can significantly increase shelter capacity, so the public homelessness response system can accommodate more people—either coming from unsheltered locations or from other precariously housed situations.[116] In one case, the overall homeless count increases (if people enter the system from, for example, a doubled-up living situation), while in the other case (an unsheltered person moving into shelter), there is no change in the overall level of homelessness.

Given mixed evidence for the efficacy of federal investments in homelessness, critics may wonder whether existing programs should see their funding increased—or even continued. A few points are worth making. First, for many people experiencing homelessness, living in a quality shelter is preferable to living unsheltered on the street. By extension, investments that fail to reduce overall levels of homelessness—but instead shift homelessness from the street into shelters—ought not be viewed as worthless or ineffective, as they're responding to people's immediate needs.

Second, that greater investments in the homelessness response system sometimes appear to pull people into that system suggests that there are many precariously housed people who desperately need housing. We argue that findings related to pull factors into homelessness imply a housing crisis that runs far deeper than headline numbers describe. If anything, these studies emphasize the necessity of continuing to provide adequate quantities of shelter and PSH—while also addressing the broader housing market conditions that create the demand for homelessness services.

Most of the studies highlighted thus far have examined the relationship between investments in the homelessness system itself (including temporary and permanent housing programs like emergency shelters, permanent supportive housing, and transitional housing) as opposed to the overall supply of affordable housing in a given region. When researchers analyzed the relationship between affordable housing built with Low-Income Housing Tax Credits and rates of homelessness within a community, they reported that while construction of affordable units did not alter the level of homelessness in a given neighborhood, it did reduce the level of homelessness at a county level.[117] This finding offers important evidence about the relationship between housing supply, affordability, and the level of homelessness in a community. Though some researchers question the efficacy of federal investments in homelessness, most agree that lower housing prices will help reduce rates of homelessness.[118] This agreement on housing costs as a mechanism to reduce rates of homelessness highlights the structural changes—beyond conventional homelessness policies and programs—needed to prevent the condition at its root.

With a broader understanding of homelessness—who experiences it, how it has changed over time, its causal drivers, its effects, and efforts to end or prevent it—we now turn our attention to the book's central purpose: explaining regional variation in rates of homelessness.

PART II

Causes

CHAPTER THREE

Individual

Near the top of an hour-long television special that aired on the Seattle-area ABC affiliate KOMO-4 in early 2019, the narrator posed a question: "What if Seattle is dying, and we don't even know it?" It's a worthy, if provocative, notion. Certainly, we would want to know what this means and whether it's the case. The documentary, *Seattle Is Dying,* a splashy feature on homelessness that would go on to make national headlines, was clear in its diagnosis. Seattle is dying, homelessness is to blame, and the homeless are to blame for their lack of housing. The *National Review* sums up the documentary's thesis by pointing to drugs, noting that "rampant and untreated and unprosecuted drug use ... [causes a] chain reaction of widespread crime and intense degradation of public places." And this, the reviewer asserts, "is the core of Seattle's decline."[1]

Seattle is far from the only city in which these concerns are voiced by observers and concerned residents. In *City Journal,* a publication of the Manhattan Institute, contributing editor Heather Mac Donald penned a 2019 article entitled, "San Francisco, Hostage to the Homeless." In an echo of *Seattle Is Dying,*

Mac Donald writes, "Failure to enforce basic standards of public behavior has made one of America's great cities increasingly unlivable."[2] Supported by jarring photographs and firsthand interviews with unsheltered San Franciscans, Mac Donald argued that the city's under-policing of drug crimes and permissive policies have encouraged many people to choose to remain homeless once they find themselves on the street—altogether contributing to a breakdown in social order and "bourgeois norms." Near the end of her diagnosis, she offers a prescription: "If San Francisco wanted to give its homeless addicts their best shot at stability, it would go after the open-air drug trade with every possible tool, including immigration law, however unlikely such a change of course is."

In this chapter, we begin the empirical portion of this book by asking whether diagnoses of homelessness like KOMO's and Mac Donald's can explain the conspicuous variation in rates of homelessness across the country. Among the explanations we consider are substance use, mental illness, poverty, and unemployment. We also address the role of "bad luck" as offered by Brendan O'Flaherty.[3] In essence, we argue that if these individual conditions have no positive statistical relationship with rates of homelessness between cities, then we can't consider these factors to be the underlying cause of regional variation in homelessness. And by definition, if they can't explain regional variation, then they can't tell us why a city like San Francisco's homelessness crisis is so much more severe than, say, Charlotte's.

THE ECOLOGICAL FALLACY

Central to this book is the concerted effort to focus our attention on differences between cities rather than those between individual people. We—perhaps like planners, policymakers, or other concerned residents—want to understand why some cities have high rates of homelessness and others do not. (Other people studying homelessness, like case managers working for service-delivery organizations, might be more interested in the pathways into and out of homelessness for a specific individual.) Without knowing anything about homelessness in the cities in our sample, one might imagine that underlying variation in their rates of homelessness might be driven by the fact that the cities in question are somehow organized differently—whether socially, politically, or economically. From a similar position of unfamiliarity, someone else might imagine that the underlying variation is driven by differences in the composition of the cities' populations. In September 2019, the Trump Administration's Council of Economic Advisors published a report on homelessness and argued as much, noting, "Severe mental illness, substance use problems, histories of incarceration, low incomes, and weak social connections each increase an individual's risk of homelessness, and higher prevalence in the population of these factors may increase total homelessness."[4] Using individual risk factors to make predictions about population-level prevalence is frequently incorrect, and in this specific case, it is.

One of the risks of analyzing social phenomena at the scale of the city is that it can lead to misleading or inaccurate conclusions about the underlying population in a given geography. Before individual-level data were widely available through databases like the Integrated Public Use Microdata Series (IPUMS), social science researchers would often leverage summary data at a broader unit of analysis—neighborhood, city, county, state, or nation—to draw conclusions about people who live in that particular location. Research has repeatedly shown that such generalizations are inappropriate and frequently incorrect.[5] These generalizations are not unique to social science research, either; rather, they're symptoms of a broader danger in statistical analysis that arises when comparing aggregate measures to their constituent parts. Broadly speaking, the phenomenon—known as the ecological fallacy—occurs when findings generated at an ecological unit of analysis (city, county, state, or nation) are mapped back to the individuals in those jurisdictions. Using individual-level data, we can (and ought to) test whether broader conclusions based on population measures of larger areas of geographic aggregation remain true for individual people who live in those areas.

A common example of an ecological fallacy stems from the analysis of literacy and immigration.[6] Imagine a study of U.S. cities that reveals, among other findings, that cities with the highest English literacy rates also have the highest rates of immigration. Based on this observation, one might conclude—and statistical averages across cities would support the conclusion—that immigrants have high levels of English literacy. But an analysis of individual-level data might suggest the opposite relationship: Since many U.S. immigrants must learn English as a second language, rates of English literacy among immigrants are lower than that of the U.S.-born population. As it turns out, on average, people simply immigrate to places with high existing rates of English literacy. Using city-level data to make assumptions about the attributes of individuals in those cities leads to an incorrect conclusion: an ecological fallacy.

In this book we are careful to avoid committing an ecological fallacy of our own. We avoid much of the risk here in our choice of subject: We don't attempt to characterize the attributes or behaviors of individual people. This is a book about cities, and our conclusions remain about cities. Certainly, given the evidence laid out in the last chapter, attributes that can sort people into groups are associated with homelessness, among them race, drug and alcohol use and abuse, mental illness, poverty status, unemployment, eviction history, and the breakdown of relationships. In this chapter, as we investigate some of these individual-level factors, we merely ask whether variation in these attributes exerts any meaningful effect on rates of homelessness at a higher level of analysis—the city or county. If levels of drug use are not disproportionately elevated in places with high rates of homelessness, we can't in good faith cite drug use as the factor that explains geographic variation.

In fact, here we ultimately identify several instances in which other researchers' individual-level findings are not echoed in city-level analyses. This doesn't mean that these researchers' findings are incorrect; it means they can't be scaled up to explain intercity differences. We know that Black and Brown people, for example, are disproportionately likely to experience homelessness, as are people who are unemployed or who have low incomes. But at the level of a city, we find that homelessness thrives in places that are disproportionately white and Asian, with high median incomes, and low levels of unemployment. We would commit an ecological fallacy by arguing that highly paid white people are more likely to be homeless.

More importantly, one of the reasons ecological fallacies are of essential importance here is that our awareness of them allows us to avoid making dangerous claims about people and their experiences. If we publish a chart illustrating a negative relationship between poverty rates and homelessness rates, for example, that doesn't mean readers can assume that poverty doesn't cause homelessness. Individual-level relationships still hold. (It would be ludicrous to argue that poverty doesn't increase one's risk of experiencing homelessness.) In other words, it's still true that we know a lot about the risk factors that cause people to become homeless at the individual level. What this knowledge doesn't allow us to do in a de facto manner is scale these observations up to the level of the population and assume we'll find correlation—much less causality.

INDIVIDUAL FACTORS

In the remainder of this chapter, we explore the relationships between a range of individual explanations of homelessness and per capita rates of homelessness across the metropolitan areas in our sample. We begin with poverty.

Poverty

One of the most intuitive explanations of homelessness is poverty. By definition, for those looking for housing, a lack of material resources to procure it is at the root of homelessness—there is little debate on the relationship between poverty and homelessness. As described by Barrett Lee and colleagues, "The poverty component, though implicit, is fundamental: Affluent individuals who unexpectedly lose their housing (to fire, flood, and the like) can replace it quickly and avoid a prolonged homeless episode."[7] And yet, while it is obvious that people experiencing homelessness are most likely poor, there are many people with low incomes who remain housed their entire lives. Therefore, it is clear that a range of factors—including poverty—converge to help explain homelessness at the individual level.[8]

To identify the role that poverty plays in explaining variation in rates of homelessness across the country, we must first
understand the landscape of poverty in the country. Within our
sample, we see significant variation in poverty rates. The level
of poverty tends to be a bit lower in the county-based CoCs, as
these areas may also include affluent suburbs. Over the thirteen
years of data in our sample, the vast majority of county CoCs
have poverty rates between 10 and 20 percent, with Santa Clara
County (California) on the low end (often just above 6 percent) and a substantial cluster of counties—including Multnomah County (Portland, OR); Los Angeles County; Hamilton
County (Cincinnati, OH); Miami-Dade County; Dallas County;
and Sacramento County—occasionally reaching annual poverty rates near 20 percent. City-based CoCs have slightly higher
rates of poverty on average, along with greater variation in rates
between cities. Other than Detroit, which saw a poverty rate
as high as 42 percent in 2012, most city-CoC poverty rates fall
between 10 and 30 percent, with San Francisco exhibiting the
lowest rate of poverty of any city in the sample.

If poverty causes homelessness, one might assume—as the
Trump administration's Council of Economic Advisors has—
that regions with high rates of poverty will also have high rates
of homelessness; that is, a disproportionate presence of poor
people in a given location will lead to disproportionate rates of
homelessness. The actual relationship, shown in Figure 7, tells a
very different story. Poverty rates are, more often than not, relatively low in places with relatively high rates of homelessness.
Somewhat surprisingly, CoCs with the highest rates of poverty
in our sample (Detroit, Miami, Dallas, Cincinnati, and Philadelphia) have some of the lowest rates of homelessness in the country. This finding suggests that homelessness—at a metropolitan

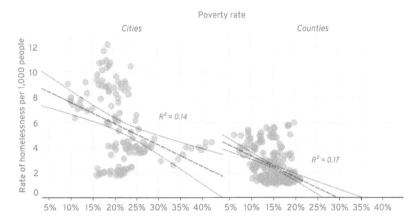

Figure 7. Percent with income below poverty level versus PIT count (per capita). Dashed lines indicate a linear regression of per capita PIT counts onto poverty rate between 2007 and 2019 for a sample of U.S. regions. Data source: HUD / U.S. Census Bureau

level—is more a symptom of affluence than of poverty.[9] In an echo of this observation, two recent studies by the consultancy McKinsey & Company highlight affluent coastal cities as the primary places in which contemporary homelessness thrives.[10] People experience poverty in every city in the country, but the consequences of being poor in a richer area appear to be more profound than they would be in a less affluent location, all else being equal.

One of the starkest examples of this relationship comes from Detroit, Michigan. Beginning in the middle of the last century, the decline of manufacturing—combined with the growth of the suburbs—reshaped this once prosperous manufacturing hub. In postwar Detroit, the automotive industry provided abundant manufacturing jobs that created and supported a strong and stable middle class. As these jobs disappeared, the city of

Detroit transformed: Economic activity slowed, unemployment increased, the population fell significantly, businesses left, and poverty rose. In *Origins of an Urban Crisis: Race and Inequality in Postwar Detroit*, historian Thomas Sugrue paints a vivid picture of the city's decline in its opening pages: "The story I tell is one of a city transformed. In the 1940s, Detroit was America's 'arsenal of democracy,' one of the nation's fastest growing boomtowns and home to the highest-paid blue-collar workers in the United States. Today, the city is plagued by joblessness, concentrated poverty, physical decay, and racial isolation."[11]

Sugrue attributes the decline of Detroit and other manufacturing cities in the United States to three different forces: loss of jobs, persistence of workplace discrimination, and racial segregation in housing. He argues that each of these forces, alone, could have had dire consequences, but when combined, they produced a devastating urban crisis that culminated in the city filing for bankruptcy in 2013. Detroit is not alone in experiencing such a decline; other manufacturing cities in the industrial Midwest and Northeast suffered a similar fate. But Detroit's decline has been the most precipitous. By 2010, over 38 percent of Detroit residents were living below the federal poverty line. That hasn't always been the case. In the 1970 census, the poverty rate in Detroit (14.9 percent) differed little from other cities in the country, including Chicago, Houston, Milwaukee, Minneapolis, San Francisco, and Seattle. In the same year, Atlanta, Boston, and Cleveland all had higher rates of poverty than Detroit. Forty years later, a substantial gap had emerged between dynamic, wealthy cities and Rust Belt victims of manufacturing decline. In the aftermath of the Great Recession, while Detroit and Cleveland saw 2010 poverty rates far above 30 percent, poverty in coastal cities like Seattle and San Francisco hovered around 13 percent. A huge gap had emerged between the metropolitan haves and the have-nots.

Despite these economic and social conditions, Detroit's level of homelessness is relatively low. Between 2009 and 2019, the per capita rate of homelessness in Detroit ranged from 2.6 per 1,000 people (in 2018) to 4.4 (in 2011)—far lower than many coastal cities, where per capita rates often exceed 10 per 1,000. These relatively low levels of homelessness challenge the prevailing narrative that homelessness is a result of poverty. As we'll argue more extensively in chapter 6, homelessness hasn't exploded in Detroit because—during the period of our study—population declines and low wages have helped keep housing abundant and relatively cheap. But as we've already seen, not all cities look like this one.

In 1970, the broad socioeconomic profiles of Boston and Detroit were remarkably similar. (Boston's poverty rate was modestly higher.) Like Detroit, Boston depended on manufacturing as its primary source of employment, and by 1970, the city had lost a significant proportion of its population as more and more people moved to the suburbs. The loss of people and jobs in Boston coincided with the deterioration of its manufacturing base. A report by the Boston Redevelopment Authority highlighted the important shift in the city's trajectory that occurred next: "To replace its shrinking industrial base the city needed to convert itself into a center of the service and finance based economy that was beginning to emerge nationwide. The concentration of world-class colleges and universities made the city a logical choice for the industries that were to eventually locate here."[12]

Today, Boston is a thriving East Coast hub known for its elite educational institutions and its leadership in industries like health care, professional services, and finance. Employment has increased dramatically in the city after falling during the 1970s. Over the past half-century, Boston built a modern economy on technological innovation and a highly educated workforce.

From 1970 to 2010, as the poverty rate in Boston increased modestly from 16 to about 20 percent, the proportion of people living in poverty in Detroit increased 2.5-fold from 15 to almost 40 percent. Yet despite the relative affluence of Boston, per capita rates of homelessness on any given night exceed 8 per 1,000, more than twice the level of Detroit. This stark contrast underscores the finding that poverty alone cannot explain regional variation in rates of homelessness—at least not in the manner that one might expect, given individual-level forces. At the level of the city, homelessness thrives amid affluence, not poverty.

Unemployment

We know from individual surveys (and common sense) that job loss can cause people to lose their housing.[13] This causal link between job loss and homelessness gets particular attention during times of economic hardship, when overall unemployment rises. During the Great Recession, analysts extensively discussed how widespread job losses could lead to higher levels of unemployment—and in turn, homelessness. In 2009, the National Coalition for the Homeless published a fact sheet on employment and homelessness, in which they noted that, "as the United States experiences the worst financial crisis since the Great Depression, the homeless population has increased significantly. The worsening economy and rising unemployment numbers emphasize a number of reasons why homelessness continues to exist and grow in exponential numbers in the United States."[14] The 2009 report stressed that while unemployment may produce a bout of homelessness, barriers associated with homelessness may also prolong a spell of joblessness and make securing new employment more difficult—the relationship could amount to a vicious cycle.[15] A decade later, the economic hardships associated with COVID-19 in 2020 have led many observers to makes similar arguments that the abrupt increase in unemployment could lead to far higher levels of homelessness than currently exist in the country. At the beginning of the pandemic, researcher Brendan O'Flaherty estimated a 40 to 45 percent increase in homelessness by the end of 2020.[16]

In our sample of cities and counties, a fairly predictable pattern emerges when analyzing unemployment between 2007 and 2019. As the economy expanded after the recession, unemployment rates decreased. By 2019, only one city in our sample—Detroit— had an unemployment rate over 10 percent. Philadelphia and Baltimore saw relatively high rates as well—over 7 percent. Among the counties in our sample, only one had an unemployment rate over 6 percent: Cuyahoga County (Cleveland). On the other side of the spectrum, we observe a number of metropolitan areas with very low unemployment rates. San Francisco, King County (Seattle), Santa Clara County (San Jose), Hennepin County (Minneapolis), Mecklenburg County (Charlotte), Miami-Dade County, and Travis County (Austin) all have unemployment rates below 4 percent. As in the case of poverty rates, we see meaningful geographic variation in unemployment rates around the country. Our question is whether this variation will help us explain why rates of homelessness differ across the United States.

Figure 8 highlights the relationship between unemployment and per capita rates of homelessness. In an illustration that mirrors the city-level relationship between poverty and homelessness, rates of homelessness are relatively low where unemployment is

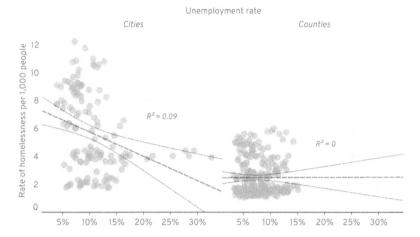

Figure 8. Unemployment rate versus PIT count (per capita). Dashed lines indicate a linear regression of per capita PIT counts onto the unemployment rate between 2007 and 2019 for a sample of U.S. regions. Data source: HUD / U.S. Census Bureau

high. It is only in areas with robust labor markets and low rates of unemployment—booming coastal cities—where homelessness is abundant.[17] In other words, rates of unemployment can't explain why coastal cities like San Francisco and Seattle have four times the rates of homelessness of Chicago. It is conceivable that rising unemployment—at a national scale—may increase average rates of homelessness throughout the nation, but higher proportions of unemployed people have no predictive value in terms of explaining regional variation.

The story of Philadelphia highlights how persistently high levels of unemployment can coexist with relatively modest levels of homelessness. In 1970, the civilian unemployment rate in Philadelphia was only 4.6 percent. Dominant employers at that time were in manufacturing, the retail trade, and professional services. As the nation writ large transitioned its economic engine from manufacturing to services, Philadelphia followed suit. From 1970 to 2011, Philadelphia's manufacturing employment fell from 187,100 to 44,475; at the same time, jobs in education and health care more than doubled to 200,051.[18] Between 1970 and 1980, the unemployment rate in Philadelphia more than doubled to over 10 percent, where it remained until spiking to nearly 17 percent during the Great Recession. By 2019, post-recession job growth had helped the city reach a multi-decade low in unemployment at just over 8 percent (still much higher than most of the other cities in our sample). And yet, despite persistent high levels of unemployment, the rate of homelessness in Philadelphia is far lower than many other cities. A cluster of postindustrial cities— like Detroit, Baltimore, and Philadelphia—exhibit far lower rates of homelessness than other East Coast cities like Washington, D.C., New York, and Boston.

Just south of San Francisco is Silicon Valley, the American epicenter of technology and venture capital. In the eighty years since William Hewlett and David Packard named their new company in a Palo Alto garage, the stretch of land has housed contemporary titans of industry, among them Apple, Yahoo, Google, and Facebook. The county that covers much of the area is Santa Clara, which includes the metropolitan area of San Jose. Its northern boundary includes Palo Alto, the home of Stanford University; the county reaches southeast along Highway 101 to the city of Gilroy. Over the last half century, this sleepy, arid stretch of land has become the economic engine of the United States—and boasts wealth and job growth that few regions can rival.[19] In 1970, unemployment rates in Santa Clara County— and its primary city, San Jose—were higher than in Philadelphia, Baltimore, Milwaukee, Chicago, and Cleveland. But unlike the story of many of the nation's manufacturing cities, Silicon

Valley's unemployment rate continued to fall over the succeeding few decades to a low of 3.9 percent in 2000 (before rising again during the Great Recession.) By 2019, the unemployment rate in Santa Clara County had fallen, once again, to less than 3.5 percent. Yet in the face of a persistently strong labor market in Silicon Valley, Santa Clara County has relatively high rates of homelessness. Among the counties in our sample, only Multnomah County (Portland), Los Angeles County, and King County (Seattle) see higher rates. As the cases of Philadelphia and Silicon Valley demonstrate, unemployment doesn't help us understand the differences between these cities' experiences with homelessness.

Mental Health

In the summer of 2019, I (Gregg) found myself on a downtown Seattle street corner, just outside the flagship Nordstrom store, waiting on a stoplight to change. Next to me were—I suspected—two tourists. As we waited for the walk signal, a man approached, speaking loudly to himself and moving erratically. We were uncomfortable. As he neared us, the traffic light changed and we crossed the street. As we walked away, I heard one of the tourists say to her friend, "I can't wait to get out of this city."

For people living in cities with large unsheltered homeless populations, this interaction may sound familiar. We don't know if the man I interacted with was experiencing homelessness or if he suffered from a severe mental illness, but all familiar indicators suggested both of these things were true. What's clear is that interactions like these can resonate emotionally with everyone involved—and they likely help construct a prevailing narrative that links homelessness and mental illness in a manner that may, or may not, be grounded in reality. Certainly, research on the topic supports an association between the phenomena—roughly 20 to 30 percent of single adults experiencing homelessness also have some form of mental illness.[20] But the number of people experiencing homelessness who have a mental illness still represents a distinct minority of the overall homeless population. In any case, given existing evidence about the relationship between mental illness and homelessness (especially unsheltered homelessness), it's worth asking whether disproportionate regional rates of serious mental illness explain disproportionate regional rates of homelessness. Are cities like Washington, D.C., and Los Angeles merely home to comparatively more people with serious mental illnesses?

To explore regional relationships between mental illness and homelessness, we depart from our sample of thirty metropolitan areas due to data limitations. Within the U.S. Department of Health and Human Services lives the Substance Abuse and Mental Health Services Administration (SAMHSA), which maintains and publishes data on substance use and mental health. Because there is limited information on these conditions collected at the city or county level, we must rely on data at the state level to capture the sufficient number of observations needed to conduct credible statistical analyses. Accordingly, in this section, we compare state-level measures of mental illness and compare them to state-level per capita rates of homelessness.

Figure 9 shows no convincing relationship between states' rates of mental illness and homelessness. (Indeed, the modest relationship that appears to exist suggests the opposite conclusion that one might expect to reach: Homelessness rates are higher where serious mental illness rates are lower.) This observation does not suggest that mental illness doesn't contribute to

Rate of serious mental illness

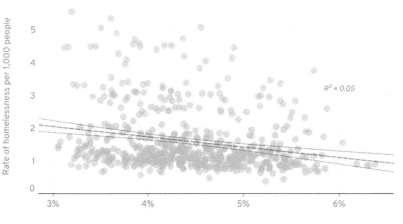

Figure 9. Rate of serious mental illness versus PIT count (per capita). Dashed lines indicate a linear regression of per capita PIT counts onto rates of serious mental illness in U.S. states between 2007 and 2019. Data source: HUD / SAMHSA

homelessness at an individual level; it implies that high rates of homelessness in certain states can't be attributed to a greater proportion of people with mental illnesses residing in those locations. Mental illness may help explain who becomes homeless within a given location, but it does not explain regional variation.

States with high rates of serious mental illness include Utah, Alabama, Colorado, Delaware, Wisconsin, Oregon, Kentucky, West Virginia, and Vermont. With the exception of Oregon, most see relatively modest levels of homelessness. On the other end of the spectrum, Hawaii has the highest per capita homelessness of the fifty states, but its rate of serious mental illness is among the lowest in the country. Other states with low levels of serious mental illness include New Jersey, Maryland, Connecticut, and Illinois, which also have relatively low levels of homelessness.

The point here is that little evidence links these two variables at the state level, and the limited association that does exist appears to suggest the opposite relationship one might expect, given what we understand about pathways into homelessness.

Drug Use

As discussed in the last chapter, drug use can be both a cause and a consequence of homelessness.[21] This nuance is often lost in public discussion of homelessness: The seeming (visible) prevalence of drug use among people without shelter is a powerful emotional touchstone inexorably linking homelessness to drugs for large segments of the general public. For analysts like Heather Mac Donald, author of the *City Journal* article cited in this chapter's introduction, the link suggests a policy response: "Go after the open-air drug trade with every possible tool."[22] For producers of the *Seattle Is Dying* documentary, too, homelessness is a drug problem that will be solved when officials confront an apparent drug epidemic in the city. In both cases, the individual-level association between drug use and homelessness implies a city-level policy response. But do regions with lower rates of drug use see lower rates of homelessness?

As in the analysis of mental illness above, we use state-level data from SAMHSA to examine the relationship between drug use and homelessness. We assess two measures of drug use, the rate of substance-use disorder (i.e., dependence on or abuse of one or more illicit drugs or alcohol) and rate of illicit drug use (see Figures 10 and 11). In each case, we observe a modest positive relationship between the two variables, but overall, substance abuse and illicit drug use explain very little variance in states' rates of homelessness: only 6 percent. (By way of comparison,

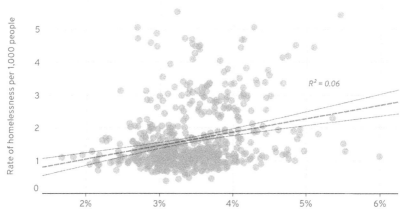

Figure 10. Rate of illicit drug use versus PIT count (per capita). Dashed lines indicate a linear regression of per capita PIT counts onto rates of illicit drug use in U.S. states between 2007 and 2019. Data source: HUD / SAMHSA

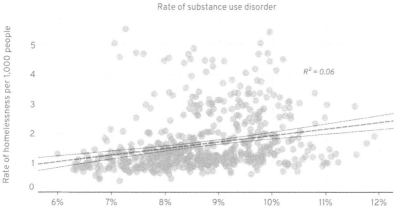

Figure 11. Rate of substance use disorder versus PIT count (per capita). Dashed lines indicate a linear regression of per capita PIT counts onto rates of substance use disorder in U.S. states between 2007 and 2019. Data source: HUD / SAMHSA

the negative relationship between mental illness and homelessness in the previous section also represented a statistical relationship in which the variable in question only explained 5 percent of the variance in homelessness rates.) We also examined state rates of use of nonprescription pain relievers (i.e., opioids) and observed a weak positive relationship that explained 2 percent of the variance in state rates of homelessness. Ultimately, none of these relationships sufficiently explains regional variation in rates of homelessness—and accordingly, none offers a corresponding policy prescription through this lens.

These findings are consistent with past research, which has found that drug use and dependency are not related to overall levels of homelessness.[23] Their implications are clear: Disproportionate rates of drug use fail to explain why certain regions see high rates of homelessness. Many drug users in New York, Washington, D.C., and Los Angeles may experience homelessness—and many may not. In all of these cases, though, overall drug use in these areas is not materially different from that in other places with far lower rates of homelessness. Accordingly, we can only conclude the disproportionate rates of homelessness in cities like San Francisco, New York, Washington, D.C., Los Angeles, and Seattle are *not* driven by more drug users residing in these locations. Something else is happening here.

Race

That a disproportionate percentage of the population experiencing homelessness in the United States identifies as Black or African American, Native/Indigenous, and/or Hispanic/Latinx should alarm Americans, but it should not surprise us. Centuries of oppression—at times blatant and violent, more frequently subtle and pernicious—have created a nation that is often unresponsive to the needs and desires of people who aren't seen as white. This discrimination, generation after generation, has made it far more difficult to build health and wealth in the country without light skin. Studies like the Center for Social Innovation's 2018 report on race and homelessness have echoed this fact: Fewer things need to go wrong in your life for you to end up losing your housing if you're Black.[24]

As cited previously, these disparities are borne out in cross-sectional and prevalence estimates of the population currently experiencing homelessness in the United States. In the language of demography or statistics, we would consider race to be a *risk factor* for homelessness, in that knowing one's race, all else being equal, tells us something about the average likelihood of that person having experienced homelessness (or experiencing homelessness in the future), given historical data. But we would not consider race or ethnicity to be a *cause* of homelessness. The odds of experiencing homelessness increase for people identified with specific races when structurally racist inequities across a range of systems—education, criminal justice, labor and housing markets, health care—interact with individual experience.

As people's experiences also interact with place, it's worth asking whether race explains any regional variation in homelessness (Figure 12). It doesn't. In fact, contrary to the individual-level associations between race and homelessness outlined above, cities in our sample with the highest relative Black populations—including Detroit and Baltimore—see some of the lowest rates of homelessness. Instead, homelessness rates are often higher in places with comparatively higher proportions of white people, including San Francisco, Boston, Portland, and Seattle. In any case, none of these statistical relationships explains much variance

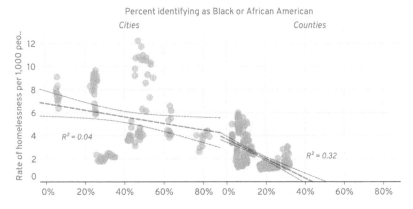

Figure 12. Percent Black/African American versus PIT count (per capita). Dashed lines indicate a linear regression of per capita PIT counts onto the proportion of persons identifying as Black or African American between 2007 and 2019 for a sample of U.S. regions. Data source: HUD / U.S. Census Bureau

in rates of homelessness across our sample, but where it does (in county CoCs), the relationship is negative; homelessness is lower where the proportion of Black/African American populations is higher. Like other individual factors, race may explain *who* becomes homeless in a given city, but it doesn't explain why one city has higher per capita rates of homelessness than another.

LUCK

A final individual risk factor for homelessness is bad luck. Brendan O'Flaherty highlights the role that luck plays in producing spells of homelessness.[25] An adverse medical event, mechanical breakdown of a car, natural disaster, or other similarly unpredictable event can drive some households into homelessness if they lack certain supports or insurance. Forms of insurance include actual private insurance policies (fire, flood, medical, etc.), social insurance, a stock of financial resources, or social capital in the form of friends or family who could provide needed support. In the absence of these formal or informal supports, bad luck can amount to the difference between being housed and unhoused.

Operationalizing luck is tricky, but basic reason suggests it should be evenly distributed throughout a society. What's not evenly distributed is the environment in which serendipity and uncertainty unfold. An unlucky event in certain markets may be more likely to produce a bout of homelessness than in places where the local context is more favorable to precariously housed adults and families. It's hardly worth writing down here, but as far as we know, no evidence suggests that high rates of homelessness in coastal cities can be attributed to a disproportionate number of unlucky people living in those cities. Rather, when someone experiences a catastrophic event, some combination of structure and individual circumstance may lead to a bout of homelessness—while in other settings, the same event won't. Understanding these structural conditions is of central concern to this book.

SUMMARY

In this chapter, we investigate numerous—and popular—individual explanations for homelessness. In a strikingly consistent fashion, none of these explanations (poverty, unemployment, mental illness, drug use, and race) explains regional variation in rates of homelessness. Homelessness is low where poverty and unemployment are greatest; neither drug use nor mental illness reliably explains regional variance; race remains an individual risk factor for homelessness that fails to explain city-to-city variation.

To digest these findings, we need to return to the discussion of precipitating events versus root causes. There is little doubt that job loss and poverty can increase the risk of homelessness for someone. But the data presented here suggest they are not root causes of a given city's homelessness crisis. If unemployment and poverty were the sole root causes of homelessness, we would perhaps expect rates of homelessness to increase in step with the prevalence of these hardships. In fact, the opposite case is true. Regions with high rates of poverty and unemployment—like Detroit, Cleveland, and Baltimore—have some of the lowest per capita rates of homelessness in the country. At its core, this observation suggests that these individual explanations of homelessness are better characterized as precipitating events. In some circumstances, job loss *can* lead to homelessness. In other settings, it doesn't. We want to understand the settings and circumstances in which these hardships occur and when—and under what conditions—they spur homelessness.

Like unemployment and poverty, mental illness and drug use—clear individual risk factors for homelessness—fail to explain regional variation in homelessness. The failure of explanation is useful for delineating the types of statements we *can't* make. For example, we can't and won't argue that Boston's comparatively high level of homelessness is the result of more people with mental illness living in the city. More generally, the findings in this chapter offer a strong case that the composition of a city's population fails to explain its rate of homelessness relative to other cities. And if individual-level factors don't explain this variation, it's worth turning our attention to other cultural or structural explanations.

CHAPTER FOUR

Landscape

In October 2018, a candidate for a seat on the Seattle City Council published and circulated a white paper online titled "The Politics of Ruinous Compassion."[1] Purporting to diagnose the city's homelessness crisis for what it was, the essay spread like wildfire, jumping from internet backrooms to the hallways of the public sector to the pages of local media. "Seattle is a city under siege," it began. The crisis wasn't a structural failing; it was an ideological success. Homelessness was collateral damage. In particular, rising rates of homelessness in recent years were a result of "a deeper, ideological war that's currently being won by a loose alliance of four major power centers: the socialist intellectuals, the compassion brigades, the homeless-industrial complex, and the addiction evangelists."[2] The candidate in question didn't win the election, but his ideas persist.

Disdain for compassionate responses isn't reserved solely for local politics. As described earlier, in 2019, the Trump administration's Council of Economic Advisors published a report titled *The State of Homelessness in America.* The stated objective of the document is remarkably similar to the purpose of our book: "This report (i) describes how homelessness varies across States and communities in the United States; (ii) analyzes the major factors that drive this variation; (iii) discusses the shortcomings of previous Federal policies to reduce homeless populations; and (iv) describes how the Trump Administration is improving Federal efforts to reduce homelessness."[3]

The report highlights four factors that explain the variation in rates of homelessness across the country, with the following pressures driving up regional rates: (i) high housing costs (attributable by the authors to overregulation of housing markets), (ii) conditions more amenable to sleeping outside, (iii) significant shelter capacity, and (iv) the overrepresentation of people in a given community who are at risk of homelessness. "Severe mental illness, substance abuse problems, histories of incarceration, low incomes, and weak social connections each increase an individual's risk of homelessness," write the authors, "and higher prevalence in the population of these factors may increase total homelessness."[4]

While such an argument seems plausible, the evidence doesn't support it. In the prior chapter, we analyzed this explanation— prevalence of individual risk factors—and found little evidence that it explains regional variation in rates of homelessness. Higher poverty rates don't imply higher rates of homelessness; substance abuse rates can't explain differences in the severity of states' homelessness. There is something else going on. In the next chapter, we test housing market explanations for homelessness and (like the administration) find that high housing costs help to explain differences in regional rates of homelessness. In this chapter, we investigate the cultural and environmental factors frequently cited as reasons for high regional rates of homelessness: local politics, the generosity of public assistance, and local weather conditions. Two of the White House's causal factors fall under this explanatory category. Namely, they argue that mild weather may encourage unsheltered homelessness—under the logic that it is easier to live without permanent shelter when weather conditions are more favorable—and that greater shelter capacity *pulls* people out of suboptimal living conditions and into shelter. Without homelessness service provision, the argument goes, people might remain precariously housed in other settings as opposed to becoming homeless (in the eyes of HUD) by entering the shelter system.

What follows from this mode of reasoning (and from local critics like that of the city council candidate cited above) is a persistent argument that certain cities have created a *culture* that encourages homelessness to thrive and persist—as a practice and a choice. The general contours of the argument suggest that temperate weather, generous social services (i.e., "welfare magnets"), and permissive local policies and politics combine to create an environment in which homelessness is left unchecked—if not, as the phrase "ruinous compassion" might suggest, promoted. Here, we test the relationships between measures of each of these cultural factors and the rate of homelessness in each city and county in our sample. We find little evidence for a correlational (much less causal) relationship.

WEATHER

One of the most common explanations that I (Gregg) hear when I discuss homelessness with people in Seattle is the weather. Homelessness is salient on the West Coast because we have relatively temperate climates that are more conducive to living without permanent shelter, the argument goes. When I push my conversation partners on Seattle's 39°F average low temperature in January and persistent winter rainfall, they usually concede that weather might not be the draw for homelessness in Seattle, but that it surely is in San Francisco, Los Angeles, and San Diego. Fair enough, I argue, but what about Texas and Florida, which have relatively low rates of homelessness but winter weather far more conducive to sleeping on the street?

The climatic argument for homelessness variation is easy to wrap one's head around—it tells a tidy story—but that doesn't mean it's right. The 2019 White House report on homelessness, at best, misleads. The authors state that "more tolerable conditions for sleeping on the streets (outside of shelter or housing) increases homelessness"—a causal claim.[5] And yet even the following sentences alter the assertion considerably: "We show that warmer places are more likely to have higher rates of unsheltered homelessness, but rates are nonetheless low in some warm places. For example, Florida and Arizona have unsheltered homeless populations lower than what would be expected given the temperatures, home prices, and poverty rates in their communities." Despite the initial sentence that draws a blanket relationship between temperature and homelessness, the subsequent text suggests a narrower link between *unsheltered* homelessness and weather—a relationship well understood in existing literature.[6]

Critical to recall in discussions of weather and homelessness is the Housing and Urban Development definition of the latter. Total homelessness in a given Continuum of Care (CoC) is the sum of the unsheltered and sheltered homeless populations (the second of which constitutes people living in emergency shelters, transitional housing, or Safe Haven domestic violence shelters—and does not include people temporarily doubled up with friends or family). Given this definition, if a person moves from outdoors into a shelter, their experience of homelessness is renamed in the eyes of the state; but it is not erased. In other words, the move does not change the total population of people experiencing homelessness: It recharacterizes it.

This distinction is essential when considering regional variation in rates of homelessness. If your goal as a researcher, policymaker, or concerned resident is to understand why homelessness is more severe in some areas than in others, we argue you must understand the entirety of the issue—and the issue is larger than unsheltered homelessness. This is not meant to minimize unsheltered homelessness; people sleeping outside are at particular risk of the physical, mental, and emotional health effects of prolonged homelessness and represent the most visible manifestation of housing instability. But by definition, everyone experiencing homelessness lacks permanent housing. That Midwestern and East Coast cities tend to have far greater shelter capacity than those on the West Coast helps to explain the relative dearth of unsheltered homelessness in places like Minneapolis, Boston, and New York. While weather may influence the level of unsheltered homelessness in a city, it also affects the *response* to homelessness in those communities. This fact helps explain why cold weather cities in the Midwest and the Northeast have robust shelter systems. Rather than cause unsheltered homelessness, weather may merely drive variation in local policy responses.

Using the data in our sample, we analyze the relationship between weather and homelessness. As is the convention in the vast majority of homelessness research, we use temperature and precipitation in January to assess the relationship in question.

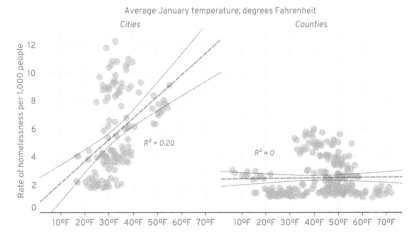

Figure 13. January average temperature versus PIT count (per capita). Dashed lines indicate a linear regression of per capita PIT counts onto average January temperatures between 2007 and 2019 for a sample of U.S. regions. Data source: HUD / NOAA

(CoCs conduct their annual point-in-time homelessness census at the end of January.) When broken out by city and county CoCs, we see a strong positive relationship between temperature and homelessness in cities and no relationship in the county CoCs (Figure 13). When we index rates of homelessness to directly compare CoCs on the same figure, we find no relationship between temperature and homelessness (Figure 14).[7] Even in our city sample, the relationship is likely an artifact driven by the coincidence that many of the city CoCs (with low rates of homelessness) are located in cold climates—including Chicago, Detroit, Indianapolis, Philadelphia, and Baltimore—and "pull down" the curve. For example, thirteen of the nineteen county CoCs in our sample have average January temperatures above 40°F. Only two city CoCs pass this threshold. When we attempt to capture ample variation in temperature and expand

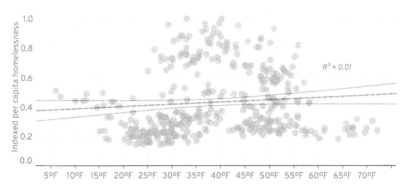

Figure 14. January average temperature versus indexed homelessness. Dashed lines indicate a linear regression of indexed rates of homelessness onto average January temperatures between 2007 and 2019 for a sample of U.S. regions. Data source: HUD / NOAA

our analysis to county CoCs (or index the sample and directly compare all regions), the temperature-homelessness relationship disappears. The dubious link between weather and *total* homeless counts is also noted in existing literature.[8]

Still, a closer look at this relationship does yield an important observation: When we break out homelessness by sheltered and unsheltered status, we see a positive relationship between January weather and unsheltered counts. The effect is particularly strong in cities (partly due to the sampling issues noted above), but it persists in counties. At face value, these data illustrate an association between temperature and unsheltered homelessness. But a central question remains as to whether average temperature in its own right uniquely and directly drives unsheltered homelessness—or whether the strong correlation in cities represents the thumbprint of some unobserved process (including, for example, the shelter-supply-response scenario outlined

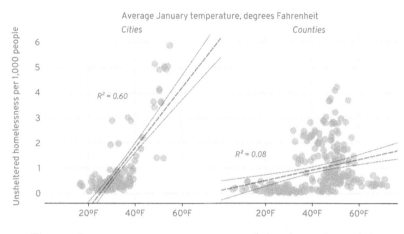

Figure 15. January average temperature versus unsheltered count (per capita). Dashed lines indicate a linear regression of per capita unsheltered PIT counts onto average January temperatures between 2007 and 2019 for a sample of U.S. regions. Data source: HUD / NOAA

above). One data point in favor of temperature driving shelter *capacity* responses to homelessness as opposed to driving unsheltered homelessness in its own right comes by way of Figure 15, which illustrates the relationship between average January temperatures and the proportion of the population experiencing homelessness in a given region that is sheltered. As might be expected if shelter capacity responds to harsh winters in places like the Midwest and Northeast, cities and counties with lower January temperatures report much higher proportions of sheltered homelessness. All told, we might say that colder weather is indeed associated with lower rates of unsheltered homelessness; but broadly speaking, temperature fails to explain variation in overall rates of homelessness throughout our sample.[9]

Even the Council of Economic Advisors softens its stance in the report's slightly more nuanced discussion. While the authors identify a strong temperature–unsheltered homelessness relationship in cold places, the relationship appears to be less convincing in warmer locales:

> Rates of unsheltered homelessness are uniformly low in cold places. In other words, the difficulty of sleeping on the streets is so high during the winter in places like Minneapolis that unsheltered homelessness is extremely rare. However, there is wide variation in rates of unsheltered homelessness in warmer places. For example, Orlando, Las Vegas, and San Francisco all have January temperatures of between 50°F and 60° degrees Fahrenheit. But their rates of unsheltered homelessness are 2, 19, and 60 per 10,000 people respectively.... It is clear that warm climates enable, but do not guarantee, high rates of unsheltered homelessness. *Thus, factors beyond climate help determine rates of unsheltered homelessness in warm places.*[10]

Far from arguing that weather can reliably explain variation in overall rates of homelessness, the report's authors note it is inadequate to even fully capture differences in unsheltered homelessness. Mother Nature—a convenient scapegoat—is not to blame.

LOCAL HOMELESSNESS RESPONSE SYSTEMS

Broadly speaking, we can split the homelessness response systems into two broad categories: those with robust shelter capacity and those with more limited shelter systems. As cited above, for example, the Midwest and East Coast includes many cities and communities that have constructed substantial shelter systems to accommodate the people in their communities who experience homelessness. Accordingly, unsheltered homelessness in many of these cities is relatively rare. The level of unsheltered homelessness in San Francisco is more than ten times that of New York and Boston, but both of the latter cities have higher overall levels of homelessness than the former. This stark difference highlights a profound distinction between homelessness responses. The East Coast model emphasizes significant shelter capacity and, in many cases, protects shelter access as a legal right.[11] By and large, West Coast cities (and some in Florida and Texas) have adopted a different approach. Shelter capacity in West Coast cities like Los Angeles, San Francisco, and Seattle is far more limited, and as a result, unsheltered homelessness is far more prevalent—even when comparing regions with similar rates of per capita homelessness.

We saw in the previous section how environmental factors like the weather may naturally guide CoCs to respond differentially to homelessness. But shelter systems serve two purposes. First, and perhaps most obviously, they provide beds and a roof to those who need them. In many cases, the shelter system offers a life-saving intervention, especially in regions with very inhospitable climates. But as critical research notes, the shelter system also serves a second purpose: concealment.[12] Homeless shelters don't end homelessness, they recharacterize it. And in doing so, they help jurisdictions *hide* people experiencing homelessness from the general public.

These purposes serve dual ends: to respond to the crisis at hand and to minimize public perception of the problem. Neither purpose serves to prevent the crisis in the first place. Nor do they cause the crisis. And yet, another argument concerning the relationship between shelter responses and homelessness—offered by many, including the Trump White House—is the notion that building additional shelter capacity encourages people to leave other suboptimal housing situations in favor of a homeless shelter; by extension, increasing rates of homelessness in a given region.

Cragg and O'Flaherty studied this phenomenon in New York City and found a modest relationship at best. The researchers tested whether rising rates of subsidized housing placements from family shelters drove entries into shelter (as families may have come to see shelters as gateways to securing permanent, subsidized housing). It wasn't the case. The researchers found that "it takes placing at least seven families into subsidized housing to draw one family into the shelter system."[13] In other words, "Better prospects of subsidized housing increase flows into the shelter system, but this effect is not nearly large enough to offset the first order effect—taking families out of the shelters reduces the number of families in them."[14] Subsequent research suggested that placements into subsidized housing "do not seem to lure large numbers of families into the shelter system."[15]

This "luring" language implies a magnet effect, whereby unstably or precariously housed people—who may not necessarily be experiencing homelessness—opt to sleep in emergency shelters for the potential service or subsidy provision on the other side. As the researchers above note, this particular magnet effect doesn't appear to hold up to scrutiny. Aside from playing to a brand of political rhetoric that alleges system-gaming on behalf of the precariously housed—the same rhetorical brand that gave us the notion of the "welfare queen"—the argument presumes some people voluntarily give up their housing in favor of the shared bathrooms, lack of privacy and storage, and often elevated noise levels that characterize many emergency shelters in the country; all for the chance that entering a shelter constitutes a step toward permanent housing support. Given crisis-response resource scarcity, such moves directly from shelter to permanent housing (subsidized or unsubsidized) are all too rare. In King County (Seattle), for example, the Department of Community and Human Services reports that only 14 percent of households exiting emergency shelters in 2019 left for some form of permanent housing (of which only a subset is subsidized).[16]

GENEROUS SOCIAL SERVICES

According to the United Nations, water scarcity may be the most visible and consequential effect of climate change.[17] As water sources dry up, millions of people who rely on that water for their existence may be forced to move. Mass migrations, and the associated social upheaval, are frightening prospects, and new settlements will be disruptive events for all those who are affected. This mass movement of people is likely to occur in the United States. One recent study estimated that a changing climate will cause 8 and 4.5 percent population reductions over the next forty-five years in the U.S. South and Midwest, respectively, as people move to more accommodating locations in the Northeast and West.[18] Imagine, during this coming period, if a policy analyst were to observe any potential or subsequent unrest or conflict in the latter regions and argue that the cause or source of these social problems was, say, the presence of fresh water as opposed to the depletion of aquifers elsewhere. *If it wasn't for this water source, we wouldn't have these problems!* The solution to a given region's instability—argues the analyst—is to restrict access to the water. Certainly, though, a more credible policy response would be to make water more available, rather than less so.

A form of this story already plays out in cities throughout the United States. Public and charitable supports—from employment centers to food banks and emergency shelters—are more frequently provided in cities, for example, than in suburban settings. Accordingly, people seeking these services are more likely to travel to cities, sometimes permanently. And some of these people don't have permanent housing. Certainly, existing research documents evidence of migration from suburban to urban locations among people experiencing homelessness.[19] Other studies have shown that mobility may indeed be related to housing instability—and that places with greater in-migration may have higher rates of homelessness because of population stresses on the housing market.[20] Importantly, though, these studies examine overall migration, not simply migration of people with low incomes or those experiencing homelessness. People move all the time, and many move to cities.

However, as concerns arise about the number of people experiencing homelessness in a given city, block, or neighborhood, some skeptical observers blame the provision of services. *Were it not for these services*—water in the desert—*these people wouldn't end up here seeking them,* the logic goes. Since these benefits and services serve as a magnet for people experiencing homelessness, we ought to remove them (as opposed to expand or better distribute their provision). *In catering to homelessness, cities encourage it,* the skeptics argue.

The social service provision debate mirrors a more general conversation about the relationship between the social safety net and homelessness writ large. Broadly, one argument along these lines suggests that a generous social safety net encourages homelessness because it draws additional people into a given city or county in search of these benefits. In practice, empirical evidence suggests the opposite relationship. For example, access to cash assistance programs reduces rather than increases homelessness.[21] Researchers have repeatedly noted that other supports and services designed to assist unhoused or precariously housed people fail to increase the reported rate of homelessness.[22] One potential exception to this finding comes from Igor Popov, who finds that investments in supports for families may increase the number of families subsequently counted in the homeless census—which suggests a latent demand for housing supports for precariously housed families.[23] The balance of the academic evidence suggests that public assistance benefits and services work to *limit* homelessness rather than accelerate the phenomenon.

In this section, we offer two analyses to test whether we see any evidence of additional "magnet" effects that may explain regional variation in rates of homelessness. The first of these assesses the generosity of public assistance benefits by state. The primary U.S. cash public assistance program is known as Temporary Assistance for Needy Families (TANF). TANF, the successor program to Aid for Families with Dependent Children (AFDC), was created in the mid-1990s as part of President Clinton's overhaul of the country's welfare system—and captures most colloquial uses of the term "welfare." A key element of the TANF program is the flexibility provided to states to determine how to spend federal money (including the maximum level of cash benefits they provide). This policy feature helps explain why TANF payments vary so substantially from state to state.[24]

Because this variation occurs at the state level, we ask whether state rates of per capita homelessness vary with the generosity of TANF benefits. In particular, because TANF benefits are only available to families, we test the relationship between benefit generosity and rates of family homelessness. We measure relative generosity by dividing a state's maximum monthly cash benefit by its median rent for a two-bedroom apartment. This ratio allows us to adjust our analysis to accommodate the fact that the cost of living varies from state to state as well. In Figure 16 below, note that there is no relationship between the relative

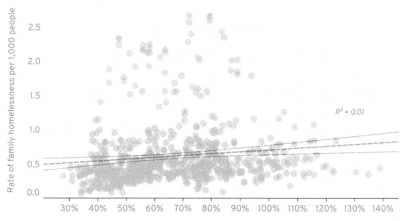

Figure 16. Benefit/rent ratio versus family PIT count (per capita). Dashed lines indicate a linear regression of family per capita PIT counts onto benefit/rent ratios in U.S. states between 2007 and 2019. Data source: HUD / Urban Institute

generosity of welfare benefits and family homelessness, as indicated by the flat, best-fit line. Indeed, our measure of the proportion of explained variation, R^2, is nearly zero.[25] If generous cash assistance drew people experiencing homelessness into a given state, we would expect to see higher per capita rates of homelessness in these places. We don't.

Because TANF does not cover all types of households (single adults are not eligible), we also ask whether certain regions are a disproportionate draw for people living in poverty as a proportion of the total share of in-migration—and whether this share of low-income in-migration varies with rates of homelessness. Social services vary by location, so people may seek to optimize public benefits by relocating, and this movement may be more prevalent for those at higher risk of homelessness. That's the theory, anyway: By providing shelter, services, and financial support, a region disproportionately attracts low-income house-holds seeking these resources. We want to know whether that's the case. Existing research, based on state homelessness data from Iowa and Michigan, has illustrated some mobility of people experiencing homelessness from suburban to urban areas within the same metropolitan area.[26] Using a national data set, George Carter also found evidence of movement from suburban to urban locations.[27] But what about between cities? Existing research, on region-to-region migration tends to find no discernible geographic trends in the movement of homeless veterans[28] or people who are unsheltered.[29] In general, homeless households are *less* mobile than housed households.[30]

Outside the academy, policy and media reports often highlight the notion that generous benefits attract people experiencing homelessness. A 2019 article in the *San Francisco Chronicle*, for example, offered answers to ninety-seven questions about homelessness.[31] Two were directly related to the issue at hand: (1) "It seems that most, if not nearly all of the homeless people in the Bay Area come here from other states due to the region's progressive politics and generous benefits. Is that true?" and (2) "Do homeless people often relocate—move to a particular city because of better services, sense of community, weather, etc.?" The responses are consistent with the findings presented in this book: "Up to 80% of homeless people become homeless in the communities they live in. Some do travel to the Bay Area because, like others migrating here, they like the weather and the liberal environment. But virtually every major city in America also claims to be a magnet for homeless people.... In San Francisco, the city found in 2019 that 55% of homeless people had reported living in San Francisco for 10 or more years, and just 6% said they'd lived in San Francisco for less than one year."

None of this is to suggest that public opinion, regional generosity, and outright compassion don't vary from region to region. On an extremely low income, it's easier to find a meal or a place to sleep in some places than in others—for more reasons than cost alone. In an article in *The Oregonian*, Lewis Davis, homeless at the time, noted, "There's a saying on the street: You have to be stupid to starve in Portland. If you sit down on any sidewalk, eventually someone brings you a meal."[32] But do people move to Portland for these meals? In the same article, the director of a local social services nonprofit argues that any city with high rates of in-migration "is going to attract all kinds of people— rich people, middle-class people, poor people. . . . I don't think I have ever met anyone who came here to be homeless. They came to find a job, and that didn't work out."

The homeless magnet story isn't reserved solely for expensive, coastal cities. A recent *Washington Post* piece explored its manifestation in Middletown, Ohio: "This small heartland city, situated almost halfway between Dayton and Cincinnati, has long had a heart. In good times and bad, it has offered a generous network of privately funded homeless shelters, drug rehabilitation facilities and soup kitchens, plus a library that promotes access for all. . . . Yet in recent months, officials and residents have begun to question whom those services are benefiting and how to shoulder the cost."[33]

Even in small-town Ohio, claims of magnet effects are ubiquitous. And that's because the argument is convenient. While conducting research on homelessness in Minneapolis while in graduate school, I (Gregg) frequently heard that the prevalence of homelessness in the city was a result of people from Chicago coming to Minnesota for its generous services and benefits. When I moved to Seattle, I heard the same argument—It's

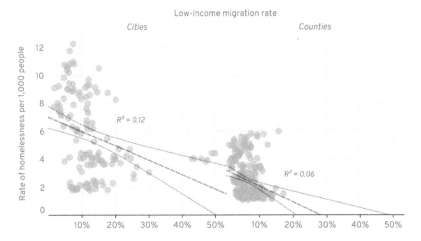

Figure 17. Low-income migration rate versus PIT count (per capita). Dashed lines indicate a linear regression of per capita PIT counts onto the low-income migration rate between 2007 and 2019 for a sample of U.S. regions. Data source: HUD / U.S. Census Bureau

people *from California* coming to Seattle for *our* benefits. As we noted above, the same argument crops up in California. And while it's impossible for every city to be a magnet, we know that some people who migrate to a given city may eventually lose their housing. The question is whether this happens disproportionately in some places more than others.

To test whether the mobility of vulnerable households helps to explain regional variation in rates of homelessness, we analyze mobility patterns across the income spectrum. In particular, Figure 17 illustrates that a region's proportion of in-migrants with incomes below the federal poverty line (out of all those moving to the region) is entirely unrelated, statistically speaking, to per capita rates of homelessness. Households with low incomes are moving to every city in our sample at similar rates. And while it's true that some poor households move to regions with high rates of homelessness, these mobility patterns don't differ from other regions. For the "welfare magnet" argument to be credible, we'd need to see evidence of disproportionate movement of low-income households to certain regions. We don't. Regions with some of the highest rates of homelessness—Washington, D.C., San Francisco, and King County—all have poverty in-migration rates of less than 4 percent. In 2019, 25 percent of households moving to Detroit were below the federal poverty line; in Philadelphia, the figure was almost 12 percent. Undermining this potential explanation for regional variation, homelessness is lowest where low-income migration is the greatest.

Combined, these two analyses suggest the mobility of poor and precariously housed households do not explain regional variation in rates of homelessness.

LOCAL POLITICAL ENVIRONMENT

A final measure of local culture is the political environment of a given metropolitan area. As highlighted in the introduction to this book, in early 2019, the Trump administration was busy blaming local, Democratic politicians for the homelessness crisis in many of the nation's coastal cities.[34] To test the credibility of this claim, we identify the political party of the mayor of each of the cities in our sample.[35] Unsurprisingly, the mayors of large U.S. cities are predominantly members of the Democratic Party. Across the cities in our sample between 2007 and 2019, 85 percent of the time, the mayor was a Democrat. Republican mayors were in control 8 percent of the time. Independents were in office around 7 percent of the sample period. (San Diego and Miami lean Republican; New York and Las Vegas have had multiple stretches of independent mayors). Democratic Party domination in most U.S. cities undermines the political argument in question: If allegedly permissive local policies implemented by Democrats are to blame for high rates of homelessness, why are rates of homelessness low in Democratic strongholds like Chicago, Detroit, and Cleveland? To subscribe to this theory, one would need to believe that the various shades of political blue explain the difference between widespread homelessness in one blue city—say, San Francisco—and relatively modest levels in another Democratic stronghold—Detroit.

To explore political explanations of homelessness further, then, we consider the common argument that certain cities have more permissive policies and ordinances regarding homelessness than others. New York City, for example, under the leadership of multiple mayors has actively pursued various degrees of police-driven responses to homelessness. The source of these policies can be traced to the 1980s, when, as in many cities around the nation, homelessness emerged as a major issue in New York City. The growing crisis prompted litigation (*Callahan v. Carey*) that ultimately forced the city to provide shelter for people experiencing homelessness—and New York became the first city with a right-to-shelter policy. In a history of homelessness in New York, Diane Jeantet summarized the response to homelessness of the three mayors who led the city during the 1980s and 1990s:

> Sometimes their policies focused only on the more dire symptoms or most visible signs of homelessness. In a 1985 decision, the late Edward Koch ordered that police remove by force anyone sleeping in the streets on freezing nights. Similarly, during the Rudy Giuliani administration, police conducted searches in public places, arresting homeless New Yorkers and taking them to shelters. . . . But when it came to actually solving homelessness—moving people beyond shelters—

Koch, David Dinkins, and Giuliani all, to a certain extent, were guided by the belief that providing permanent housing to shelter residents would only serve to draw more people to the shelter system.[36]

I (Gregg) first became interested in the issue of homelessness while working in New York as an investment banker in the mid-1990s. I lived on the Upper West Side of Manhattan and rode the subway each day down to the financial district in lower Manhattan where my office was located. At that time, Rudy Giuliani was mayor, and he was committed to "cleaning up" New York. On my morning subway rides, it wasn't uncommon for me to see police officers pull a sleeping person off the train. These moments helped me to understand what "cleaning up" meant: It was a spatial solution to the problem. To ensure that Manhattan was safe and pleasant for tourists and the professionals who called it home, the city moved people experiencing homelessness elsewhere. This response didn't end anyone's experience with homelessness; it moved that experience to a different location. It's possible that the people I saw dragged off trains were brought to emergency shelters. I don't know. But I do know what strong enforcement of homelessness looks like in a big U.S. city.

From a political perspective, Giuliani's strict enforcement was broadly praised. Popular narratives acknowledged that New York was more pleasant for tourists and residents, and Giuliani, therefore, deserved the credit. If we ignore the plights and common humanity of those without housing—and we hide them from view—it is far easier to arrive at this conclusion. Williams Cole, in a critique entitled "Against the Giuliani Legacy" wrote: "Reporting on our city [New York] makes it clear Rudy Giuliani has won a war of perception concerning how he has 'cleaned up New York' and changed its very fabric. One recent example from the *Montreal Gazette* gushes, 'It's easy to see why Rudy Giuliani is the most popular mayor in New York history. Not only has Rudy cleaned the streets, he's cleaned them up . . . taken the pimps and pushers off the streets and made them safe again . . . and chased the homeless and the squeegee kids away.'"[37]

Spatial solutions to homelessness aren't reserved solely for cities run by Rudy Giuliani. Aggressive enforcement of anti-homeless law persists in some of the most progressive cities in the nation. In their book *Banished*, Katherine Beckett and Steve Herbert chronicle the policing of homelessness in U.S. cities, notably Seattle, and observe that the evidence of banishment and exclusion from public spaces for people experiencing homelessness in Seattle contradicts the pervasive narrative of soft, permissive progressive governments as the driver of homelessness in coastal cities: "Seattle is one of the pioneering cities in the use of banishment as a social control strategy."[38] The authors explore the effects of this form of social control:

> We suggest that banishment as policy is futile and counterproductive. Although its use serves many short-term interests—including those of police, prosecutors, and private capital—it is nonetheless a policy failure. Its futility lies in the reality that many of those pressured to relocate are hard-pressed to do so. They are deeply attached to the places from which they are banned, for multiple reasons. . . . Banishment is also counterproductive because it imperils efforts by the socially marginal to integrate with mainstream society. . . . Furthermore, banishment does nothing to resolve any of the underlying conditions that generate social marginality, such as poor employment prospects, inadequate affordable housing, or the challenges of addiction. To the extent that cities increasingly rely on banishment as a putative solution to disorder, they will succeed only in displacing some individuals from one location to another and in rendering the lives of the disorderly more difficult.

Its increased use therefore deserves to be questioned and significantly curtailed.[39]

Despite a lack of empirical evidence in support of the thesis that stronger policing of homelessness is the key to limiting its prevalence, these ideas persist at most levels of government and in a broad array of public forums. The recent White House report on homelessness draws a link between policing of local ordinances and high levels of unsheltered homelessness: "One potential factor is differences in city ordinances and policing practices, as these policies would directly affect the tolerability of living on the street and predict the aggregate number of unsheltered homeless people. Some States more than others engage in more stringent enforcement of quality of life issues like restrictions on the use of tents and encampments, loitering, and other related activities."[40] The authors provide scant evidentiary support for this assertion. If shelter capacity remains fixed, aggressive enforcement results in the shuffling of people experiencing homelessness around a city. (One only need look at the movement of homeless encampments from neighborhood to neighborhood following "street sweeps" to see the point here.) For the permissive policies argument to carry any water, we'd need to see evidence that stronger policing and more restrictive ordinances reduce rates of homelessness, whether intra- or inter-regionally. That evidence is nonexistent. The White House report cites Brendan O'Flaherty from his 1996 book, *Making Room: The Economics of Homelessness*, in support of more aggressive policing. But the broader context of O'Flaherty's comments suggests an entirely different interpretation: "Asking the police to be more aggressive—arresting panhandlers and people sleeping unobtrusively in public places—is futile. Police officers—as a routine matter, which is what counts—won't do it, and homeless people, since jail is warm, wouldn't be deterred much if they did. I'm not arguing that the police should do nothing. Aggressive but nonpunitive referral is a positive strategy; it has a record of reducing street homelessness and the attendant costs it imposes on other people."[41]

The point here is that so-called soft policing isn't to blame for the homelessness crises in many cities. It's possible that tougher responses from law enforcement may move visual evidence of homelessness to less apparent locations (i.e., out of Grand Central Station in New York City), but they won't alter the total number of people experiencing homelessness.[42]

While local policies and their enforcement play a major role in local responses to homelessness, one can't discount the important role that courts have also played. As cited earlier, the *Callahan v. Carey* case forced New York City to create a shelter system for its growing homeless population—a model that has been replicated nationwide. More recently, a lawsuit originating in Boise, Idaho, raised the fundamental issue about who has a right to public spaces. In 2009, a group of people experiencing homelessness, represented by Idaho Legal Services, Latham & Watkins LLP, and the National Center on Homelessness and Poverty filed a complaint against the city of Boise after having been ticketed for violating a city ordinance that prohibited sleeping outside. The plaintiffs argued that because there was no place for them to sleep, the ordinance constituted cruel and unusual punishment. Ultimately, lawmakers changed the rule in question in such a manner that prohibited citations when the shelter system was at capacity. (And even following the change in the law, on appeal, the Ninth Circuit determined that the rule was unconstitutional.) Boise appealed to the Supreme Court, but the high court refused to hear the case—thereby preserving its unconstitutionality throughout the Ninth Circuit, which includes states with high levels of unsheltered homelessness, including Washington, Oregon, and California. While the topic invites philosophical, moral, and legal questions concerning the relationship between residents and the state, for the time being, criminalizing homelessness is not the law of the land (in the Ninth Circuit). As such, cities must think beyond a narrow view of policies and ordinances designed to punish the unhoused: to broader considerations about the availability of housing for those who need it. After the Supreme Court refused to hear the case—preserving the rulings of the Ninth Circuit—Executive Director Maria Foscarins at the National Homelessness Law Center remarked: "We're thrilled that the Court has let the 9th Circuit decision stand so that homeless people are not punished for sleeping on the streets when they have no other option. But ultimately our goal is to end homelessness through housing—which is effective and saves taxpayer dollars—so that no one has to sleep on the streets in the first place. We hope the 9th Circuit decision will help communities find the political will to put that housing in place. Housing, not handcuffs, is what ends homelessness."[43]

SUMMARY

Cultural and environmental arguments about homelessness are compelling. Weather and politics are easy scapegoats when critics seek to assign blame for a homelessness crisis that exacts a significant toll on people and a broader community. But little evidence supports these lines of argument. Certainly, one can trace a connection between the insufficient federal housing support for low-income households over the last four decades and increasing precarity among many low-income households.[44] Existing research also draws a strong link between federal disinvestment and overall levels of homelessness. But it fails to explain regional variation.

Locally, neither public-assistance generosity—which varies at the state level—nor the mobility of low-income households helps us understand why homeless rates differ across the country. Despite arguments to the contrary, existing literature fails to confirm the argument that more aggressive policing and enforcement solve homelessness. At best, criminalization of homelessness relocates a housing crisis from one region to another. ("Out of sight, out of mind" hardly constitutes a comprehensive response to housing instability.) And just as criminalization relocates homelessness, weather patterns recharacterize it. While weather and climate may help to explain why some cities have robust shelter systems, temperature fails to explain overall rates. Refuting these arguments forces regions to confront the reality that the crisis of homelessness is not entirely outside their control (as it would be if the weather were to blame). Homelessness is a direct result of how we construct and operate our cities.

CHAPTER FIVE

Market

U.S. News and World Report publishes an annual ranking of the states in the union. To sort the list, the magazine compiles scores on a range of factors, including quality of "health care, education, the economy, infrastructure, opportunity, fiscal stability, crime and corrections, and the natural environment." In 2019, Washington took the top spot. In forty-eighth place was Mississippi, which scored near the very bottom in many categories, including health care, education, the economy, and infrastructure.[1] That Mississippi would score low on an arbitrary list of states is unsurprising—so much so that residents of neighboring states are quick to sigh "Thank God for Mississippi" when confronted with ranked lists of states, because their states frequently rank above Mississippi.[2]

But in perhaps a somewhat unexpected result, when the measure is homelessness, Mississippi is alone at the head of the class. That a state known for its poverty, poor educational system, and inferior health care would lead the nation with the lowest per capita of homelessness seems to strain credulity. But Mississippi is also cheap. Evan Horowitz, in an article in the *Boston Globe*, analyzed the income and homelessness relationship and reached a similar conclusion: "Rich states have more homeless people. It's not an iron-clad rule, just a loose tendency, but it cuts sharply against the grain of economic expectation."[3] "Homelessness is largely about the price of homes," he writes. "Mississippi and Alabama are cheap places to live." With the invisible hand at work, states with lower median incomes tend to see cheaper housing costs—and vice versa. Washington, which enjoyed the top position in the *U.S. News and World Report* ranking, had at the time the fifth-highest per capita rate of homelessness in the country. Washington and Mississippi are far from outliers. Instead, they help to begin to illustrate the fundamental argument of this book: Homelessness is a housing problem.

Earlier chapters suggest that neither individual factors nor local culture and politics explain regional variation in rates of homelessness. We now turn to more fundamental structural drivers of this phenomenon: housing market conditions. In contrast to popular narratives concerning the causes of homelessness, abundant academic research provides credible links between housing markets and housing instability. As a result, a challenge has arisen to reconcile seemingly contradictory evidence—between anecdote and research. The complexity (and general inaccessibility) of the academic evidence base doesn't help. Broadly speaking, scholarly communication has failed to inform or shift public perception of the nature of the country's homelessness crisis, thereby opening the door for more readily interpretable (and emotional) explanations like drug use and mental health. But we argue the contradictions in question only emerge if we blur units of analysis. Throughout this book, we've sought to stress that attributing city-level findings to individuals—or vice versa—will often lead to imprecise (or flat-out wrong) diagnoses. At the level of the city (or county), we've demonstrated that individual and cultural explanations fail to explain regional variance, even where they might offer explanations for why a given person lost their housing. Risk factors don't imply root causes.

We now turn to a range of housing market explanations.

HOUSING COST BURDEN

A common narrative deployed to explain homelessness draws on the concept of housing cost burden: the percentage of one's household income that goes toward rent. The higher your burden, the greater your risk of homelessness. This logic generally goes uncontested—and for good reason. For example, in the 2016 *State of the Nation's Housing,* published by the Joint Center for Housing Studies at Harvard University, the authors note that "housing cost burdens are a fact of life for a growing number of renters. These burdens put households at risk of housing instability and homelessness, particularly in the nation's high-cost cities."[4] Other researchers have identified specific thresholds for median housing cost burdens that, upon crossing, boost rates of homelessness in cities.[5] And these findings make sense. There is little doubt that higher rent burdens increase precarity for vulnerable households.

It's worth investigating, though, the extent to which housing cost burdens can explain the intercity variation in rates of homelessness currently under the microscope. To test these relationships, we first consider the association between median gross rent as a percentage of household income (among renters) and per capita rates of homelessness. As Figure 18 illustrates, there

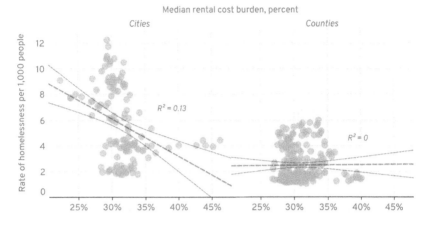

Figure 18. Median gross rent as a percentage of household income versus PIT count (per capita). Dashed lines indicate a linear regression of per capita PIT counts onto median rental cost burden between 2007 and 2019 for a sample of U.S. regions. Data source: HUD / U.S. Census Bureau

is no clear correlation between these variables. In fact, in our data set, the relationship is mildly negative. This finding seems counterintuitive.

Part of what's going on here is that there is a tight relationship between housing costs and incomes within a given metropolitan area. Consider the distribution of median rent burdens: The vast majority of cities and counties in our sample have median rental burdens between 26 and 34 percent. The tight distribution demonstrates that rents tend to scale with incomes, and, therefore, even places with high median housing costs do not *necessarily* have high cost burdens. Cost burdens in San Francisco and Seattle are near the national average, and some of the highest median cost burdens for renters are found in lower-cost cities like Detroit. The story in Detroit and other postindustrial cities is one of low rents coupled with very low incomes—so low that we observe relatively high housing cost burdens for renters. When combined with the low rates of homelessness, a city like Detroit helps to explain the slightly negative (but otherwise unsubstantial) relationship between cost burdens and homelessness. And, as always, note that we're interested in inter-regional variation here. For a given household, a high cost burden indisputably increases the risk of homelessness.

A critic might argue that *median* rent burden offers an inappropriate measure when studying homelessness, not least because households at the median are at very little risk of homelessness. A more appropriate question might be whether implied housing cost burdens faced by low-income households predict homelessness.[6] Figure 19 depicts the relationship.

Again, this relationship fails to provide a credible explanation. Low-income renters in Philadelphia have higher cost burdens (54 percent across the whole sample) than similarly situated low-income renters in New York (50 percent), San Francisco (40 percent), and Seattle/King County (40 percent). By every definition of the word, these burdens are unaffordable. And some renters have it worse, putting up to 70 or 80 percent of their incomes to housing costs. But if the housing market is to blame for regional variation in rates of homelessness, this common housing fraction—frequently blamed for homelessness—doesn't provide the explanation we seek.

Recent research offers more nuance. Chris Glynn and colleagues used data from all CoCs in the country—a much broader sample than the one we use in this book—and found evidence of inflection points in the relationship between housing cost burdens and community levels of homelessness.[7] According to their analysis, rates of homelessness rise sharply once housing cost burden exceeds 30–34 percent. This threshold makes

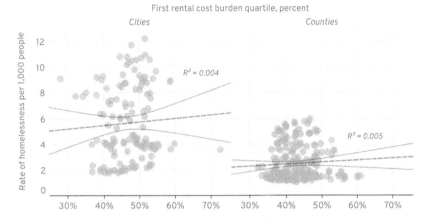

Figure 19. First-quartile housing cost burden versus PIT count (per capita). Dashed lines indicate a linear regression of per capita PIT counts onto the first rental cost burden quartile between 2007 and 2019 for a sample of U.S. regions. Data source: HUD / U.S. Census Bureau

sense, especially given the 30 percent cutoff often deployed to signify whether a household is indeed "cost burdened." Importantly, the researchers' analysis employed statistical methods to control for variation along dimensions other than housing cost burden, including population size and poverty rates, in addition to allowing for the relationship between these variables and the outcome variable of interest—rates of homelessness—to be nonlinear. Doing so allowed the researchers to isolate the effect of a given variable (in this case, housing cost burden) while holding others constant and to identify the existence of the inflection points in question. Certainly, we agree that higher cost burdens lead to higher rates of homelessness at the individual level. And if we control for other factors, within a given community, rising housing cost burdens (especially past the inflection points identified by Glynn et al.) will lead to higher community-level homelessness. Within our sample of thirty CoCs (representing most of the largest MSAs in the country), though, housing cost burden doesn't help explain regional variation.[8]

ABSOLUTE RENT LEVELS

As demonstrated above, the housing cost burden fraction (rent divided by income) fails to explain regional variation in rates of homelessness. But let's deconstruct the fraction into its component parts. In chapter 3, we tested a meaningful correlate of the denominator and found a negative relationship between poverty and rates of homelessness. High poverty regions do not have high rates of homelessness. Poverty may lead to homelessness at the individual level, but it does not explain regional variation. We now consider the numerator of the burden fraction: housing costs. Do *absolute* rent levels explain variation?

Unsurprisingly, the landscape of our sample illustrates substantial variation in rents across CoCs. Consistent with expectations, a number of cities in the industrial Midwest—Detroit, Indianapolis, St. Louis, Cuyahoga County (Cleveland), and Hamilton County (Cincinnati)—have low median rents (below $750). On the other end of the spectrum are a handful of expensive coastal cities and counties. Boston, San Francisco, King County (Seattle), San Diego County, and Washington, D.C., all see median monthly rents between $1,500 and $2,000. The highest rental costs in our sample are in Santa Clara County (Silicon Valley), where median rents are nearly $2,300/month; over three times the level of Rust Belt cities. These stark differences highlight the radically different consequences of poverty depending on where one lives.

Consider the graphs in Figure 20. Unlike many previous analyses presented in this book, the relationship between the

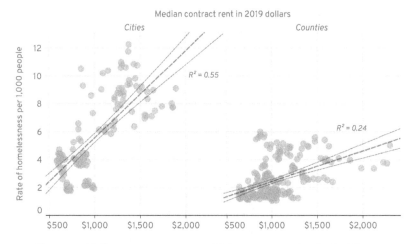

Figure 20. Median contract rent versus PIT count (per capita). Dashed lines indicate a linear regression of per capita PIT counts onto median contract rent between 2007 and 2019 for a sample of U.S. regions. Data source: HUD / U.S. Census Bureau

variables in question is convincingly positive—and captures the intuitive relationship between housing markets and homelessness that we might expect at first blush. In city CoCs, the relationship between rents and homelessness is drastic; in county CoCs (i.e., regions with less urban concentration), the relationship is substantial but slightly less pronounced. Our measure of explained variation (R^2) is significantly higher than we've observed elsewhere.

In Figure 21, we also consider the relationship between rents at the twenty-fifth percentile and rates of homelessness. Precariously housed adults and families rarely rent at the fiftieth percentile, so just as was the case in our test of housing cost burden, it's worth examining low-income rents. As the graphic demonstrates, the story is the same. Places with higher rents at the twenty-fifth percentile have higher rates of homelessness.[9]

Figure 21. First-quartile rent versus PIT count (per capita). Dashed lines indicate a linear regression of per capita PIT counts onto the first rent quartile between 2007 and 2019 for a sample of U.S. regions. Data source: HUD / U.S. Census Bureau

These findings invite an obvious question: Why do absolute rents explain regional variation, but housing cost burden doesn't? One plausible explanation comes from the fact that for households with extremely low incomes, the absolute level of rent is far more important. If you're a cost-burdened renter at the upper end of the income spectrum, you can choose to spend less on housing if the need arises. If you're a cost-burdened renter at the lower end of the income spectrum, that's not true: Rents don't drop to zero. Instead, they hit a floor determined by the local housing context and the rules that govern housing quality; eventually, you're living in the cheapest housing available (and we're left asking a question about low-income housing supply).

This part of the story is a double-edged sword. On a relative basis, the quality of housing in the United States is very high. Housing units of inadequate quality are rare, and levels of quality don't differ meaningfully between subsidized and market-rate units.[10] This national move toward high-quality housing unquestionably represents a positive change relative to prior eras, when housing quality represented a major public concern.[11] At the same time, because of the well-documented link between housing quality and price, increased quality—in a somewhat perverse result—may limit the supply of "naturally occurring" affordable rental housing due to higher prices and may increase the cost of new, affordable units.[12] Certainly, rules must govern housing quality and safety. But this contradiction highlights a logical inconsistency in the U.S. approach to affordable development: We mandate a minimum level of quality but fail to provide sufficient resources to households who can't afford the housing constructed or maintained at this standard.

In sum, we believe that this finding—the importance of absolute rents—speaks to a basic and intuitive fact: For a highly impoverished household, it is likely easier to access housing in Detroit or St. Louis, where median rents are between $600 and $700 per month, than in San Francisco and Santa Clara County, where costs are three to four times higher. Affordable housing that meets basic standards is accessible in some locations, but not others. There are more ways to "make it work" in St. Louis. Minimum wage labor, public assistance, and support from family and friends can be enough to help you get by. Such supports—which also exist in more expensive cities—are woefully inadequate given the cost of housing.

RENTAL MARKET VACANCY RATES

The final variable we investigate is rental market vacancy rates— that is, the proportion of available rental units in a given region at any given point in time. In 2019, numerous CoCs had rental market vacancy rates in excess of 8 percent, including Atlanta, St. Louis, Mecklenburg County (Charlotte), Dallas County, Clark County (Las Vegas), and Hillsborough County (Tampa)—representing a more accommodating rental market for housing. That same year, the availability of rental housing was severely constrained in several markets, among them the list of usual suspects, including San Francisco, Boston, New York, Santa Clara County, Los Angeles County, and King County (Seattle). But there's a surprising addition to this list, as well: Detroit.

In the decade since the Great Recession, rental vacancies in Detroit have fallen considerably. In 2010, Detroit had a rental market vacancy rate of nearly 14 percent: the highest rate in our sample. Over the ensuing nine years, the vacancy rate fell by over ten percentage points to less than 4 percent, placing Detroit in the same company as San Francisco and New York. Explaining this precipitous decline requires a closer look at post-recession Detroit. Indeed, both total population and the total number of housing units have fallen in the city since 2007. Most substantial, though, are the city's levels of unoccupied, vacant housing units. Over this period, between 25 and 30 percent of all units were unoccupied. To understand the city's tight rental market in the context of a quarter of all housing units being vacant, it is important to note that most of these unoccupied units are not available for lease. Many units are abandoned—and therefore not included in the active housing stock in the city. As population and employment levels have stabilized in Detroit over the last decade, housing has become scarcer; and serious concerns have arisen regarding rising housing instability and homelessness in the years to come.[13] Through 2019, rental costs remained low, but if rental housing scarcity continues to persist, we'd anticipate upward pressure on rents—which will further pun-ish many low-income households residing in this city. Detroit has a hidden advantage, however, that few other cities with tight rental markets enjoy: Detroit's vacant units offer the potential for refurbishment and could then be brought back into the hous-ing system. As Robin Runyan wrote in *Hour Detroit,* "With nearly 81,000 off-market vacant units, the city of Detroit does have suf-ficient housing stock."[14]

Outside the somewhat anomalous case of Detroit, we observe a strong, somewhat intuitive relationship between vacancy rates and rental costs (see Figure 22). Because rents tend to be higher when vacancy rates are low (all else being equal), we're ulti-mately measuring different aspects of a related phenomenon; these variables aren't independent of one another. This relation-ship is well known and has been observed by researchers in the fields of economics and real estate for decades.[15] As it relates to the topic of homelessness, given the relationship between two variables, we would expect to see higher rates of homelessness where vacancy rates are low.

Indeed, graphically and statistically, as shown in Figure 23, vacancy rates join rental costs as the only variables that explain regional variation in homelessness.[16] Because these variables are intimately related—vacancy rates help to predict housing costs—we don't attempt to rank the variables in terms of their relative impact on rates of homelessness.[17] Rather, we present these analyses as two examples of how related housing market dynamics explain why some regions have high rates of home-lessness while others don't. While beyond the scope of the base analyses in this book, we also conducted a series of multivari-ate models—statistical analyses that attempt to explain vari-ance in per capita rates of homelessness using more than one

Figure 22. Median rent versus rental vacancy rate. Dashed lines indicate a linear regression of rental vacancy rates onto media contract rent between 2007 and 2019 for a sample of U.S. regions. Data source: U.S. Census Bureau

Figure 23. Rental vacancy rate versus PIT count (per capita). Dashed lines indicate a linear regression of per capita PIT counts onto the natural log of rental vacancy rate between 2007 and 2019 for a sample of U.S. regions. Data source: HUD / U.S. Census Bureau

explanatory variable at once—that demonstrate similar results. Rents and vacancies continue to have significant explanatory power even after controlling for the effects of a range of different variables, including poverty, income, housing cost burden, population, age, race/ethnicity, gender, household structure, housing tenure, and inequality. Generally speaking, these housing market effects are strongest when seeking to explain indexed rates of per capita homelessness (i.e., when we place counties and cities on equal footing). They also tend to persist in so-called area fixed effects models whereby we seek to explicitly understand intra-regional variation over time. Comparatively speaking, these multivariate and fixed effects models suggest that vacancy rates appear to persist more strongly intra-regionally and rent effects persist more strongly inter-regionally.

To further explore the relationship, the following graphic plots first-quartile rental market vacancy rates against per capita rates of homelessness (Figure 24). (First-quartile vacancy rates come from measuring the vacancy rate of the market for units with rents between zero and the twenty-fifth percentile of regional rent.) Unsurprisingly, vacancy rates of cheaper rental units predict rates of homelessness, as well. While vacancies for these units appear to have slightly less predictive power than the overall market vacancy rates, because the difference is modest, one shouldn't draw too many conclusions here. The point is that the housing market— as a whole—helps create the conditions in which homelessness varies from region to region. It's not merely a shortage of low-income housing: It's an overall housing shortage that matters. As we discuss in the final chapter of this book, that fact doesn't imply that exclusively building luxury condos will solve a region's housing challenges—far from it. Housing doesn't magically "filter" or trickle down to low-income households. It is essential, therefore,

Figure 24. First-quartile vacancy rate versus PIT count (per capita). Dashed lines indicate a linear regression of per capita PIT counts onto the natural log of the first rental vacancy rate quartile between 2007 and 2019 for a sample of U.S. regions. Data source: HUD / U.S. Census Bureau

to ensure sufficient housing for the lowest-income households. But, as these figures demonstrate, tight housing conditions persist throughout the income spectrum and therefore, boosting the production of housing at all levels will relieve some of the pressure in these tight, expensive housing markets.

UNDERSTANDING THE MARKET

If we attribute regional variation in homelessness to housing market dynamics—rent levels and vacancy rates—as the previous analysis suggests we ought to, we need to understand why some cities have high housing costs and low vacancy rates while others do not. To do so, we need to understand how the forces of supply and demand shape the housing stock in a particular city or region. In the next chapter, we provide a more detailed analysis, but we provide a brief discussion here.

It is common among people who subscribe to structural explanations of homelessness to draw a link between population growth and homelessness. This connection makes intuitive sense. Rapid increases in employment and population may bring wealthy people to a community and displace existing residents. This problem is one of demand: As population and wages increase, the demand for housing grows. Indeed, housing scholars identify the key drivers of housing demand as income, population, and household formation.[18] Given the employment and population booms in cities like San Francisco, Seattle, and Washington, D.C., it would be easy to blame increasing rates of homelessness on these demand dynamics. But further investigation suggests that focusing solely on the demand side of the equation is inadequate. Many cities and counties with high rates of population growth fail to see high per capita rates of homelessness. In our sample, we observe—in Figure 25—only a modest positive relationship between population growth and homelessness in cities and virtually no relationship in counties.[19]

While the correlations in the previous chart tell a broad story about the population-homelessness relationship (or lack thereof), the case of Mecklenburg County (Charlotte), North Carolina, offers an illustration of a rapidly growing metropolitan area where rising demand has not produced scarce housing (when compared to other high-growth cities). Driven by a diverse economy, the population of Mecklenburg County grew by 28 percent from 2007 to 2019—one of the fastest growing large counties in the country. By comparison, King County (Seattle), home to a tech-driven population boom, grew by only 21.5 percent over the same period. The growing population of

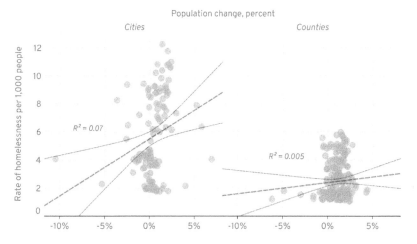

Figure 25. Change in population versus PIT count (per capita). Dashed lines indicate a linear regression of per capita PIT counts onto population change between 2007 and 2019 for a sample of U.S. regions. Data source: HUD / U.S. Census Bureau

the Charlotte region works for large employers in financial services, health care, and retail. And indeed, population growth has created a sharp increase in the demand for local housing. But while rents have risen during this expansion, vacancy rates have remained elevated, thanks to the quick and substantial construction of new housing. Over the period covered in our study, the average vacancy rate in Mecklenburg County hovered near 7 percent, and the number of occupied rental housing units increased by over 43 percent—a dramatic increase. Given sufficient housing resources, rates of homelessness have remained relatively low compared to many other fast-growing regions in the country. Over the study period, rates of homelessness in Mecklenburg have ranged from a low of 1.4 per thousand (in 2017) to 3.1 (in 2010)—well below the rates of other fast-growing counties, such as Multnomah (Portland) and King (Seattle).

Why, in response to substantial population growth, was Charlotte able to build a substantial number of new housing units? And why do other boomtowns like San Francisco and Seattle face chronic shortages of housing, even as population and employment continue to rise? More generally, why do some cities respond to growth by adding additional housing units, while other cities continue to operate with limited supplies of housing? To understand what's going on here, it's critical to recognize the concept of housing supply elasticity. In economics, price elasticity of supply refers to how responsive ("elastic") the supply of a given good or service is to a change in its price. The price elasticity of supply of housing, then, measures the change in housing supply in response to a change in the price of housing. When prices increase significantly, an elastic market will, in response, construct a large amount of housing, while an inelastic market will produce relatively fewer units. Urban economists have calculated local housing supply elasticities for cities across the United States, and cities with inelastic housing supply tend to have significant topographical constraints (like water and mountains) and/or restrictive regulatory environments that prevent rapid construction.[20] Large cities with inelastic housing supplies include New York City, Los Angeles, San Francisco, Seattle, and Miami. The urban economist Albert Saiz lists Houston, Austin, Charlotte, Kansas City, and Indianapolis as cities with the most elastic housing supply in the country.

In inelastic markets, increases in the demand for (and prices of) housing won't result in a robust supply response, thereby exacerbating existing housing market pressures. The relatively elastic housing supply of Charlotte, on the other hand—driven by an accommodating topography and a less restrictive regulatory environment—helps explain why, in response to a local economic boom, construction increased substantially, housing costs failed to spike to the extent they have in other regions, and rental market vacancies remain higher than in many other cities experiencing booms.

Because of the importance of rental market vacancy rates in this analysis, it is important to investigate the concept more deeply. Even in places with low vacancy rates, many units are often vacant. (We saw one version of this phenomenon in Detroit above.) A recent article out of the Bay Area proclaimed: "San Francisco has nearly five empty homes per homeless resident."[21] This fact feels like a contradiction—and at face value, it is. And while the San Francisco calculation is technically correct—the numbers are right there on the American Community Survey (ACS)—it points to a central challenge of operationalizing the concept of vacancy: that of how to measure the idea in a manner that captures the housing market to which a given renter might actually be exposed. To shed light on this question, let's break down vacant units in San Francisco using data from the ACS.

The "vacant" units referenced by the author of the San Francisco article aren't vacant in the sense that a potential buyer or renter could secure one of them. Many are already rented or purchased but remain vacant for a portion of the year; others are seasonal or vacation homes. The ACS offers a catch-all "Other Vacant" category, too, which includes units "held for occupancy by a caretaker or janitor, and units held for personal reasons of the owner."[22] There's undoubtedly a story of excess and waste to be told here, but it is a story of vacancy writ large—and not one of rental vacancies. Table 1 shows the actual breakdown of vacant units in San Francisco in 2017.

TABLE I

Summary of Vacant Units: San Francisco, 2017

Total Housing Units	397,566
Occupied Units	360,323
Owner-occupied	131,576
Renter-occupied	228,747
Vacant Units	37,243
For rent	8,292
Rented, not occupied	1,428
For sale, only	1,244
Sold, not occupied	4,157
Seasonal, recreational, or occasional use	10,603
Other vacant	11,519
Homeowner Vacancy Rate	0.9%
Rental Vacancy Rate	3.5%

As the table demonstrates, for potential renters in San Francisco, there are a limited number of options. The rental vacancy rate is calculated by dividing the total number of rental units available for rent (8,292) by the sum of that value and the number of occupied rental units (228,747). The quotient produces the rental market vacancy rate—in this case, 3.5 percent.

In San Francisco, more than twenty-two thousand units are vacant for "Seasonal" or "Other" reasons. Thus, by the broad definition of "vacant," there are enough units to house all people experiencing homelessness in the city, but that's not the same thing as saying San Francisco has sufficient housing for all of its residents and it just needs to allocate the housing more efficiently. In reality, the number of *rentable* rental units is remarkably low. We can't efficiently allocate our way out of this problem.

Still, 8,292 potential units available for rent sounds like a large number. Why so many rental vacancies in a city with such significant demand for housing? The answer lies in studies of housing markets. Scholars have repeatedly identified a "natural vacancy rate" for rental housing between 4 and 5 percent.[23] Just as economists consider there to be a natural rate of unemployment—below which there is a shortage of labor—the natural vacancy rate indicates the level at which the rental market is in equilibrium. Given the normal frictions and transitions of any housing market, it is impossible for every unit to be occupied at once. People move and units are vacated, occasionally for an extended period. Vacancy rates above the natural rate indicate a market with surplus units, while markets operating below the natural rate have a housing deficit. Rather than suggesting an abundance of housing units ready to be occupied by the precariously housed, San Francisco's 3.5 percent rental market vacancy rate indicates a market in deficit—in dire need of additional rental units to meet the needs of its growing population.

Urban economics literature helps provide an important link between the two variables of interest in this chapter: rental market vacancy rates and absolute levels of rents. Dozens of studies have highlighted a strong theoretical and empirical relationship between these two variables. According to Kenneth Rosen and Lawrence Smith, variations "in the vacancy rate around some natural rate of vacancy exert a significant influence on the rate of change of the price of rental housing services."[24] Subsequent research has refined Rosen and Smith's analysis but reached consistent conclusions.[25] The story is straightforward enough. When housing market conditions are tight and vacancies are limited, rents in a region receive upward pressure. Accordingly, the absolute rent levels tested in this chapter can be partially explained by the prevailing vacancy rates in a given locale (and not necessarily the other way around).

The housing market factors outlined in this chapter—in particular, absolute rents and vacancy rates—provide a credible explanation for regional variations in homelessness. As noted previously, this finding does not suggest that individual factors do not matter. Instead, it suggests that household risk factors may produce a spell of homelessness in some settings and circumstances but not in others. Context matters. Vulnerable households live in every city of the country; the difference in *rates* of homelessness can be attributed to structural factors associated with the housing market. Individual factors may help explain who becomes homeless in a tight housing market like Seattle, but they fail to explain why the city has five times the rate of homelessness of Chicago.

It's worth noting that while these market factors help to explain the differences we're after, they don't capture everything. Statistically, even after taking housing into account, plenty of meaningful regional variation remains unexplained. But it would be shocking if rents explained 100 percent of variance. Homelessness is a complex social phenomenon involving the lived experiences of hundreds of thousands of people; it is not a function of one or two variables. (If it were, policy solutions to housing instability would likely be more readily available.) In other words, by no stretch of the imagination do housing market variables explain all variation in the manifestation or experience of homelessness across cities around the country. Certainly, other research examining within-area changes over time has identified a positive relationship between rents and homelessness.[26] And yet even within a given city, there may be circumstances in which housing costs rise and the rate of homelessness does not. Brendan O'Flaherty highlights two such periods—one in New York, and one in Los Angeles—where such an outcome occurred.[27]

But these market factors are still useful. That so much regional variance is captured by a handful of straightforward measurements suggests there's something fundamental at play here. And to the extent that cities and counties are in a position to affect structural change, understanding these fundamental relationships remains critical to crafting the most appropriate response to the crisis.

Our analysis can also consider other upstream explanations for the variation that we observe. One such structural factor that has been implicated as a potential driver of homelessness is income inequality. Existing research demonstrates that inequality helps to explain both homelessness and the vastly different housing market conditions that we observe throughout the United States. As described in our first chapter, O'Flaherty highlighted the relationship between income inequality and homelessness in his 1996 book. Importantly, he drew a link between income inequality and the housing market dynamics that produce high rates of homelessness.[28] While we argue in this book that housing market factors explain variation in rates of homelessness, income inequality helps us understand why housing market conditions are more conducive to homelessness in some locales than others. Recent research from Thomas Byrne, Benjamin Harwood, and Anthony Orlando provides just such a link. In a sample of 239 communities in the United States (a far larger sample than the one we include in our book), income inequality—as measured by Gini coefficients—has a *causal* relationship with rates of homelessness.[29] In other words, the pronounced income inequality seen in many U.S. cities helps to produce an environment with high housing costs and modest incomes where homelessness flourishes. In our sample of thirty large metropolitan areas, we do not find a strong link between income inequality and per capita rates of homelessness—it is present in city CoCs, but not in county CoCs. This is likely due to the fact that many of the cities in our sample have relatively high rates of income inequality. In other words, there isn't enough variation here. The much larger sample used by Byrne and colleagues includes far greater variation in levels of inequality and therefore provides more opportunity to explore this relationship. We conclude that income inequality may not explain regional variation among the largest and most unequal cities (those metropolitan areas in our sample), but it does help to explain why homelessness is much worse in communities where income inequality is high.

PART III

Conclusion

CHAPTER SIX

Typology

In a recent article for Bloomberg CityLab, Benjamin Schneider highlights how the "modern" notion of homelessness that began in the 1980s differs from prior eras, in which the experience was isolated to skid rows and single-room occupancy hotels (SROs). Describing this earlier, more limited scope of homelessness in prior generations, Nan Roman, chief executive of the National Alliance to End Homelessness, suggests in the article that "there were people with mental illness, lots of people with substance abuse disorders, lots of poor people, all the same issues, but there was not widespread homelessness." In contrast, when describing the modern manifestation, Roman states: "What changed was the housing."[1] In particular, scarce and expensive housing—a condition that has become more prevalent in the United States over the last few decades—has produced a crisis greater in scope. This much is in broad agreement with what you've read so far. But as also described throughout this book, challenging housing market conditions are not evenly distributed throughout the country: Housing is more expensive and less readily available in some places. In this chapter, we begin to examine why these market conditions vary so considerably.

At the University of Washington, I (Gregg) teach a course that covers key questions in urban economics: *Why do cities exist? Why is land in cities more expensive than in rural areas? Why do some cities grow while others shrink?* In the class, one of my favorite exercises is to ask students to guess the Zillow Home Value Index—a measure of home values in a given geographic area— for Cleveland, Ohio. To frame the conversation, I let them know that the equivalent estimate for Seattle is about $750,000. After giving them a moment to think, I invite students to shout out their answers: "$250,000!" "$175,000!" $300,000!" "$150,000!" Every time I deploy this exercise, I hear a similar distribution of responses. Inevitably, I get to shout back—"You are all WAY TOO HIGH!"—and to incredulous and quizzical looks, I disclose that the Zillow Home Value Index for Cleveland was about $50,000 in 2017 and had grown to just over $60,000 by 2019. The students are shocked. The index is less than 10 percent of the price of a home in Seattle. When I tell them the equivalent figure in San Francisco is nearly $1.4 million, the stark differences between U.S. housing markets become abundantly clear.

To understand the roots underlying the drastic variation in housing costs around the country, we note that housing in the United States is currently understood as a commodity: something that can be bought, sold, or traded and that fluctuates in price as a function of its supply and demand. Accordingly, in this chapter, we take a closer look at the demand for and supply of housing, as well as the powerful private and public forces that help shape each term. We argue that an analysis focused exclusively on the demand for housing is insufficient—just as are attempts that solely encompass the supply side.

DEMAND

Foundational studies from housing economics suggest that the primary drivers of housing demand include population growth, employment, and income.[2] The relationship between these factors is intuitive: All else equal, more people with more money will increase the demand for housing. By implication, regions with the greatest demand will be those with growing populations and rising employment and incomes—when primary employers in a given city create new, high-paying jobs, housing demand rises in kind. But a key question is what types of organizations are most responsible for employment gains? And the answer is largely the private sector. As of December 2019, only 15 percent of all non-farm jobs were with federal, state, and local governments.[3] Accordingly, over 85 percent of all employment is in the private sector, making private-sector employment the primary driver of housing demand in a given location.[4] A notable exception comes from our nation's capital, where almost 30 percent of employment is in the public sector, where the ebb and flow of government employment can have a major effect on the demand for housing in the metropolitan area.

Naturally, governments influence housing demand through more means than direct employment—largely via a toolkit that can expand or restrict employment and population growth. Local governments in particular frequently seek to actively cultivate an environment that promotes job growth, often operating under the logic that job-market health promotes rising incomes, wealth accumulation, and, by extension, a larger tax base. Indeed, these factors tend to be prized above other regional characteristics as markers of a successful metropolitan area. Accordingly, states and cities frequently invest directly in or provide other incentives to private companies in order to boost local employment. Especially in regions where jobs are in short supply, local governments often incentivize businesses with tax breaks to open a new plant or facility—thereby providing jobs for residents and, in theory, improving the local economy. Benjamin Austin and colleagues argue that place-based policies designed to increase employment in economically depressed locations could indeed yield positive results for municipalities.[5] In general, questions about place-based policies—most notably state and local business tax incentives—revolve around cost-benefit considerations: Namely, are the economic benefits and positive spillover effects worth the loss in tax receipts? The evidence, as summarized by Cailin Slattery and Owen Zidar, suggests—in many cases—no.[6]

Recently, a high-profile example of the quest for local employment played out nationally. In 2017, Amazon announced its intention to open a second corporate headquarters (HQ2, as it was called) somewhere in North America. The second location would represent an equal to the only home the e-commerce giant has known since its founding: Seattle. The lure of thousands of high-paying jobs and a highly educated workforce was tempting for many cities. But as Derek Thompson highlighted in an article for *The Atlantic*, Amazon wanted something in return: "several billion dollars in tax incentives and a potential face-lift to the host city."[7]

The heavy price tag did little to dissuade cities from entering the HQ2 sweepstakes: 238 cities submitted proposals, with approaches ranging from creative to outlandish. Nicky Woolf, in an article for the *New Statesmen*, called the process "The Hunger Games for cities" and highlighted some of the more absurd approaches: "A group representing Tucson, Arizona delivered a 21-foot cactus by truck to Amazon's Seattle office. The city council of Stonecrest, Georgia, voted simply to hand over 345 acres of land for the tech giant to build its own municipality, a new town which would be called Amazon City. The night before the filing deadline, New York Mayor Bill de Blasio lit every light he could, from the rooftops of One World Trade and the Empire State Building to all of the city's wifi hotspots, in Amazon's signature shade of orange."[8]

Beyond these gimmicks, Woolf also noted a range of significant provisions included in various proposals. Chicago offered a scheme in which Amazon could recoup 50 percent of all income taxes paid by Amazon employees; Boston and San Francisco offered teams of taxpayer-funded city workers to serve the company; Atlanta offered a dedicated train car on its subway system. Altogether, many jurisdictions offered tax concessions and other incentives valued at more than $5 billion.[9]

In response to these concessions, many critics wondered why local jurisdictions should offer considerable tax breaks to prosperous corporations like Amazon in the first place. Thompson highlighted three reasons cities and states should end this practice: (1) corporate giveaways may be redundant—that is, the company in question is likely to select a given location regardless of offered benefits; (2) companies may not deliver the anticipated job growth (see the Foxconn debacle in Wisconsin);[10] and (3) it's "ludicrous for Americans to collectively pay tens of billions of dollars for huge corporations to relocate *within the United States*."[11] When Amazon ultimately selected New York and Northern Virginia to jointly house two new headquarters, many wondered whether the company had really needed such a drawn-out process to create new homes in the country's financial and political hubs.

Indeed, this process is worth further examination. After collecting initial submissions, Amazon released a final list of twenty potential HQ2 destinations, which included expected candidates like Washington, D.C., New York, and Los Angeles, but also much smaller cities like Indianapolis and Pittsburgh. At the time, many argued there was little chance Amazon would select a small city like Indianapolis given the massive shock such a selection would have on the region's real-estate markets—and the challenge of attracting top technology talent to the middle of Indiana. But Indianapolis's relatively long odds didn't stop the city from assembling a benefits package to entice Jeff Bezos and his company. And in the years following its design and submission of the proposal in question, the Indiana Economic Development Corporation—which worked on the proposal with the Indianapolis Chamber of Commerce—has refused to release details of the proposal. This refusal prompted a lawsuit that demands its public release, including details of any tax breaks offered to Amazon.[12]

Why the reluctance to release the proposal? Certainly, the city likely fears the backlash that many communities faced when they disclosed the scope of the incentives offered to one of the wealthiest companies in the world.[13] But concern about corporate handouts and potential misuse of public funds wasn't the only concern raised during the HQ2 process. An important counterargument to the bid process raised the potential *negative* consequences of Amazon coming to town. Much of the tech talent would likely need to be imported, and the resulting population boom could present big challenges for the community. Seattle, for many, was the canary in the coal mine. The tech boom that has brought tens of thousands of employees to Seattle has changed the city in material respects.[14] Critics pointed to congestion, sky-high housing prices, displacement, and homelessness—and drew a causal arrow connecting Amazon's rise with Seattle's housing squeeze. These concerns are broadly summarized by Slattery and Zidar in their evaluation of state and local business incentives: "How much do these policies improve the well-being of underemployed and low-income workers? Are the most distressed places able to attract firms with tax incentives? . . . At the local level, is the newly attracted firm stimulating hiring of local residents who were previously unemployed and working in low-wage jobs? Or as was argued in the case of Amazon's proposal for putting a headquarters in New York City, are all the good jobs going to people moving in from other locations, leaving locals with more congestion and higher prices?"[15]

Some cities anticipated these concerns in their proposals to Amazon. Minneapolis, for example, offered far lower tax benefits than did other cities—largely to ward off potential negative implications for existing corporate residents (including Target Corporation) and the fiscal implications of large tax incentives. After Minneapolis was not included as a finalist for HQ2, *The Minnesota Daily* expressed relief in an editorial: "Having to provide incentives as high as $7 billion in order to win the bid is a legislative and political burden; one the state might not have been able to match. Additionally, housing has been a point of contention in the Twin Cities because of rapid growth. Affordable housing and gentrification were a hot button issue in the municipal elections during the fall, and the problems facing the city in this regard would grow if Amazon touched down in Minnesota."[16]

Amazon's search for a second headquarters highlights the manners in which public and private forces contribute to the demand for housing. Local governments are not powerless in this arena; many times, they actively work to stimulate the local economy, and by extension, prod the demand side of the equation. In other words, rather than sitting on the sideline as labor and housing markets run their course, governments actively stimulate or limit the demand for housing. Local policymakers must navigate the tension of maximizing employment and income while minimizing the potential consequences of stimulative policies and programs. The case of Minneapolis illustrates a city concerned about these potential consequences. And while it's clear the economic trajectories of many Rust Belt cities—characterized by declining employment, incomes, and population—are to be avoided, the consequences of hyper-growth (as seen in Seattle and other boomtowns) offer a cautionary tale to other cities.

There's a contradiction at play here. Local jurisdictions tend to be eager to bring new jobs to a community. They offer incentives, issue permits, and fast-track construction of new buildings. Less frequently over the course of a given job-courting routine are municipalities made to think about where these new employees will live. Indeed, by and large, while economic development agencies actively bring employers and employees to a region, they take a laissez-faire approach to housing these employees. Noting this disconnect, Stephen Norman, executive director of the King County Housing Authority, quipped, "Homes are where jobs go at night."

SUPPLY

Like the demand for housing, its supply is determined by a range of public and private actors. Certainly, since the vast majority of housing in the United States is constructed privately, housing supply necessarily depends on the actions of private firms. And absent government support or subsidies, in a vacuum, housing will tend to be constructed where it can be built profitably. But housing isn't built in a vacuum. Governments actively stimulate or restrict supply through a range of policies and programs designed to incentivize production or govern the production process.

As demonstrated in the previous chapter, the development of housing doesn't depend solely on population growth. Some high-growth regions construct plenty of housing; others seem to have persistent housing shortages. To think through the manners in which housing supply differs from region to region, we emphasize the concept of supply elasticity—the degree to which the supply of housing changes given a change in its price. As outlined by Albert Saiz, two primary factors drive a community's supply response: the geographic attributes of an area (including mountains and bodies of water) and the local regulatory environment. Both factors can promote greater housing production or restrict it. In a somewhat cruel irony, the topographical attributes that make some cities desirable also make it difficult to accommodate growing populations. According to Saiz's estimates of supply elasticity, the ten cities with the least responsive housing-supply responses all border either water or mountains. Regions with the most elastic (responsive) supply tend to be found in flat, land-locked locations, where geographic barriers to new housing construction are scant.[17]

Despite the importance of topography, researchers and policymakers generally pay more attention to Saiz's second factor: regulations. Fair enough—geography tends to be fixed within a given city. Accordingly, *changes* to a supply response (i.e., changes to a market's supply elasticity) are often solely a function of the local regulatory environment. One of the most hotly debated topics in the current environment is the notion of single-family zoning. Residential zoning is one of the seemingly innocuous rules and regulations that has played a major role in the housing crises that are gripping cities around the nation. Broadly, zoning regulations help explain why multifamily housing isn't more abundant in Seattle, for example: It's illegal on roughly 70 percent of the residential parcels in the city.[18] Seattle isn't alone in its reliance on single-family homes to house its residents. A recent article in *The New York Times* highlighted that zoning outliers like New York City and Washington, D.C.—in which only 15 and 36 percent of parcels are respectively zoned single-family—stand in stark contrast to many other cities in the country—including Los Angeles, Minneapolis, and Charlotte—where over 70 percent of residential land is reserved for single-family homes. The authors call single-family zoning "practically gospel in America, embraced by homeowners and local governments to protect neighborhoods of tidy houses from denser development nearby."[19]

As cities grow, challenges associated with a reliance on single-family homes become more and more apparent. In the absence of zoning reform, most growth must be accommodated by the small minority of parcels that permit multifamily housing. In rapidly growing areas, the approach is simply untenable—and accordingly, some jurisdictions, including Minneapolis and the state of Oregon, have recently taken steps to ban single-family zoning. (Such a ban does not actually outlaw single-family homes; rather it bans zoning that precludes the construction of multifamily dwellings on any parcel.) Advocates see these kinds of zoning reforms as key tools to address the housing shortages apparent in many U.S. cities.

But zoning isn't the only regulatory impediment to greater housing development. A frequently complex regulatory approval process also explains why construction—both single-family and multifamily—is difficult to pursue even where it is legally permitted. Examples of other regulatory constraints include building codes and various forms of land use restrictions, among them minimum lot sizes, height limits, setbacks, and open-space requirements.[20] Researchers at the University of Pennsylvania have leveraged these factors to develop an index that measures the stringency of land use regulations: the Wharton Residential Land Use Regulation Index. Saiz employed this index—combined with his topographical analysis—to generate the estimates of housing supply elasticity we reference throughout the following sections.

To the extent that policies follow politics, below the surface of an otherwise benign regulatory landscape is a swath of often contentious local politics that complicate efforts to change the way cities are physically structured. One of the hallmarks of American society is homeownership. Over time, roughly two-thirds of U.S. households have owned their own condominium or single-family home, and home equity is the largest source of wealth for most U.S. households.[21] A logical consequence of this reality is that households seek to preserve (or grow) the value of their home equity by any means necessary. William Fischel coined the phrase the "Homevoter Hypothesis" to describe the ways in which homeowners support the value of their most important asset via political participation and the exertion of control over local governments. Fischel summarized: "My contribution is to point out that one of the fundamental changes has been to make homeowners acutely defensive about changes in land use that might possibly affect their home's value. . . . It might be better for all concerned if homeowners could again see their homes as steady investments and good places to live rather than a way to get rich."[22]

A conspicuous example of Fischel's hypothesis comes by way of homeowners opposing new residential development.[23] In *Generation Priced Out: Who Gets to Live in the New Urban America*, Randy Shaw highlights a generational conflict whereby younger generations—who struggle to afford housing in many cities— support greater residential development. Baby boomers, on the other hand, the primary beneficiaries of the generational home- equity lottery, "have enjoyed soaring home values by prevent- ing the construction of new housing in their communities."[24] The contentious debate around eliminating single-family zon- ing provides real-time examples of the Homevoter Hypoth- esis at work. Single-family homeowners—even self-described political progressives—may aggressively oppose zoning changes that would bring multifamily housing to their neighborhoods. In this manner, we can understand single-family zoning as exclusionary—and the current debate as highlighting how homeowners seek to preserve the exclusive character of their neighborhoods. Common bogeymen deployed to oppose zoning changes include congestion, inadequate infrastructure, crowded schools, and changes to "neighborhood character." (Note that character arguments often drove the active, publicly buoyed racial segregation of U.S. cities' public and private housing.)

No place exemplifies the challenges of new housing con- struction better than California. In *Golden Gates: Fighting for Housing in America*, Conor Dougherty demonstrates how local politics and special interests converge to prevent or limit hous- ing development. In 2015, then governor of California Jerry Brown proposed streamlining the construction process for new housing in exchange for commitments to reserve units for lower-income households. Dougherty describes the fate of the potential deal:

As the proposal made its way through the capitol, cities, environmental groups, and construction unions all rose up against it. Each of these groups wanted different things—cities wanted more say over what could be built where, environmentalists wanted more environmental reviews, and unions wanted a prevailing wage guarantee that favored workers—but what united them was a fear that if building was easier, they would lose their leverage over projects. That was why housing law was so hard to streamline: A complicated process was full of political profit. Negotiations broke down and the governor's proposal died.[25]

Dougherty's description is important. Zoning, code, and review often appear as banal, fixed facets of the development process, but behind these regulations are people. Their interests and political interactions shape the viability of any idealized policy crafted to accommodate growing populations.

LOCAL CONTEXTS

As we noted in the previous chapter, some housing-market conditions are less forgiving than others, and these differences help to explain variation in rates of homelessness. Thus far, here, we've suggested that the price elasticity of supply of housing helps to explain variation in these market conditions. But elasticity alone is insufficient to explain whether we might consider a given region's supply to be *adequate.* Adequacy or sufficiency judgments about a housing market naturally require the consideration of both the demand for housing *and* the associated supply response. Consider Figure 26, which plots cities' post-recession population growth rates versus their housing supply elasticities. We have placed ellipses around similar cities as a first step toward developing an explanatory typology:

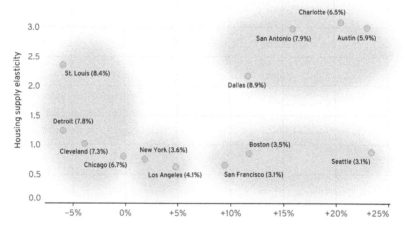

Figure 26. Population growth versus housing supply elasticity. Dots indicate U.S. cities; parentheses indicate 2010-2019 rental vacancy rates. Data source: U.S. Census Bureau / Saiz (2010)

The figure suggests four different groups of cities. On the left, we see St. Louis, Detroit, Cleveland, and Chicago—all of which have flat to negative population growth. Each of these cities also has a relatively low rate of per capita homelessness. In other words, in terms of housing supply and vacancy rates, supply elasticity doesn't matter nearly as much where there is limited demand. Without population growth, markets aren't pressured to increase housing supply. Existing housing supply is generally adequate, as demonstrated by the relatively high vacancy rates in each location. But in this group of cities, we still see variation; St. Louis has a higher supply elasticity than Detroit, Cleveland, or Chicago. The difference here can be attributed to topography: a key input to the supply elasticity formula. Because Detroit, Cleveland, and Chicago all border Great Lakes, these metropolitan areas can only expand in one direction—away from the water. Landlocked St. Louis doesn't have this constraint. By implication, if population growth were to ramp up in Chicago, Detroit, and Cleveland, it's possible their housing markets could tighten (with higher prices following after existing vacant units have been occupied). As described in the prior chapter, we're already seeing evidence of this in Detroit. We would expect St. Louis, due to its favorable topography, to be slightly more accommodating.

Moving counterclockwise in the graphic, the next category of cities includes New York and Los Angeles. The two largest cities in the country have similar dynamics. They have enormous populations, exhibit modest growth, and have low supply elasticities. As cited previously, these dynamics help to explain the high housing costs and low vacancy rates observed in these cities. As we know, rates of homelessness are also high in both cities. Note that from a supply-elasticity standpoint, Chicago doesn't differ meaningfully from New York or Los Angeles. The difference is that Chicago is no longer a growing city—and as a result, doesn't experience the same housing pressures.

In the lower-right corner of the graphic are the coastal boomtowns of Boston, Seattle, and San Francisco. These cities are marked by high population growth and low supply elasticities— a dangerous combination for renters. The logical outcomes are housing markets with high rents and low vacancies. (All three cities have vacancy rates below four percent.) It should come as no surprise to readers by this point that these locations also see high rates of homelessness.

The final grouping of cities resides in the upper-right portion of the graphic: cities with high growth and high supply elasticity. These Sun Belt cities see population growth rates similar to those in Seattle and San Francisco, but what sets them apart from their coastal peers is a robust supply response: We would expect cities with high supply elasticities to expand housing supply more rapidly as populations grow, and the high rental vacancy rates in these cities provide evidence that they do. This observation helps explain why the robust population growth in Charlotte, North Carolina, has not produced the harsh housing-market dynamics that exist in other growing metros like San Francisco and Seattle. Given these dynamics, we propose grouping cities as shown in Table 2.

This typology summarizes the prior analysis by linking population–elasticity relationships with their subsequent implications for homelessness. Two types of cities are associated with lower relative rates of homelessness: those in the Rust Belt and those in the Sun Belt. For Rust Belt cities, population loss or stagnation drives a more accommodating housing market. Given that housing is a durable asset, as population falls, housing availability rises. In these circumstances, housing supply often outpaces demand, producing lower rents and higher vacancy rates. The case of Rust Belt cities provides compelling evidence that reasonably abundant and affordable housing precludes homelessness, even in regions where poverty is prevalent.

The second type—Sun Belt cities—includes growing metro areas in the South like Austin, Charlotte, Dallas, and San Antonio. Each of these cities has experienced double-digit percentage population growth since the end of the Great Recession. Unlike Rust Belt cities, these cities have robust economies and growing populations. How do these vibrant cities manage to maintain relatively lower rates of homelessness? As these cities have grown and demand for housing has increased, they've

TABLE 2

A Typology of Cities: Growth, Housing Responses,
and Homelessness

Type		Rate of Homelessness
I	Rust Belt (low to negative growth)	Low
II	Sun Belt (high growth; elastic supply)	Low
III	Megacities (modest growth; inelastic supply)	High
IV	Boomtowns (high growth; inelastic supply)	High

followed with a robust supply response, maintaining moderately priced housing and medium-to-high vacancy rates despite the growth.[26]

The other two categories—growing megacities and boomtowns—share a common denominator: inelastic housing supplies. As we know from Figure 26, low supply elasticity isn't a problem when population growth slows or turns negative—consider the case of Chicago. But unlike Chicago, New York and Los Angeles have continued to grow, albeit at a relatively modest pace; and this growth has continued to pressure the housing market, given the very limited supply response in these cities. Accordingly, rents remain elevated and vacancy rates are low. As unaccommodating housing market conditions continue to apply pressure to a wide range of precariously housed households, high rates of homelessness persist.

The final group in our typology of cities are boomtowns—currently illustrated by the cases of Boston, Seattle, and San Francisco. These cities embody the perfect storm for housing instability and homelessness: high growth, low supply elasticity, high housing costs, and extremely low vacancy rates. It's in this manner that homelessness can thrive amid affluence. The troubling conundrum for local leaders in these cities is how to respond. They tend not to aspire to become the next Detroit or Cleveland—cities marked by population loss. Population growth, high wages, and a robust economy are generally considered markers of a successful city. But what if these very attributes are also responsible for the homelessness crisis that exists in these cities? We, and many others, have already presented a case about the relationship between affluence and homelessness at the metropolitan level.[27] All else being equal, we might normatively say that prosperity is indeed a desirable goal for a municipality to pursue on behalf of its residents. We shouldn't expect cities to actively impede prosperous opportunities. How, then, can these communities house the thousands of people who continue to move to these cities—as well as the people who already live there?

We also note that our typology aligns well with other statistical models of cities that have sought to cluster regions as a function of their socioeconomic and housing profiles. Glynn and colleagues, for example, grouped regions based on trends in rates of homelessness, population, and affordability. The model identified six clusters of CoCs, each of which tended to correspond to geographic regions (despite geographic data not being offered to the clustering algorithm). These regions are in rough agreement with ours: namely, one encompasses the Midwest, Mid-Atlantic, and parts of the southeast (i.e., including our Rust Belt cities), another includes New England, Florida, the mountain west and central United States (including our Sun Belt), and a third includes most of the West Coast and large East Coast cities like Boston and Washington, D.C. (combining our Types III and IV, megacities and boomtowns).[28]

We don't claim that all cities fit neatly into the above typology; nor do we suggest that cities remain in the same category indefinitely. Indeed, we note early evidence that Austin may be transitioning out of the Sun Belt category as housing production begins to lag and rates of homelessness begin to rise. A recent white paper from the Kinder Institute for Urban Research at Rice University suggests that such persistently high population growth is beginning to strain the Sun Belt cities previously known for abundant housing and relatively low costs. Without appropriate planning and policy responses, these cities risk a rise in housing cost burden and income inequality.[29] And we don't expect the housing market conditions we observe over the period of our study (2007–2019) to persist in perpetuity.

Indeed, as described by David Collier and colleagues, our typology includes "ideal" categories or types and isn't intended to cover all possible examples.[30] (Readers will note that not all cities in our sample are included in our typology.) We deploy ideal types to highlight fundamental relationships and their implications. In this case, we've sought to illustrate the relationship between population growth (demand) and supply elasticity—and, in turn, how those forces converge to produce the housing market dynamics that help explain regional variation in rates of homelessness. Given the conundrum above, then—that cities are incentivized politically to pursue an economic agenda that, without careful housing market calibration, will also spur housing instability—the burning question is what to do about it. The next chapter offers a vision for what this calibration might look like and how cities and our nation might go about nurturing an environment that affords it.

CHAPTER SEVEN

Response

Barack Obama once remarked that, as president, he didn't get to make any easy decisions: "If it was an easily solvable problem, or even a modestly difficult but solvable problem, it would not reach me, because, by definition, somebody else would have solved it."[1] The executive branch is a broad, multifaceted system employing over four million skilled professionals, each of whom are faced with countless decisions on a daily basis. Few of these reach the Oval Office.

The subnational management of and response to broad social problems operate similarly, in that by the time regions grapple with them—really grapple with them—the decisions to make are often intractably difficult. If they weren't, they'd have been made by now. In the case of a dangerous roadway intersection, concerned residents might write a letter to a councilmember, the elected official might alert the appropriate department, and after studying the intersection in question, agency staff might install a stoplight—solving the problem via the governmental infrastructure established to respond to exactly such problems. But many problems are bigger than stoplights. Underfunded agencies can lack sufficient resources, some problems require coordinated action across multiple agencies (at multiple levels of government), and others can suffer from lack of consensus about whether a given issue merits a governmental response in the first place.

Homelessness persists due to all three of these challenges. It is costly, its response requires participation and engagement from a variety of federal and local agencies, and public opinion buoys a robust debate about whether the government ought to respond to what's often perceived as an individual problem. While many talented and committed professionals have devoted their lives to preventing, mitigating, and ending homelessness, a half million people are still without housing on any given night in the country (a number that understates the true scale of the problem). This fact is not for want of talent or energy responding to the crisis at hand: Rather, the structural impediments outlined in this book have prevented enduring progress toward housing for all.

In this final chapter, we offer a prescription. Unlike other scholarship that describes the various tools that can be used to prevent and end homelessness, we take a broader view. Certainly, the research that analyzes the outcomes of a range of different interventions is important and worthy of your attention—but there are publications that provide greater detail on those topics than we do here.[2] Rather, we highlight issues we argue are higher-order concerns: public perception, funding, and placing the problem within a broader societal context. We also write for a broad audience, including policymakers tasked with preventing and ending homelessness, concerned residents who don't understand why so many people remain unhoused, and funders wondering how to make impactful investments.

Those who work on this issue know that long-run prevention of homelessness rests in greater access to housing—more afford-able units and income supplements to bridge the affordability gap. The near-term is more complicated.

Given the inadequate resources dedicated to ending home-lessness, the short-run is characterized by policymakers and practitioners being faced with a stream of difficult resource-allocation decisions. *Do we increase shelter capacity? Do we invest in diversion? Do we emphasize rapid rehousing or permanent supportive housing?* Scarcity forces these decisions upon us. These questions are critically important, and their answers are deeply consequen-tial to the people seeking shelter and housing decisions through the homelessness crisis response system. But if a given housing program is found to be the most effective and efficient response to homelessness, and only 5 percent of the people in a munici-pal response system can access the program due to housing and resource constraints, its overall utility drastically falls. An unfor-tunate by-product of this reality is the questioned efficacy of many contemporary homelessness responses. We take issue with this conclusion—that our response system has failed—because ample evidence suggests that many of these housing programs do work for some people. In reality, the approaches that work have not been sufficiently scaled to the magnitude of the crisis. That is the failure. Until we solve the fundamental problems of political will, resource commitment, and a lack of understand-ing of the issue as structural in nature, homelessness will persist.

THREE TENSIONS

In addition to the general impediments shared across many walks of policymaking outlined above, policy challenges unique to homelessness deserve further attention. In particular, within the community of people working to end homelessness, we note three core tensions that arise in the design of the most appropriate policy response: namely, short- versus long-term solutions, public versus private efforts, and in the case of the former, federal versus local responsibilities. We address these tensions in order to provide context for a policy vision presented later in this chapter.

Short- versus Long-Term Solutions

Most broadly, we might consider policy responses to homelessness to vary along temporal lines. While emergency shelters respond to the crisis at hand, permanent housing (whether public, private, subsidized, or unsubsidized) offers, by definition, a long-term end to a household's emergency. But it takes time to build housing. And given the severity of the public-health risks of experiencing homelessness—not least in cold climates—municipal shelter investments undoubtedly save lives.

Indeed, given the robust emergency shelter systems that have been constructed on the East Coast, the question of where the marginal dollar should be invested is easier: Resources should be used to expand the supply of permanent housing solutions. On the West Coast (and certain locations in Texas and Florida), where unsheltered homelessness is more conspicuous, community leaders must wrestle with the decision of whether to create greater shelter capacity in an effort to get people off the street or to invest in long-run housing solutions. Investments in permanent housing will, by definition, allow the current crisis of unsheltered homelessness to persist while developers undertake the relatively slow process of constructing permanent housing.

Further complicating efforts to resolve this tension is bureaucratic fragmentation. It is unlikely that a single municipal department is tasked with allocating the marginal dollar to, say, shelters versus affordable housing construction. In reality, human services departments tend to oversee shelter systems and homelessness services, public health departments and behavioral health providers mitigate the physical risks related to unsheltered homelessness, and planning departments and housing offices tend to address the regional housing supply. Differentially allocating money to various aspects of the response is complicated by this structure.

But as is the case in many of the tensions that we present, there's somewhat of a false dichotomy at work here. Ultimately, regions need both reactive and proactive policies and programs to respond to the housing crises they're facing—and those they may face in the future. Without a diverse portfolio of temporary and permanent housing opportunities, regions necessarily fail to respond to the needs of some of their constituents. Politically, as well—and homelessness is undeniably political—it is often expedient to invest in temporary solutions for the purpose of demonstrating quick, tangible (ostensible) progress and garnering the public trust necessary for long-term investment. (As we noted earlier, one role of emergency shelters is to hide people experiencing homelessness from people with housing.) The pressure to demonstrate progress is particularly acute on the West Coast, where many residents—voters—are growing increasingly frustrated with the state of unsheltered homelessness.

All told, while we acknowledge the critical importance of investing in emergency response systems to meet the needs of people sleeping outside, generally we advocate for policy and budgeting decisions that privilege the development of permanent housing solutions. Both approaches have merit, but only the latter will mitigate future stress on the former.

Public versus Private

In the United States, the private market serves as an allocation mechanism for most of the goods and services Americans consume or use; housing included. There are a few notable exceptions—public education, public health care (Medicare and Medicaid), and public safety among them—but, in general, most households rely on the private market to provide for both necessary and elective consumption. Housing—and the fact that millions of U.S. households lack affordable housing—highlights one of the shortcomings of an economic system that almost exclusively relies on market allocation. Economist Charles Lindblom wrote extensively about the relationship between markets and society, and his words are as relevant today as they were a half century ago: "A market is like a tool: designed to do certain jobs but unsuited for others. Not wholly familiar with what it can do, people often leave it lying in the drawer when they could use it. But then they also use it when they should not, like an amateur craftsman who carelessly uses his chisel as a screwdriver."[3]

Lindblom's point is far from normative. He's not arguing that markets are good or bad. Rather, he makes the case that markets work well for some activities and not others; and that it is vitally important to recognize when each is the case. Here, we argue that relying (solely) on the private market to solve our affordable housing crisis is like relying on Lindblom's chisel to screw hinges to a door. Certainly, we hope that private developers will continue to build great amounts of market-rate housing, because these units can help to reduce overall pressure on the market.

With the help of subsidies and tax credits, some of these developers may also contribute to the stock of housing that is affordable to more people. But when it comes to supplying housing for people with little to no income, the tool of the private market is not well-suited to the task.

Consistent with this logic, there is a growing recognition that the private sector alone cannot solve the affordable housing crisis that plagues many communities in the United States. Observers on both ends of the political spectrum have arrived at a similar conclusion, albeit by different paths. On one side, critics argue that a host of regulatory constraints (building codes, environmental regulations, lengthy permitting processes, zoning restrictions, parking minimums, and highly paid union labor) have made the construction of housing too expensive. Eliminating these constraints would allow the private market to produce a greater supply of housing that is more affordable to more people. The other side of the debate suggests that relying on for-profit developers to supply housing to those with little to no ability to pay is like trying to jam a square peg into a round hole. That's what the public sector is *supposed* to do, anyway. One of the roles of the government is to provide a basic safety net for households that includes access to core needs like food, health care, and shelter—so the argument goes.

There's some truth to both of these critiques. Housing *is* too expensive to construct. Unlike most other industries in the United States, it appears to be immune to technological advancements. Virtually every other product built or assembled today—cars, televisions, computers, spacecraft—is done so more quickly and more cheaply than it was fifty years ago. In many cases, costs have fallen while functionality has increased exponentially. A glaring example is in the processing power of computers; a modern iPhone has one hundred thousand times the processing power of the computer that NASA used to send people to the moon in 1969.[4] Yet despite perennial promises of low-cost, modular units and advances in materials and construction technology, we still build houses largely the same way we did when Neil Armstrong first stepped onto the lunar surface. Continued efforts to improve construction efficiency are critically important. This lack of technological and operational advancement makes the debate about public versus private provision of housing even more difficult.

Here, we argue developers are right, at least insofar as we agree that their profit incentives tend not to be aligned with the goals of affordable housing supply responses. Under capitalism, we don't expect corporations to self-organize in a benevolent manner to produce thousands of new rental units for people on fixed incomes in every major city in the country—not if such development isn't profitable. Left unchecked, market conditions are likely to continue to evolve such that developers will fail to supply sufficient levels of affordable housing for the population that needs it. These facts imply a need for a strong public action. And any public intervention will necessitate a dual thrust. First, the precariously housed need support, either in the form of cash assistance or rental subsidies. Second, the low end of the market in particular requires a robust supply response. Either approach alone is likely insufficient. Rental assistance is essential, but subsidies and time-limited vouchers don't work if the units aren't there.

Critically, we argue for a paradigm shift in how we think about housing. Rather than conceptualizing housing as solely a private good—one procured through market transactions—housing must be de-commodified. Shelter is fundamental to human survival and demands a different treatment than iPhones. A path toward a sustainable housing system requires a decoupling of a portion of the housing stock from the market, especially for households with the lowest incomes. In practice, this decoupling can be facilitated through public and nonprofit ownership of a portion of the multifamily housing stock. This approach doesn't preclude a role for the private sector; it notes that a reliance on private development alone won't address the dual crises of affordable housing and homelessness.

Local versus Federal

If we accept the premise that the public sector has a major role to play in homelessness and housing system improvement, a third tension arises regarding the relative responsibilities of national and subnational (i.e., state, regional, county, and city) governments. Complicating this debate is the fact that needs are not evenly distributed geographically, whether within a nation, state, or county. Accordingly, a common refrain is why states with low levels of per capita homelessness should subsidize homelessness-response programs in other states. The same argument often plays out locally, with suburban and rural regions often unwilling to commit revenue toward an issue that is most visible in the urban core.

We are unconvinced that the spatial distribution of homelessness should prevent or limit the response at any level of government. Aid is often unevenly distributed—consider agricultural subsidies and natural disaster relief—and, indeed, works best when it flows to areas of the greatest need. We argue the various organizational tiers of government each have distinct roles to play in an appropriate homelessness response. The federal government, for example, has financial resources that far exceed those of state and local governments due to federal taxation and the ability to raise large sums of money through debt issuance by the U.S. Treasury. This scale can facilitate substantial investments in housing—in the form of direct housing development, production subsidies, and tax credits—that far exceed the capacity of state and local jurisdictions. Expansions of existing federal programs (including housing vouchers) to cover all eligible households would provide substantial support to low-income households.

At the state and local level, governments can leverage a range of tools to promote housing for all. The strategies are neither new nor novel. State and local subsidies targeted to the households with the greatest needs have proven to be effective at limiting homelessness. At the beginning of the first New York City mayoral terms for both Michael Bloomberg and Bill de Blasio, the *New York Times* editorial page urged both mayors-elect to fund housing rental subsidies for households facing homelessness. The editorials called for city as well as state resources to fund the effort.[5] Beyond such subsidies, financial investments in affordable housing and permanent supportive housing would make a significant difference. Local governments can also bolster their emergency shelter systems where appropriate. Importantly, states, counties, and cities can also deploy a range of regulatory tools targeting tenant protections and ease of construction (including eviction protections, rent stabilization, zoning changes, and the streamlining of various permitting and review processes). In other words, a carefully calibrated policy strategy—implemented across all levels of government—is key to ensuring policy tactics align with revenue generation and the politics necessary to see the work through. We take a deeper dive into this strategy in the sections that follow.

In particular, we seek to provide a roadmap for addressing *and* preventing the crisis at hand. Homelessness is by no means inevitable. (The country's success in radically reducing veteran homelessness offers one illustration of this fact.) Our prescription, informed by conversations with experts and our own research, requires three, interrelated steps: (1) changing public perceptions of homelessness, (2) raising adequate resources to fund needed programming and investments, and (3) applying a systems approach to our understanding of the issue. These steps are not to be taken sequentially: All must operate in unison. Building a credible response to homelessness on one or two legs of this stool alone is impossible.

CHANGING PERCEPTION OF THE PROBLEM

In 2006, two psychologists published a study of brain responses to human images. The authors sought to build a stronger understanding of prejudice, and in doing so, showed study participants pictures of people and objects that differed along a variety of characteristics—from college students to heroin users to Olympians and people experiencing homelessness.[6] Given prior models of stereotyping behavior, the researchers predicted that study participants' brain activity—as measured by cerebral blood flow—would be notably different when viewing pictures of members of extreme social out-groups, including presumptive addicts and people experiencing homelessness. In particular, the researchers expected members of these out-groups to be "dehumanized," whereby humanization of others corresponded to brain activity consistent with social cognition. Indeed, this pattern of neural activation was present when viewing images of people from every social category *except* extreme-out groups, suggesting that "extreme out-groups may be perceived as less than human." Brain activity when viewing the latter images was also consistent with neural fingerprints of disgust.

The point here is that even social neuroscience documents the dehumanization of people experiencing homelessness—and when we don't see one another as human, we don't ascribe dignity to one another. This severe form of othering necessarily hampers policy efforts because it erects a psychological wall between the allegedly deserving and the allegedly undeserving. Throughout U.S. history, policymakers (and their constituents) have drawn a bright line in social policy between those who deserve support and assistance and those who don't. Won't "bailing out" the latter only further incentivize bad behavior? Debates about social welfare frequently hinge on this question. Even Franklin D. Roosevelt, architect of the New Deal, struggled with providing aid to those who needed it. In his 1935 State of the Union address, Roosevelt articulated his concerns with state welfare—even in the midst of the nation's most dire economic depression:

> A large proportion of these unemployed and their dependents have been forced on the relief rolls. The burden of the Federal Government has grown with great rapidity. We have here a human as well as an economic problem. When humane considerations are concerned, Americans give them precedence. The lessons of history, confirmed by the evidence immediately before me, show conclusively that continued dependence upon relief induces a spiritual disintegration fundamentally destructive to the national fiber. To dole our relief in this way is to administer a narcotic, a subtle destroyer of the human spirit. It is inimical to the dictates of a sound policy. It is in violation of the traditions of America. Work must be found for able-bodied but destitute workers.[7]

When combined with the psychological evidence presented above, this deep-seated U.S. suspicion of public assistance further complicates efforts to prevent and end homelessness in the country. These challenges are nontrivial. But they also suggest a path forward, in that they imply that a successful psychological and social response will do two things: First, a successful response will embrace homelessness as structural in nature, as opposed to a product of bad decisions or social deviancy; and second, it will see the people unhoused by this structure as fully human. We mean the word *successful* here instrumentally. Public perception shapes politics. Homelessness isn't a winning issue for local politicians—indeed, more frequently it functions as a political lightning rod that makes coordinated public responses to the problem more challenging. Even if the money were available, the political will might not exist.

Recent scholarship on the public perceptions of homelessness offers a reason for optimism in this fight. Compared to surveys conducted in 1990, public opinion in 2016 suggested greater levels of compassion and liberal attitudes than existed a quarter-century earlier.[8] A follow-up study analyzed the underlying causes of homelessness: structural causes (lack of affordable housing, lack of government supports, and the economic system), intrinsic causes (laziness and irresponsible behavior), and health causes (mental illness, substance abuse, and physical illness).[9] The most prevalent responses regarding causes were mental illness, substance use, and lack of affordable housing. But respondents differed meaningfully on their causal assessments based on age, gender, income, education, and political affiliation. The encouraging news from the standpoint of this book is that there is meaningful understanding that affordable housing plays a significant role in the homelessness crisis, but attributing homelessness to structural causes is strongly associated with affiliation with the Democratic party. In addition, believing that structural causes explain homelessness is inversely related to income. Therefore, higher income people are far less likely to believe that a lack of housing is the root of homelessness. While this research provides reasons for optimism about the public's understanding of the problem and willingness to make investments to address it, there is a significant segment of the population that continues to blame individuals and their underlying health conditions.

Currently, federal dollars earmarked for a homelessness response largely flow out of the Department of Housing and Urban Development, but the local recipients of these dollars are most frequently the local governmental agencies responsible for behavioral health care, senior services, and—to the extent they're concerned with housing at all—emergency responses to homelessness, like shelter. Locally speaking, homelessness dollars are human services dollars, because homelessness is, by implication, a human problem. The bureaucratic machinery mirrors popular belief. But if homelessness is indeed a housing problem, as we argue here, this organizational paradigm would suggest a policy lens entirely out of focus. It would also further suggest that shifting public attitudes on and understandings of homelessness are fundamental to the housing solutions we're after. To move from a place of iterative improvement to true systems change, we argue the country requires a reorientation in the manner it conceptualizes (and accordingly approaches) the problem in the first place. If homelessness continues to be seen exclusively as a personal problem—and not one of structure—policy prescriptions will remain reactive in nature. If we want to do more than treat the symptom, we must come to understand the necessity of a coordinated housing response.

The required social change isn't limited to public perceptions of homelessness. It also implies a reframing of housing. We need homeowners who are willing to advocate and vote for increased housing density; people who are willing to live with less space; a move away from the penchant for single-family homes—particularly in our nation's cities. And yet, at the same time, there's a danger in exclusively advocating for people to jettison the default American dream of white-picket-fence home ownership—not least because homes are still the largest assets people own. Homeownership can be a tool to close the racial wealth gap; homeownership must remain on the table. What, then, does it mean to align personal politics with a coordinated housing response? When cities seek to alter residential zoning in order to create more housing density, residents can support these efforts. Concerned residents in Minnesota, for example, recently formed the group Neighbors for More Neighbors to advocate for an end to exclusionary practices like single-family zoning. "Lots of people want to live here," said Janne Flisrand, one of the founders of the group. "It's a great city to live in. And we have used our city policies to keep people out."[10] The work of Neighbors for More Neighbors as well as other YIMBY ("Yes In My Back Yard") movements have been critical in efforts to increase multifamily zoning in cities around the nation. Rather than leaving advocacy to those who are struggling with the current regulatory framework, beneficiaries of the status quo can stand up for affordability and accessibility.

SUFFICIENT RESOURCES

Just like housing, homelessness is expensive. Costs rise as people who lose their housing and remain unhoused stress a range of municipal systems, including public safety, criminal justice, public health, and emergency medicine. Estimates suggest the public costs associated with homelessness range from $30,000 to $100,000 per person per year.[11] New York City, for example, spends roughly $3 billion per year on homelessness and has a one-night count of 78,000, which corresponds to about $40,000 per person.[12] Other studies have noted the cost savings of permanent supportive housing: A recent study out of Australia, for example, found that supportive housing lowered the annual use of government services by people experiencing homelessness from $48,000 to $35,117 annually (including the cost of the supportive housing in question).[13] Approaches like Housing First—in which shelter resources precede any treatment services or other programmatic supports—have produced significant cost reductions when compared to traditional homelessness services.[14] But rather than a merely reactive system that responds to the crisis at hand, we seek a proactive approach that prevents homelessness in the first place and ensures people can retain their housing when they regain it. Adequate and affordable housing is at the core of this better system—implying the need for substantial resources to fund the capital investments needed to construct and develop it.

While the costs of homelessness are high on an individualized basis, federal spending is relatively modest. In fiscal year 2019, direct federal spending on homelessness via HUD, Health and Human Services, the Veteran's Administration, and other ancillary agencies totaled about $6.5 billion. When including funding for rental assistance and other housing support for low-income households (i.e., tenant-based and project-based vouchers and Community Development Block Grants), the total rises to just over $44 billion. Finally, adding in other federal housing assistance (including public housing and HOME—a program that provides funds to local jurisdictions for rental subsidies, housing rehabilitation, and new construction), the amount reaches roughly $55 billion. By way of comparison, the discretionary portion of the federal budget in 2019 was $1.3 trillion, so these expenditures represent roughly 4.2 percent of all discretionary spending. On top of this spending, the federal government also issued about $9.5 billion in Low-Income Housing Tax Credits to promote the development of affordable housing. Summing it all, the federal government commits about $65 billion in support of low-income housing needs in the country each year. Compare this sum to lost tax receipts from the home mortgage interest tax deduction, which allows homeowners to deduct mortgage interest from their federal income taxes. Prior to the 2017 tax reform package, the mortgage interest tax deduction cost the federal government nearly $70 billion in lost revenue. Under the new tax law, that number has fallen to about $30 billion, as fewer households now benefit from this deduction. Even after this major change, the federal government commits a sum equal to 50 percent of all federal funding on low-income housing support to a single program that exclusively benefits high-income homeowners. (The government does, however, provide support to low-income households through a range of other social safety-net programs, including cash assistance, medical coverage, and food support, and any expansion or extension of these programs would, by definition, bolster the financial position of households at risk of experiencing homelessness.)

Calculating spending at the state and local level for housing and homelessness is more complicated. Because federal funds flow to states and cities, the expenditures announced by these jurisdictions also include the funds provided by the federal government. City budgets, too, include funds appropriated from their own states. This complex web of funding sources certainly complicates the analysis. This confusion prompted one California legislator, David Chui—a Democrat from San Francisco—to introduce a proposal requiring the state to account for every dollar spent on homelessness within the state.[15] But there are clear examples in which state (as opposed to federal) funds are committed directly to housing and homelessness. In 2018, voters in California approved Propositions 1 and 2, which authorized $4 billion in bonding capacity for affordable housing and $2 billion in borrowed funds to construct supportive housing for people with serious mental illness, respectively.

Local jurisdictions, too, invest directly. In 2016, Los Angeles voters approved a referendum to spend $1.2 billion over ten years to construct housing for the homeless. In particular, the dollars were earmarked for the construction of 1,000 new units of housing, each year, for a total of 10,000 units over the decade. But by the end of 2019, only 1 percent of those units were ready to be occupied, prompting frustration and criticism.[16] According to City Controller Ron Galperin, "the ten year plan . . . hasn't lived up to its promise because of the high price of construction, stalled approvals and regulatory barriers."[17] In 2016, the expected costs for these units ranged from $350,000 to $414,000. In reality, median costs have clocked in at $531,000, and only 7,640 units are expected to be constructed. The adjustments imply a contribution from this source of funding at $157,000 per unit (or about 25 percent of the total cost). Presumably the city is using debt funding (mortgages) to fund the remaining portion of the construction costs. And even in the best of circumstances, 10,000 units over ten years in a city with a homeless population that exceeds fifty thousand people on any given night seems inadequate. But what is the right number?

It's difficult to point to a single number required to end homelessness. When the global management consulting firm McKinsey & Company strove to quantify the resources needed to end homelessness in Seattle/King County, they estimated the total housing supply that would be needed to accommodate the extremely low-income (ELI) households—those earning less than 30 percent of area median income (AMI)—that currently lack affordable housing. The McKinsey report called for a total of thirty-seven thousand new housing units, which didn't address the needs of other low-income households earning between 30 and 50 percent of AMI. Despite the narrow focus of the analysis, the cost is still substantial: "Using a conservative set of assumptions, ending homelessness in King County would therefore cost between $4.5 billion and $11 billion over ten years, or between $450 million and $1.1 billion each year for the next ten years. To put it another way, ending homelessness in King County would require spending two to four times the approximately $260 million currently spent on homelessness and ELI housing in the region."[18]

It is important to note that the McKinsey estimate is the total sum needed to develop thirty-seven thousand housing units. It assumes the development is entirely equity financed, so upon completion, the county—or whatever entity funded the construction—would own the units free and clear without any mortgage. Obviously, public sources of funds could be leveraged with property mortgages to limit the level of public financing required. But if McKinsey is right, and thirty-seven thousand units are needed to end homelessness in King County, the recent proposal in Los Angeles—to construct ten thousand units over

ten years—appears woefully inadequate indeed. McKinsey estimated up to $11 billion over ten years would be required to fill
the gap, while the Los Angeles proposal provided $1.2 billion—
in a county with four times the homeless population of King
County. If we broadly apply the McKinsey math and methodology (a gross generalization to be sure) to Los Angeles, the jurisdiction would need $20–$45 billion. These figures highlight the
scale of the issue and the resources that are needed to address it.
If regions with substantial populations experiencing homelessness continue to nibble around the edges of the problem (if we
can call $1.2 billion over ten years nibbling), there is little hope
for a sustainable solution.

Because much of current local spending in a region like
King County is devoted to the crisis response, a relatively small
amount is dedicated to housing development and rental assistance for extremely low-income households. The funds needed
to construct this housing are well above current spending levels.
And while McKinsey's price tag is daunting, the region has
made large investments in the past. In 2016, voters in the Puget
Sound region approved a $54 billion, twenty-five-year plan to
extend public transit throughout the region, including via light
rail and bus rapid transit. One could easily argue that housing is
just as critical of an infrastructure investment as public transit:
essential for a growing region. Of course, this argument requires
community members to conceptualize housing—particularly
housing for low-income households—as a public good rather
than a private commodity.

The U.S. Census Bureau conducts an annual survey of state
and local finances. This survey provides detail on dollars that
flow to states from the federal government, as well as the total
funds generated within the state. The results tell an interesting

story about revenue generation. In California—the largest state budget in the nation—just over 17 percent of all revenue at the state and local levels comes from the federal government. Of the general revenue raised statewide, about 56 percent comes from state-level (as opposed to local) sources. Total general revenue per capita (from both state and local sources) is about $9,800. The state of Washington, on the other hand, generates about $1,000 less in general revenue per capita, and only 14.6 percent of its total revenue comes from federal sources. Massachusetts relies heavily on state revenue: Over 64 percent of all general revenue in the state is raised at the state level, but per capita general revenue is comparable to Washington and California (at roughly $9,300). These states differ meaningfully from a lower-tax jurisdiction like Texas. Texas generates $6,611 per person in general revenue, which is split relatively evenly between state and local sources. Federal sources account for 16.5 percent of total revenue in Texas.

While an additional $1 billion per year to end homelessness in the Puget Sound region may sound daunting, it need not be. Let's consider this amount from both a national and local perspective. To fund an additional $1 billion in Washington annually, total revenue generation per capita from state and local sources would need to rise to $9,026 per person—a 1.5 percent increase from its current level—still far below the per capita figures raised in both California and Massachusetts. At the scale of the federal government, the number is also relatively small. To turn to a previous example, eliminating the mortgage interest deduction for homeowners would free up $30 billion, which, if dedicated to homelessness and housing initiatives, would represent roughly a 60 percent increase in federal funding for low-income households. Washington's per capita share of that increase would produce $660 million of additional funding each year—two-thirds of the total amount required even in McKinsey's most costly estimate.

At the federal level, greater appropriations to HUD could also support an expansion of the voucher program or further investments in affordable housing development. With interest rates at historic lows, the U.S. Treasury could provide extremely low-interest loans to local housing authorities to support the acquisition or construction of affordable housing. No agency can borrow as cheaply as the U.S. government. The federal government could also raise the value of the tax credits it issues to help fund the development of affordable housing. The Low-Income Housing Tax Credit program has funded the construction or rehabilitation of over three million housing units since its inception in the 1980s. Despite the program's complexity and frequent inefficiencies, it remains the primary tool used to fund affordable housing in the United States, and it ought to be improved.

Notwithstanding the various federal options to increase funding for housing services, there still remains the fact that the need for resources is not evenly distributed throughout the country. As described to us by researcher Jill Khadduri, one option for marrying federal resources to the regional housing needs would be to implement an add-on to the LIHTC program in which states or local jurisdictions could get additional tax credits if they provide a local match. Under such a program, only those localities with a need and desire for additional affordable housing production would participate in the program, and they would need to invest their own resources in order to get additional federal support. It's a creative proposal that could generate additional federal support for housing with improved targeting.

State governments rely on income, property, and sales taxes to fund operations, but the mix in each state varies considerably. A report from the Institute on Taxation and Economic Policy (ITEP) found that the vast majority of states have regressive tax policies: Low-income households pay a higher percentage of their income in taxes than high earners. Washington State has the most regressive tax regime, followed closely by Texas and Florida. A hallmark of regressive tax systems is the reliance on sales and excise taxes with limited or no state income tax. In the ITEP report, researchers found that implied tax rates from sales and excise taxes are 7.1 percent for the bottom one-fifth of the income distribution, 4.8 percent for the middle 20 percent of earners, and only 0.9 percent for the top 1 percent.[19] The top 1 percent of earners in Washington pay a 3 percent tax rate as a share of household income (including all state and local taxes), while the poorest 20 percent face a 17.8 percent rate. The lack of a state income tax is a major culprit for the regressive nature of taxation in Washington. It shouldn't be a surprise that two of the wealthiest people in the country—Bill Gates (Microsoft) and Jeff Bezos (Amazon)—call Washington home. Correcting these regressive tax regimes would provide an opportunity for increased, and more equitable, revenue generation for many states. This is easier said than done.

At the local level, similar challenges exist when trying to generate additional funding for social services. In 2018, the Seattle City Council proposed a "head tax" designed to raise $275 per employee from local businesses that earned at least $20 million the prior year. Amazon—though part of the initial negotiations—publicly announced its opposition to the tax and threatened to halt construction in Seattle in response. This threat warped the narrative, and business interests quickly rallied around the "No

Tax on Jobs" movement formed to oppose the tax. The council ultimately abandoned the proposal. An article in *The Atlantic* highlighted the fractured politics at play: "They [city council members] say big companies like Amazon have held the city hostage by refusing to engage in a discussion about new revenue streams to fund affordable housing, and that though they might have quashed this effort, they have put forward no solutions for the city's problems. Business leaders, meanwhile, say they're fed up with a constant stream of taxes that have done little to solve Seattle's growing homelessness crisis."[20]

The head tax debacle was frustrating on all sides. Corporations were upset at being targeted; the city felt their hands were tied in terms of being able to raise additional revenue. Economist Jared Bernstein summarized the challenges in a *Washington Post* editorial citing tax analysts Steve Rosenthal and Richard Auxier: "How are fiscally constrained cities supposed to find revenue as their populations and services grow?"[21] Bernstein argues that given: (a) the state of Washington's prohibition on taxing income or wealth, (b) Amazon's nonexistent federal tax bill, (c) the fact that the head tax would have cost Amazon $10 million per year—in the face of first-quarter 2018 net income of $1.6 billion, and (d) growing needs in Seattle related to housing affordability and homelessness—pursuing additional revenue at the local level is wise:

> Do these facts provide a rationale for asking large businesses to help pay for a serious social problem like homelessness? These companies are better known for putting out their hands for tax breaks in exchange for the added economic activity they bring to places where they locate. But while such activity is welcomed by many, it also creates greater demand for public services, for schools, police, infrastructure, maintenance, etc. It also raises housing prices in these

areas. So yes, I think there's a solid rationale for asking them to offset some of the social costs to which they contribute.

The head tax may have been improperly designed, whether from a taxation or perception perspective (or both). But denying local jurisdictions the right to raise revenue also appears short-sighted. Incomes and wealth are staggering in the Puget Sound and Bay Area regions: The inability to fund social programs doesn't stem from a lack of funds—it stems from a lack of will.

SYSTEMS APPROACH

Harvard Business School is a forerunner in the use of the case-study method in management education. Cases help students learn key concepts of finance, marketing, strategy, and operations. One of the most famous of these cases is the National Cranberry Cooperative case—more commonly, just the "Cranberry Case"—which "describes the continuous flow process used to process cranberries into juice and/or sauce." Students must "analyze process flows to determine where the bottlenecks are and to decide how, and whether, to expand capacity."[22] Long story short: The cranberry operation needed greater drying capacity so the delivery trucks would not need to wait around for the plant to finish processing the wet berries. For thousands of students over the last three decades, the Cranberry Case has highlighted the importance of systems and how they work: how a single bottleneck can disrupt an otherwise successful operation. Ultimately, the case teaches that disappointing operational outcomes might be attributable to factors upstream in a system.

Aside from its real, often traumatic manifestation as human experience, homelessness is a system, too. Or at least its socio-economic and bureaucratic contexts form one. People flow into snaking lines of waitlists. They wait for supportive housing openings or vouchers for months, all while looking for their own housing on the private market and watching other people, deemed of "higher priority," get fast-tracked into units that somehow materialize. Rental markets ebb and flow; the homelessness and housing systems bump up against others: education, incarceration, health care. And as was the case with the flow of cranberries through the plant, plenty of changes could improve—maybe even eliminate—the problems with the system. By definition, waitlists for housing programs would be shorter if fewer people lost their housing in the first place. And in cases in which people do lose their housing and subsequently seek assistance through a city or county's homelessness crisis-response system, their experience with that system would be greatly improved if more housing options (subsidized or unsubsidized) were ready to receive them. The operationalization and management of homelessness is a function of bureaucracy and systems thinking. These systems warrant improvement. Many warrant reimagination writ large.

The homelessness system is somewhat circular, as it begins *and* ends with housing. When we think about some abstract notion of *system improvement*, then, this thinking must also begin and end with housing. Much of this book has sought to illustrate the fundamental ability of housing markets to shape cities' relationships with homelessness. Accordingly, we're active in our prescription. Improving the flow through crisis-response programs and reforming their gatekeeping roles are necessary moves toward an efficient system, but these iterative improvements pale in comparison to the additive value of the housing supply response (as well as income supplements and rental subsidies) required to ensure people have secure, private, and warm places to sleep at night. An *efficient* crisis-response system isn't necessarily an *equitable* system—much less one that guarantees people always have the housing they need, when they need it. In other words, if homelessness is a housing problem, wringing efficiencies out of the current emergency shelter system alone won't solve it. Jurisdictions must also ensure that people remain housed in the first place—and if a household does find itself seeking shelter, jurisdictions must ensure ample housing exists on the other side of the crisis response.

From the systems perspective, the availability of affordable housing plays a determinative role in both inflow to homelessness and outflow from homelessness. But housing policy prescriptions for each of these transitions vary substantially: Preventing people from losing their housing in the first place is a vastly different exercise than ensuring safe and healthy movement through crisis-response programs and the securing of new affordable housing as quickly as possible. And each is essential. If we consider the homelessness system to encompass three stages—inflow, in which precipitating events like job loss interact with structural factors like housing affordability; response, in which people interact with programs like coordinated entry services and emergency shelters; and outflow, in which they (ideally) return to permanent, affordable housing—it's clear each stage warrants its own unique set of investments. Critically, investing in the response stage without ensuring adequate capacity for outflow begets a situation in which jurisdictions merely warehouse people in a shelter system indefinitely. No investment in shelters is sufficiently large to end homelessness without affordable housing on the other side.

We address these three stages more deeply in turn.

Stage One—Inflow

By definition, the first stage in this system involves the loss of permanent housing. This loss can be immediate—in the case of an eviction with no subsequent options—or it can be a long, drawn-out process in which a household moves from apartment to couch to car, until they have exhausted all of their housing options. Either way, these events signify *entry* into the homelessness system. From a process standpoint, mitigating the flow into homelessness is essential: People remain housed, and people currently unhoused are more likely to be able to access housing programs.

It's at the inflow stage that many large structural challenges—poverty, lack of affordable housing, racism and other forms of discrimination, inadequate health care, and inequities in education and employment—most readily make themselves known. These factors converge to make some households more vulnerable to housing loss than others. With an eye toward helping mitigate this convergence, we highlight two important areas of focus. First, researchers have highlighted the important role that income supplements play in preventing a spell of homelessness. Such supplements may come in the form of permanent housing subsidies, temporary payments, diversion dollars ("flex funds"), or more fundamental changes, like an expansion of the Earned Income Tax Credit program, which provides cash payments to low-income households via the income tax system.[23] Such cash buffers help households who would otherwise lose their housing as a result of a one-time crisis or emergency. The expansion of housing voucher programs to cover all eligible households in the country would also meaningfully expand the purchasing power of millions of people with low incomes. Extensive research has documented the success that vouchers have had in preventing and ending homelessness.[24] Second, especially in cities with expensive and scarce housing, housing-supply investments targeting households with the lowest incomes—0 to 30 percent of AMI—are paramount. Expensive, tight housing markets provide very little margin for households at risk: One negative episode or a spell of bad luck can quickly turn into housing loss.

Efforts to expand the supply of housing require deep investment from federal, state, and local governments. Broadly speaking, these investments could include direct support for development or acquisition, but they could also come in the form of a more robust Low-Income Housing Tax Credit program—the primary tool currently used to fund the development of affordable housing—as well as housing trust funds, land banks, and shared equity homeownership models. In all cases, the goal here ought to be creating a stock of de-commodified housing and land that resides outside the private market. Note that de-commodified housing doesn't necessarily connote *public* housing (though it may). Nonprofit ownership, too, implies an understanding of housing that is divorced from a profit motive. There are also important initiatives focused on the preservation of affordable housing; for example, the King County Housing Authority has purchased over seven thousand housing units since 1991 in an effort to preserve affordability in perpetuity.[25] Such action doesn't increase the overall supply of housing, but it does increase the stock of housing that isn't subject to market forces and pricing. Furthermore, without more multifamily zoning and the density that comes with it, growing cities will have no place to house new residents—which will further displace low-income households and place additional pressure on already expensive housing. The necessary zoning reforms probably imply limiting the degree of single-family zoning in a given city. In addition, local governments can work to ensure that the regulatory hoops that developers must jump through are limited such that basic protections exist, but that housing can still be permitted and constructed in a timely fashion. Finally, the public and private sector alike must pay greater attention to alternative forms of housing (including single-room occupancies) and new construction technologies. As discussed previously, the construction industry is one of the few that has shown little to no efficiency gains over the last half-century.

In the short run, prevention programs are essential to limiting inflow. From a policy-design perspective, prevention is hard, because there's often no way of knowing what would have actually happened to a participating household if a given prevention program hadn't existed in the first place. This natural absence of a real comparison group—a counterfactual—makes program evaluation difficult; and consequently, prevention programs have been plagued over the years by accusations of inefficiency. And there's some truth to these claims. Of the population at risk of homelessness at any given point in time, only a few households actually lose their housing—again, consider the size of the U.S. population below the poverty line versus that experiencing homelessness—and targeting those select households may be next to impossible. However, emerging (but perhaps unsurprising) evidence suggests certain prevention programs like some forms of emergency cash assistance, housing subsidies, and other services do ultimately limit the incidence of homelessness.[26] These programs should be supported and scaled.

Stage Two—Crisis Response

When most people think about "the homelessness system," they are likely thinking about stage two in our model. Coordinated entry facilities, emergency shelters, day shelters for the unsheltered homeless, Safe Havens, transitional housing, rapid rehousing, and permanent supportive housing programs form the response system's constituent pieces. Most public investment in homelessness as a distinct spending priority concerns this stage. Broadly speaking, we can think about this system as serving two overarching goals: (a) providing basic needs and keeping people safe during a crisis, and (b) helping people to move beyond the crisis. Mats on the floor in a congregate emergency shelter may provide some basic needs for residents, but on their own, they may fail to materially move people toward permanent housing.

Other elements of the system attempt to move people out of it. And this is where the analysis gets more difficult. Because of the temporary nature of some of these programs (notably transitional housing and rapid rehousing), some program participants may return to the homelessness response system when housing opportunities or subsidies end.[27] The effectiveness of these programs is also likely to vary by region: Unsurprisingly, a time-limited rental subsidy on the private market is more likely to be effective in more accommodating markets. Permanent supportive housing, on the other hand, is, by definition, permanent—but it is also more expensive. The cost implies a tradeoff: Jurisdictions can serve fewer people successfully. And this is where financial constraints and the limited stock of housing units for use by permanent supportive housing programs limit its potential. Further complicating homeless-housing decisions is the fact that not everyone needs something like permanent supportive housing. In fact, most people who experience homelessness don't—other supports and assistance are sufficient.

These portfolio decisions are important, but a broader challenge for communities is the decision of whether to allocate resources to the crisis-response system—stage two—at all or to invest in upstream prevention efforts and the affordable housing needed for people to end their homelessness. By and large, CoCs have focused intently on the efficiency of their crisis responses. These efforts have sought to ensure that households receive the services most appropriate for their needs and circumstances—and that enough services exist in the first place. And while these operational changes can precipitate real improvements, there is a limit to their reach. In the case of many regions with high rates of homelessness, the tremendous inflow into the crisis-response system has overwhelmed many of the benefits that might have been realized from the operational efficiencies gained. Trying to optimize a shelter system during periods of great inflow is like repairing a smoke alarm in a house that's on fire. As someone we spoke to on this topic stated, "We can't efficiency our way out of this."

A tangible example of this phenomenon comes by way of the Family Homelessness Initiative funded by the Bill and Melinda Gates Foundation.[28] Over the last twelve years, the foundation has invested tens of millions of dollars to improve the crisis response system for families in the Puget Sound region. The initiative has focused on three core principles: prevention and diversion (short-term assistance, landlord mediation, and other emergency supports), coordinated entry (a single point of contact for families as they seek support from the homelessness response system), and rapid rehousing (placing families in permanent housing as soon as possible). Findings of the program have demonstrated favorable results for the families and the system that serves them.[29] At the same time, the level of family homelessness in the region has continued to rise. This fact highlights that the benefits of well-funded and carefully implemented programs targeting the crisis response system can be overwhelmed by robust inflow into the system.

It can also be overwhelmed by a lack of outflow. Setting aside debates about the relative efficacy of transitional housing, rapid rehousing, and permanent supportive housing, program success is predicated on the existence of a unit someone can move into or retain. Without enough units—regardless of ownership and operation—none of these programs can provide sufficient pathways out of the response system. It's like plugging a bathtub while the water is still running: The water will rise. Limited opportunities to *exit* the shelter system—or leave the streets—turn the response system into a warehouse for people experiencing homelessness. Rather than serving as a soft, temporary landing for people who lose their housing, the system becomes a more permanent reality. We need an exit.

Stage Three—Outflow

Outflow, as introduced above, is essential to a properly functioning system. In addition to representing housing solutions for people experiencing homelessness, exits from the response stage also free up capacity and resources for others entering that stage. Certainly, all the efforts outlined in the first stage—those that provide income support and increase the stock of affordable housing—would help facilitate outflow. But here, we also draw attention to the unique stock of permanent housing specifically designated for people who have previously experienced homelessness (especially chronic homelessness; and including permanent supportive housing). Unlike temporary rental supports, transitional housing, and rapid re-housing, permanent supportive housing isn't time-limited, and it often includes further

services and supports for residents who need them. Therefore, we view this intervention as a critical element of our third
stage—not just as another feature of the crisis response system.

Over the past few years, the communities in our sample have
greatly increased the stock of permanent housing units in their
portfolio: a welcome development. Given the cost-effectiveness
arguments offered earlier in this chapter, we encourage the continued funding and construction of permanent supportive housing units. Some people leaving the crisis-response system may
reside in permanent supportive housing for a decade or more
before leaving for housing in the private market (either subsidized or unsubsidized); others may live in permanent supportive
housing for the rest of their lives. Fixed incomes or disabilities might preclude some people from attaining private-market
housing. When we cease to view housing as a commodity and
instead as an essential component of human life and dignity, a
diversity of housing solutions makes more sense.

Despite the welcome increase of permanent units, the supply of this form of housing remains drastically limited, and this
scarcity serves as a critical bottleneck with knock-on effects for
the overall system. Without more permanent supportive housing units to serve the population of (often chronically homeless)
people who need them, many CoCs—bound by requirements
to prioritize housing for those with the greatest medical need
and barriers to housing—ultimately opt to refer potential permanent supportive housing occupants to time-limited housing
programs (like rapid rehousing) with fewer supportive services.
When renters can't retain their rapid rehousing leases at the end
of a subsidy period, they may fall back into homelessness. Meanwhile, rental subsidies have been exhausted, and people who
might have been able to hold on to those leases are instead on

a waiting list, sleeping in shelters. In this manner, lack of sufficient permanent supportive housing can frustrate the efforts of a crisis-response system that may have otherwise worked for more people.

By definition, permanent supportive housing is designed to help people with service needs. But there are other people experiencing homelessness—without such needs—for whom a long-term subsidy, like a voucher, would provide access to much-needed housing. Providing permanent supportive housing units to people without the relevant service needs implies a mismatch. Communities need a portfolio of housing options (from short-term subsidies to long-term subsidies *and* permanent supportive housing) to ensure people can find the right housing—efficiently and effectively. In other words, with respect to housing supply, communities require not only a sufficient number of permanent supportive housing units, but also private units that households can access via rental subsidies. Housing must reflect the diversity of shelter and service needs of the people living in it.

Local responses to homelessness during the COVID-19 pandemic offer a reason for optimism in the fight against homelessness. As described earlier, many jurisdictions leased hotel and motel rooms for people experiencing homelessness in order to provide safety and to limit virus outbreaks in congregate settings such as emergency shelters. Given the success of many of these programs, local governments around the country have taken steps to acquire hotels and motels in order to create additional permanent or temporary housing options for households that need them. Large-scale purchases of these buildings have the potential to meaningfully increase the stock of affordable units in a community. The depressed prices for hotel properties during the COVID-19 pandemic presented a unique opportunity for jurisdictions to increase housing capacity at lower prices than would be typical: a meaningful silver lining of the otherwise tragic pandemic.

The three interrelated elements presented above—shifting public perceptions of homelessness, committing far greater resources to meet the scale of the problem, and broadening our understanding and management of what constitutes the homelessness system—suggest bold, paradigmatic shifts in the manner in which the country addresses homelessness. But such personal and public investments are possible. A recent example shows us as much: The case of the U.S. response to veteran homelessness offers a template for how the three constituent elements of this vision can come together to form a sustainable housing response. Since 2009, homelessness among former members of the U.S. armed services has fallen by nearly 50 percent—and this rapid decline is no accident.[30] Political will, funding, and effective use of the broader homelessness response system has dramatically reduced the population of veterans without housing.

Why did we do it? And what, exactly, did we do? Given the poor treatment of veterans who returned from the Vietnam War a generation ago, great political concern arose to prevent repeating the same mistakes for those who served in the wars in Iraq and Afghanistan. But theories of the policymaking process itself also help explain the substantial federal commitment to ending homelessness among veterans. Policy scholars Helen Ingram and Anne Schneider developed the concept of social construction of target populations as a way to understand why certain populations receive benefits and support throughout the policymaking process while others do not.[31] The researchers argue that one can predict how a given subpopulation will benefit from policy-making based on two variables: their power and their social construction. Plotting these two variables against one another creates a matrix of four categories: Advantaged (high power and positive social construction), Contenders (high power and negative social construction), Dependents (low power and positive social construction), and Deviants (low power and negative social construction). Small-business owners and first responders might be examples of Advantaged populations; oil-company executives are Contenders; Dependents include widows and orphans; and Deviants would include drug dealers and other criminals.

The matrix helps us understand the difference between homeless veterans and homeless civilians (and the political will that follows in the response to each). Veterans experiencing homelessness have a favorable social construction. As former soldiers, they occupy the Advantaged category. As veterans who have lost their housing, they occupy the Dependent category: worthy beneficiaries of support. Yet without this view into someone's past—without psychological or social assumptions of whether someone *ever* occupied the Advantaged category—the default political (and policymaking) assumption of civilian homelessness is the Deviant category. Given a negative social construction and no power, civilians experiencing homelessness receive far less de facto attention and support throughout the policymaking process. We see evidence of this dynamic in public opinion research on homelessness. Jack Tsai and colleagues conducted a national online survey and found that the general public was more supportive of homelessness funding for the veteran population than for nonveteran adults who experience homelessness.[32]

But the social construction of veterans only explains part of the story. There was also a lot of money. A white paper from the Department of Veterans Affairs states, "Ending Veteran Homelessness has been a priority of this Administration and VA that has resulted in an unprecedented commitment of resources, planning and commitment directed toward this goal. This initiative was announced in 2009 and incorporates six core elements: outreach and education, treatment, enhancing income/employment/benefits, community partnerships, prevention, and providing housing and supportive services. Over $2.6 billion has been committed to this initiative to date [2009–2014], resulting in substantial increases in the housing stock available to support homeless Veterans."[33]

Ultimately, policymakers, agency staff, and nonprofits knitted together a broad system of housing support to deliver effective programs and resources to those who needed it. The system constituted far more than shelter: A combination of rapid rehousing, housing vouchers, and permanent supportive housing services—along with a fleet of other ancillary efforts to ensure people were housed outside the crisis response—were carefully integrated to ensure program success.[34] A new, growing focus on communities attaining "functional zero" veteran homelessness, in which regions must prove the number of veterans experiencing homelessness each month is smaller than its average monthly housing rate, ensures such communities apply a systems lens to policymaking: Inflow has to be smaller than outflow, so you've got to focus on both upstream and downstream interventions. Some cities have achieved this functional zero measure for both veteran homelessness and chronic homelessness, and emerging evidence has illustrated that upstream interventions (like diversion and engagement with other systems) can ensure that homelessness can indeed be prevented before it manifests in full.[35]

Access to housing—independent of one's ability to pay—is the bedrock of these policy successes. From the veterans example, we know that investments in housing, rental subsidies, and systems thinking can substantially reduce the population of people experiencing homelessness. The question is whether we will extend the same focus, attention, and resources to the rest of the population without stable housing. At the time of this writing, the answer to that question remains unclear. Despite extensive research highlighting the drivers of the U.S. homelessness crisis, perceptions of the issue still break along partisan, perceptual, and anecdotal lines. Which makes sense. This is a book about cities, but homelessness is about people. And for all the reasons described above, it's easy to fall back on narratives about people, especially the narratives that stir emotion.

But these narratives aren't enough; they don't get at the roots. In naming homelessness as a structural problem, with its roots in affordable housing, we hope to provide concerned readers with direction. Our attempt here has been to think through the substantial variation in rates of homelessness observed throughout the country, inviting the question of why homelessness is so prevalent in some cities, but not others. *This* question should give us pause, not least because it suggests intent. People design cities and structure markets. They can also choose to change them.

NOTES

CHAPTER 1. BASELINE

1. Melissa Santos. "Across the Entire State, WA Voters Rank Homelessness as the No. 1 Issue Lawmakers Must Address," *Crosscut*, January 2020, https://crosscut.com/2020/01/across-entire-state-wa-voters-rank-homelessness-no-1-issue-lawmakers-must-address.

2. Data retrieved from: https://trends.google.com/trends/explore?date=todaypercent205-y&geo=US&q=homeless,inequality,racism,poverty,climatepercent20change and https://trends.google.com/trends/explore?date=todaypercent205-y&geo=US&q=homeless,inequality,racism,poverty,discrimination.

3. United States Government Accountability Office, *Homelessness: Better HUD Oversight of Data Collection Could Improve Estimates of the Homeless Population* (Washington, DC: GAO, July 2020). https://www.gao.gov/assets/710/708090.pdf.

4. National Center for Education Statistics, Table 204.75a, Homeless Students Enrolled in Public Elementary and Secondary Schools, by Grade, Primary Nighttime Residence, and Selected Student Characteristics: 2009–10 through 2016–17, https://nces.ed.gov/programs/digest/d19/tables/dt19_204.75a.asp?current=yes.

5. Vincent A. Fusaro, Helen G. Levy, and H. Luke Shaefer, "Racial and Ethnic Disparities in the Lifetime Prevalence of Homelessness in the United States," *Demography* 55, no. 6 (2018): 2119–28; Katherine H. Shelton, Pamela J. Taylor, Adrian Bonner, and Marianne den van Bree, "Risk Factors for Homelessness: Evidence from a Population-Based Study," *Psychiatric Services* 60, no. 4 (2009): 465–72; Jack Tsai, "Lifetime and 1-Year Prevalence of Homelessness in the US Population: Results from the National Epidemiologic Survey on Alcohol and Related Conditions-III," *Journal of Public Health (United Kingdom)* 40, no. 1 (2018): 65–74.

6. Pam Fessler, "Trump Continues Criticism of Democrats on Homelessness, but Hasn't Intervened," National Public Radio, January 2, 2020, https://www.npr.org/2020/01/02/793134351/trump-continues-criticism-of-democrats-on-homelessness-but-hasnt-intervened.

7. Ezra Klein, *Why We're Polarized* (New York: Avid Reader Books, 2020).

8. When comparing King County (Seattle) to Cook County (Chicago) and City of San Francisco to City of Chicago.

9. Applied Survey Research, *Count Us In: Seattle/King County Point-In-Time Count of Persons Experiencing Homelessness 2019*. Seattle, WA: Applied Survey Research, 2019.

10. Brendan O'Flaherty, "Wrong Person and Wrong Place: For Homelessness, the Conjunction Is What Matters," *Journal of Housing Economics* 13 (2004): 1–15.

11. Meghan Henry, Rian Watt, Anna Mahathey, Jillian Ouellette, and Aubrey Sitler, *The 2019 Annual Homeless Assessment Report (AHAR) to Congress: Part I* (Washington, DC: The U.S. Department of Housing and Urban Development: Office of Community Planning and Development, 2020).

12. Santos, "Across the Entire State."

13. Applied Survey Research, "Count Us In."

14. The only exceptions are small portions of Alabama, Arkansas, and Oklahoma that are not covered by a CoC.

15. Henry et al., *The 2019 Annual Homeless Assessment Report (AHAR) to Congress: Part I*; Josh Leopold, Dennis Culhane, and Jill Khadduri, *Where Do Homeless People Come From? Movement of Households from Their*

Prior Residences into Homeless Residential Facilities in Michigan in Iowa (Rockville, MD: Abt Associates, 2020).

16. Given the statistical uncertainty (and evolving methodology) of PIT counts, we are especially attuned to outliers in our sample. For the purpose of this book, we have excluded three statistical outliers: Detroit's 2007 and 2008 counts, as well as Travis County's 2007 count. The early years of the PIT counts in these cities were substantial outliers compared to the counts that appeared in subsequent years. We also exclude data from Atlanta prior to 2014 and from Miami-Dade County prior to 2013 due to administrative changes affecting the geographic boundaries of these CoCs.

17. Henry et al., *The 2019 Annual Homeless Assessment Report (AHAR) to Congress: Part I.*

18. Gregg Colburn, Rachel Fyall, Samantha Thompson, Taquesha Dean, Christina McHugh, Pear Moraras, Victoria Ewing, and Sarah Argodale, "Impact of Hotels as Non-Congregate Emergency Shelters," November 2020. https://kcrha.org/wp-content/uploads/2020/11/Impact-of-Hotels-as-ES-Study_Full-Report_Final-11302020.pdf

19. David Gutman and Sydney Brownstone, "Proposed King County Budget Includes New Sales Tax for Housing, 450 Job Losses," *Seattle Times*, September 22, 2020. https://www.seattletimes.com/seattle-news/politics/proposed-king-county-budget-includes-new-sales-tax-for-housing-450-job-losses/.

20. Emily Benfer, David Bloom Robinson, Stacy Butler, Lavar Edmonds, Sam Gilman, Katherine Lucas McKay, Lisa Owens, Neil Steinkamp, and Diane Yentel, *The Covid-19 Eviction Crisis: An Estimated 30–40 Million People Are at Risk* (Washington, DC: National Low Income Housing Coalition, 2020), https://nlihc.org/sites/default/files/The_Eviction_Crisis_080720.pdf.

21. Benfer et al., *The Covid-19 Eviction Crisis.*"

22. Henry et al., *The 2019 Annual Homeless Assessment Report (AHAR) to Congress: Part I.*

23. Ibid.

24. "What Does Ending Homelessness Mean?" United States Interagency Council on Homelessness, June 4, 2018. https://www.usich.gov/goals/what-does-ending-homelessness-mean/.

CHAPTER 2. EVIDENCE

1. Henry et al., *The 2019 Annual Homeless Assessment Report (AHAR) to Congress: Part I.*

2. J. B. Wogan, "While Homeless Veterans Get Housing, Rest Are Left in the Cold." Governing: The Future of States and Localities, January 29, 2016, https://www.governing.com/topics/health-human-services/gov-veteran-homelessness-obama-washington.html.

3. Marybeth Shinn and Jill Khadduri, *In the Midst of Plenty: How to Prevent and End Homelessness* (Hoboken, NJ: Wiley, 2020).

4. Brendan O'Flaherty, *Making Room: The Economics of Homelessness* (Cambridge, MA: Harvard University Press, 1996), 3.

5. "Extremely low income" is defined as incomes below the federal poverty line or below 30 percent of area median income. Andrew Aurand, Dan Emmanuel, Daniel Threet, Ikra Rafi, and Diane Yentel, *The GAP: A Shortage of Affordable Homes* (Washington, DC: National Low Income Housing Coalition, 2020).

6. Some state and local supports contribute to the stock of subsidized housing, but those programs are not reflected in these estimates.

7. The 2018 difference between median contract rent (what renters sign up for) and median gross rent (what they pay including utilities) in Hennepin County in 2018 was $93.00, based on 2018 ACS 1-Year estimates.

8. Aurand et al., *The GAP.*

9. Rapid rehousing, while considered a permanent form of housing per HUD, is a time-limited program that lacks permanence.

10. Henry et al., *The 2019 Annual Homeless Assessment Report (AHAR) to Congress: Part I.*

11. Jeffrey Olivet, Marc Dones, Molly Richard, Catriona Wilkey, Svetlana Yampolskaya, Maya Beit-Arie, and Lunise Joseph, "SPARC Phase One Study Findings," https://center4si.com/wp-content/uploads/2018/03/SPARC-Phase-1-Findings-March-20181.pdf. Needham, MA: C4 Social Innovations, 2018

12. Shinn and Khadduri, *In the Midst of Plenty.*

13. Randall Kuhn and Dennis Culhane, "Applying Cluster Analysis to Test a Typology of Homelessness by Pattern of Shelter Utilization: Results from the Analysis of Administrative Data," *American Journal of Community Psychology* 26, no. 2 (1998): 207–32.

14. Other researchers have used slightly different terminology—Roger Nooe and David Patterson for example, refer to first-time, episodic, and chronic homelessness—but the principle is the same. Roger M. Nooe and David A. Patterson, "The Ecology of Homelessness." *Journal of Human Behavior in the Social Environment* 20, no. 2 (2010): 105–52.

15. Bruce G. Link, Ezra Susser, Ann Stueve, Jo Phelan, Robert E. Moore, and Elmer Struening, "Lifetime and Five-Year Prevalence of Homelessness in the United States," *American Journal of Public Health* 84, no. 12 (1994): 1907–12.

16. Chris Glynn and Emily B. Fox, "Dynamics of Homelessness in Urban America," *Annals of Applied Statistics* 13, no. 1 (2019): 573–605.

17. National Law Center on Homelessness and Poverty, *Don't Count on It: How the HUD Point-in-Time Count Underestimates the Homelessness Crisis in America* (Washington, DC: National Law Center on Homelessness & Poverty, 2017), https://www.nlchp.org/documents/HUD -PIT-report2017.

18. Glynn and Fox, "Dynamics of Homelessness in Urban America."

19. Kim Hopper, Marybeth Shinn, Eugene Laska, Morris Meisner, and Joseph Wanderling, "Estimating Numbers of Unsheltered Homeless People through Plant-Capture and Postcount Survey Methods," *Innovations in Design and Analysis* 98, no. 8 (2008): 1438–42.

20. Glynn and Fox, "Dynamics of Homelessness in Urban America."

21. Anna Kondratas, "Estimates and Public Policy: The Politics of Numbers," *Housing Policy Debate* 2, no. 3 (1991): 629–47.

22. United States Government Accountability Office, *Homelessness: A Complex Problem and the Federal Response*, Washington, DC: United States General Accounting Office; Kondratas "Estimates and Public Policy."

23. Richard B. Freeman and Brian Hall, "Permanent Homelessness in America?," *Population Research and Policy Review* 6, no. 1 (1987): 3–27; Kondratas, "Estimates and Public Policy."

24. Freeman and Hall, "Permanent Homelessness in America?"

25. Kondratas, "Estimates and Public Policy."

26. Freeman and Hall, "Permanent Homelessness in America?," 20.

27. U.S. Department of Housing and Urban Development, *The Annual Homeless Assessment Report to Congress* (Washington, DC: U.S. Department of Housing and Urban Development, Office of Policy Development and Research, 2007).

28. Fusaro et al., "Racial and Ethnic Disparities in the Lifetime Prevalence of Homelessness in the United States"; Shelton et al., "Risk Factors for Homelessness"; Tsai, "Lifetime and 1-Year Prevalence of Homelessness in the US Population."

29. O'Flaherty, "Wrong Person and Wrong Place," 1.

30. Brendan O'Flaherty is far from the only scholar to highlight the importance of understanding interactions that produce homelessness. Deden Rukmana argues that intercity (typically focused on structural issues) and intracity (typically focused on the individual) data are complementary and help to provide a more complete understanding of homelessness. Deden Rukmana, "The Causes of Homelessness and the Characteristics Associated with High Risk of Homelessness: A Review of Intercity and Intracity Homelessness Data," *Housing Policy Debate* 30, no. 2 (2020): 291–308. Deborah Cobb-Clark and colleagues, like O'Flaherty, describe homelessness as an unfortunate combination of (i) personal disadvantage, such as poor health, addiction, and unemployment; (ii) structural factors, such as limited public assistance, housing market dynamics, and constrained employment opportunities; and (iii) bad luck. Cobb-Clark et al. argue that bouts of homelessness and, importantly, the length of time that people spend homeless are a function of these three factors and how they interact. Deborah Cobb-Clark, Nicolas Herault, Rosanna Scutella, and Yi-Ping Tseng. "A Journey Home: What Drives How Long People Are Homeless?," *Journal of Urban Economics* 91 (2016): 57–72.

31. Dirk W. Early, "A Microeconomic Analysis of Homelessness: An Empirical Investigation Using Choice-Based Sampling," *Journal of Housing Economics* 8 no. 4 (1999): 312–27; Greg A. Greenberg and Robert A. Rosenheck, "Mental Health Correlates of Past Homelessness in

the National Comorbidity Study Replication," *Journal of Health Care for the Poor and Underserved* 21, no. 4 (2010): 1234–49.

32. Thomas Byrne, Dan Treglia, Dennis P. Culhane, John Kuhn, and Vincent Kane, "Predictors of Homelessness among Families and Single Adults after Exit from Homelessness Prevention and Rapid Rehousing Programs: Evidence from the Department of Veterans Affairs Supportive Services for Veteran Families Program," *Housing Policy Debate* 26, no. 1 (2015): 252–75.

33. Early, "A Microeconomic Analysis of Homelessness"; Greenberg and Rosenheck, "Mental Health Correlates of Past Homelessness."

34. Early, "A Microeconomic Analysis of Homelessness."

35. Dirk W. Early, "The Determinants for Homelessness and the Targeting of Housing Assistance," *Journal of Urban Economics* 55, no. 1 (2004): 195–214.; Greenberg and Rosenheck, "Mental Health Correlates of Past Homelessness."

36. Daniel H. Castellanos, "The Role of Institutional Placement, Family Conflict, and Homosexuality in Homelessness Pathways among Latino LGBT Youth in New York City," *Journal of Homosexuality* 63, no. 5 (2016): 601–32.

37. Debbie S. Bates and Paul A. Toro, "Developing Measures to Assess Social Support among Homeless and Poor People," *Journal of Community Psychology* 27, no. 2 (1999): 137–56.

38. Mark LaGory, Ferris Ritchey, and Kevin Fitzpatrick, "Homelessness and Affiliation," *The Sociological Quarterly* 32, no. 2 (1991): 201–18; Erika R. Lehmann, Philip H. Kass, Christina M. Drake, and Sara B. Nichols, "Risk Factors for First-Time Homelessness in Low-Income Women," *American Journal of Orthopsychiatry* 77, no. 1 (2007): 20–28.

39. Angela R. Fertig and David A. Reingold, "Homelessness among At-Risk Families with Children in Twenty American Cities," *Social Service Review* 82, no. 3 (2008): 485–510.

40. Kevin Corinth and Claire Rossi-de Vries, "Social Ties and the Incidence of Homelessness," *Housing Policy Debate* 28, no. 4 (2018): 592–608.

41. Early, "A Microeconomic Analysis of Homelessness."

42. Jeffrey Draine, Mark S. Salzer, Dennis P. Culhane, and Trevor R. Hadley, "Role of Social Disadvantage in Crime, Joblessness,

and Homelessness among Persons with Serious Mental Illness," *Psychiatric Services* 53, no. 5 (2002): 565–73; Greenberg and Rosenheck, "Mental Health Correlates of Past Homelessness."

43. Greenberg and Rosenheck, "Mental Health Correlates of Past Homelessness."

44. Shinn and Khadduri, *In the Midst of Plenty*. Certainly, that a prior history of incarceration makes it more difficult to attain a job and a rental lease—and that individual attributes like race are structurally associated with higher rates of incarceration—suggests we ought to understand criminal history as an attribute that interacts with broader structural factors, as well.

45. Sam Allgood and Ronald S. Warren, "The Duration of Homelessness: Evidence from a National Survey," *Journal of Housing Economics* 12, no. 4 (2003): 273–90.

46. Ibid.

47. Seena Fazel, Vivek Khosla, Helen Doll, and John Geddes, "The Prevalence of Mental Disorders among the Homeless in Western Countries: Systematic Review and Meta-Regression Analysis," *PLoS Medicine* 5, no. 12 (2008): 1670–81; Shinn and Khadduri, *In the Midst of Plenty*.

48. Early, "A Microeconomic Analysis of Homelessness"; Dick W. Early, "An Empirical Investigation of the Determinants of Street Homelessness," *Journal of Housing Economics* 14, no. 1 (2005): 27–47; Greenberg and Rosenheck, "Mental Health Correlates of Past Homelessness."

49. Marybeth Shinn, Daniel Gubits, and Lauren Dunton, *Behavioral Health Improvements over Time among Adults in Families Experiencing Homelessness* (Washington, DC: Office of Planning, Research and Evaluation (OPRE), 2018).

50. Michael J. Dear and Jennifer R. Wolch, *Landscapes of Despair: From Deinstitutionalization to Homelessness* (Princeton, NJ: Princeton University Press, 1987).

51. O'Flaherty, *Making Room*; Shinn and Khadduri; *In the Midst of Plenty*.

52. Stephanie Hartwell, "Deviance over the Life Course: The Case of Homeless Substance Abusers," *Substance Use and Misuse* 38, no. 3–6

(2003): 475–502; Guy Johnson and Chris Chamberlain, "Homelessness and Substance Abuse: Which Comes First?," *Australian Social Work* 61, no. 4 (2008): 342–56; Joanne Neale, "Housing and Illicit Drug Use," *Housing Review* 46, no. 5 (1997): 104–6; Joanne Neale, "Homelessness amongst Drug Users: A Double Jeopardy Explored," *International Journal of Drug Policy* 12, no. 4 (2001): 353–69.

53. Gerhard Glomm and Andrew John, "Homelessness and Labor Markets," *Regional Science and Urban Economics* 32, no. 5 (2002): 591–606.

54. Lorraine R. Reitzel, Nicole A. Short, Norman B. Schmidt, Lorra Garey, Michael J. Zvolensky, Alexis Moisiuc, Carrie Reddick, Darla E. Kendzor, and Michael S. Businelle, "Distress Tolerance Links Sleep Problems with Stress and Health in Homeless," *American Journal of Health Behavior* 41, no. 6 (2017): 760–75.

55. Henry et al., *The 2019 Annual Homeless Assessment Report (AHAR) to Congress: Part I.*; Angela L. Hudson, Kynna Wright, Debika Bhattacharya, Karabi Sinha, Adeline Nyamathi, and Mary Marfisee, "Correlates of Adult Assault among Homeless Women," *Journal of Health Care for the Poor and Underserved* 21, no. 4 (2010): 1250–62; Ray M. Merrill, Rickelle Richards, and Arielle Sloan, "Prenatal Maternal Stress and Physical Abuse among Homeless Women and Infant Health Outcomes in the United States," *Epidemiology Research International* (2011): 1–10; Kimberly A. Tyler, and Rachel M. Schmitz, "A Comparison of Risk Factors for Various Forms of Trauma in the Lives of Lesbian, Gay, Bisexual and Heterosexual Homeless Youth," *Journal of Trauma & Dissociation* 19, no. 4 (2018): 431–43; Kimberly A. Tyler, and Rachel M. Schmitz, "Child Abuse, Mental Health and Sleeping Arrangements among Homeless Youth: Links to Physical and Sexual Street Victimization," *Children and Youth Services Review* 95, April (2018): 327–33; Margot B. Kushel, Jennifer L. Evans, Sharon Perry, Marjorie J. Robertson, and Andrew R Moss, "No Door to Lock: Victimization among Homeless and Marginally Housed Persons," *Archives of Internal Medicine* 163 (2003): 2492–99.

56. Bates and Toro, "Developing Measures to Assess Social Support"; Fertig and Reingold, "Homelessness among At-Risk Families with Children"; LaGory et al., "Homelessness and Affiliation"; Erika R. Lehmann et al., "Risk Factors for First-Time Homelessness

in Low-Income Women,"; Ami Rokach. "The Lonely and Homeless: Causes and Consequences," *Social Indicators Research* 69 (2004): 37–50.

57. Kevin M. Fitzpatrick, Mark E. LaGory, and Ferris J. Ritchey, "Dangerous Places: Exposure to Violence and Its Mental Health Consequences for the Homeless," *American Journal of Orthopsychiatry* 69, no. 4 (1999): 438–47; Mimi M. Kim, Julian D. Ford, Daniel L. Howard, and Daniel W. Bradford, "Assessing Trauma, Substance Abuse, and Mental Health in a Sample of Homeless Men," *Health and Social Work* 35, no. 1 (2010): 39–48; Adam M. Lippert and Barrett A. Lee, "Stress, Coping, and Mental Health Differences among Homeless People," *Sociological Inquiry* 85, no. 3 (2015): 343–74.

58. Martha R. Burt, "Homeless Families, Singles, and Others: Findings from the 1996 National Survey of Homeless Assistance Providers and Clients," *Housing Policy Debate* 12, no. 4 (2001): 737.

59. Michael Cragg and Brendan O'Flaherty, "Do Homeless Shelter Conditions Determine Shelter Population? The Case of the Dinkins Deluge," *Journal of Urban Economics,* 46 (1999): 377–415; Brendan O'Flaherty and Ting Wu, "Homeless Shelters for Single Adults: Why Does Their Population Change?" *Social Service Review* 82, no. 3 (2008): 511–50; Shinn and Khadduri, *In the Midst of Plenty.*

60. Maria Hanratty, "Do Local Economic Conditions Affect Homelessness? Impact of Area Housing Market Factors, Unemployment, and Poverty on Community Homeless Rates," *Housing Policy Debate* 27, no. 4 (2017): 640–55; Seungbeom Kang, "Beyond Households: Regional Determinants of Housing Instability among Low-Income Renters in the United States," *Housing Studies* (2019).

61. Jacob William Faber, "On the Street during the Great Recession: Exploring the Relationship between Foreclosures and Homelessness," *Housing Policy Debate* 29, no. 4 (2019): 588–606; Sarena Goodman, Peter Messeri, and Brendan O'Flaherty, "Homelessness Prevention in New York City: On Average, It Works," *Journal of Housing Economics* 31 (2016): 14–34.

62. Thomas Byrne, Ellen A. Munley, Jamison D. Fargo, Ann E. Montgomery, and Dennis P. Culhane, "New Perspectives on Community-Level Determinants of Homelessness," *Journal of Urban Affairs* 35, no. 5 (2013): 607–25; Jamison D. Fargo, Ellen A. Munley,

Thomas H. Byrne, Ann Elizabeth Montgomery, and Dennis P. Culhane, "Community-Level Characteristics Associated with Variation in Rates of Homelessness among Families and Single Adults," *American Journal of Public Health* 103, SUPPL. 2 (2013); Hanratty, "Do Local Economic Conditions Affect Homelessness?"; John M. Quigley and Steven Raphael, "The Economics of Homelessness: The Evidence from North America," *International Journal of Housing Policy* 1, no. 3 (2001): 323–36; Steven Raphael, "Housing Market Regulation and Homelessness," in *How to House the Homeless*, ed. Ingrid Gould Ellen and Brendan O'Flaherty (New York: Russell Sage Foundation, 2010), 110–40.

63. Quigley and Raphael, "The Economics of Homelessness"; Raphael, "Housing Market Regulation and Homelessness."

64. Kevin Corinth, "The Impact of Permanent Supportive Housing on Homeless Populations," *Journal of Housing Economics* 35 (2017): 69–84; Kevin Corinth and David S. Lucas, "When Warm and Cold Don't Mix: The Implications of Climate for the Determinants of Homelessness," *Journal of Housing Economics* 41, August (2017): 45–56.

65. Fargo et al., "Community-Level Characteristics"; Glynn and Fox, "Dynamics of Homelessness in Urban America"; Hanratty, "Do Local Economic Conditions Affect Homelessness?"; Barrett A. Lee, Townsand Price-Spratlen, and James W. Kanan, "Determinants of Homelessness in Metropolitan Areas," *Journal of Urban Affairs* 25, no. 3 (2003): 335–56; Raphael, "Housing Market Regulation and Homelessness."

66. Corinth, "The Impact of Permanent Supportive Housing on Homeless Populations"; Fargo et al., "Community-Level Characteristics," Glynn and Fox, "Dynamics of Homelessness in Urban America"; Hanratty, "Do Local Economic Conditions Affect Homelessness?"; Lee et al., "Determinants of Homelessness in Metropolitan Areas."

67. Byrne et al., "New Perspectives on Community-Level Determinants of Homelessness."

68. Quigley and Raphael, "The Economics of Homelessness."

69. Fargo et al., "Community-Level Characteristics," Glynn and Fox, "Dynamics of Homelessness in Urban America."

70. Ibid.

71. Fargo et al., "Community-Level Characteristics"; Hanratty, "Do Local Economic Conditions Affect Homelessness?"

72. Byrne et al., "New Perspectives on Community-Level Determinants of Homelessness."

73. Ibid.

74. Ibid.

75. Hanratty, "Do Local Economic Conditions Affect Homelessness?"

76. Glynn and Fox, "Dynamics of Homelessness in Urban America."

77. Chris Glynn, Thomas H. Byrne, and Dennis P. Culhane, "Inflection Points in Community-Level Homeless Rates," unpublished paper, available at http://works.bepress.com/dennis_culhane/228/.

78. Glynn and Fox, "Dynamics of Homelessness in Urban America."

79. Veronica Harnish, "I've Been Homeless 3 Times. The Problem Isn't Drugs or Mental Illness—It's Poverty," *Vox*, March 8, 2016, https://www.vox.com/2016/3/8/11173304/homeless-in-america.

80. Ibid.

81. Byrne et al., "Predictors of Homelessness among Families and Single Adults"; Marah Curtis, Hope Corman, Kelly Noonan, and Nancy E. Reichman, "Life Shocks and Homelessness," *Demography 50*, no. 6 (2013): 2227–53; Faber, "On the Street during the Great Recession; Brendan O'Flaherty, "Homelessness as Bad Luck: Implications for Research and Policy," in *How to House the Homeless*, ed. Ingrid Gould Ellen and Brendan O'Flaherty (New York: Russell Sage Foundation, 2010), 143–82.

82. Curtis et al., "Life Shocks and Homelessness," 2227.

83. M. Bowen, T. Marshall, A. Yahyouche, V. Paudyal, S. Marwick, K. Saunders, S. Burwood, and D. Stewart, "Multimorbidity and Emergency Department Visits by a Homeless Population: A Database Study in Specialist General Practice," *British Journal of General Practice* 69, no. 685 (2019): E515–25; Seena Fazel, John R. Geddes, and Margot Kushel, "The Health of Homeless People in High-Income Countries: Descriptive Epidemiology, Health Consequences, and Clinical and Policy Recommendations," *The Lancet* 384, no. 9953 (2014): 1529–40; Jill S. Roncarati, Travis P. Baggett, James J. O'Connell, Stephen W. Hwang, E. Francis Cook, Nancy Krieger, and Glorian Sorensen, "Mortality among Unsheltered Homeless Adults in Boston, Massachusetts, 2000–2009," *JAMA Internal Medicine* 178, no. 9 (2018): 1242–48.

84. Bowen et al., "Multimorbidity and Emergency Department Visits"; Fazel et al., "The Health of Homeless People."

85. Jennifer Adams, Robert Rosenheck, Lauren Gee, Catherine L. Seibyl, and Margot Kushel, "Hospitalized Younger: A Comparison of a National Sample of Homeless and Housed Inpatient Veterans," *Journal of Health Care for the Poor and Underserved* 18 (2007): 173–84.; Bowen et al., "Multimorbidity and Emergency Department Visits"; Margot B. Kushel, Sharon Perry, David Bangsberg, Richard Clark, and Andrew R Moss, "Emergency Department Use among the Homeless and Marginally Housed: Results from a Community-Based Study," *American Journal of Public Health* 92, no. 5 (2002): 778–84.

86. Kushel et al., "No Door to Lock"; Hudson et al., "Correlates of Adult Assault among Homeless Women"; Merrill et al., "Prenatal Maternal Stress."

87. Bowen et al., "Multimorbidity and Emergency Department Visits"; Fazel et al., "The Health of Homeless People."

88. Fitzpatrick, LaGory, and Ritchey, "Dangerous Places; Lippert and Lee, "Stress, Coping, and Mental Health."

89. Ellen L. Bassuk and Lynn Rosenberg, "Psychosocial Characteristics of Homeless Children and Children with Homes," *Pediatrics* 85, no. 3 (1990): 257–61; Yvonne Rafferty and Marybeth Shinn, "The Impact of Homelessness on Children," *American Psychologist* 46, no. 11 (1991): 1170–79; Leslie Rescoria, Ruth Parker, and Paul Stolley, "Ability, Achievement, and Adjustment in Homeless Children," *American Journal of Orthopsychiatry* 61, April (1991): 210–20.

90. Bassuk and Rosenberg, "Psychosocial Characteristics of Homeless Children and Children with Homes"; Rafferty and Shinn, "The Impact of Homelessness on Children."

91. Daniel S. Miller and Elizabeth H. B. Lin, "Children in Sheltered Homeless Families: Reported Health Status and Use of Health Services," *Pediatrics* 81, no. 5 (1988): 668–73; Rafferty and Shinn, "The Impact of Homelessness on Children."

92. Miller and Lin, "Children in Sheltered Homeless Families."

93. Rafferty and Shinn, "The Impact of Homelessness on Children"; Rescoria et al., "Ability, Achievement, and Adjustment in

Homeless Children"; B. T. Zima, K. B. Wells, and H. E. Freeman, "Emotional and Behavioral Problems and Severe Academic Delays among Sheltered Homeless Children in Los Angeles County," *American Journal of Public Health* 84, no. 2 (1994): 260–64.

94. J. J. Cutuli, Christopher David Desjardins, Janette E. Herbers, Jeffrey D. Long, David Heistad, Chi-Keung Chan, Elizabeth Hinz, and Ann Masten, "Academic Achievement Trajectories of Homeless and Highly Mobile Students: Resilience in the Context of Chronic and Acute Risk," *Child Development* 84, no. 3 (2013): 841–57; John Fantuzzo and Staci Perlman, "The Unique Impact of Out-of-Home Placement and the Mediating Effects of Child Maltreatment and Homelessness on Early School Success," *Children and Youth Services Review* 29, no. 7 (2007): 941–60; Janette E. Herbers, J. J. Cutuli, Laura M. Supkoff, David Heistad, Chi-Keung Chan, Elizabeth Hinz, and Ann S. Masten, "Early Reading Skills and Academic Achievement of Students Facing Poverty, Homelessness, and High Residential Mobility," *Educational Researcher* 41, no. 9 (2012): 366–74; Rafferty and Shinn, "The Impact of Homelessness on Children"; Zima et al., "Emotional and Behavioral Problems."

95. Tyler and Schmitz, "Child Abuse, Mental Health and Sleeping Arrangements among Homeless Youth."

96. Rokach, "The Lonely and Homeless: Causes and Consequences."

97. Ann G. Smolen, "Children Born into Loss: Some Developmental Consequences of Homelessness," *Journal for the Psychoanalysis of Culture and Society* 8, no. 2 (2003): 250–57.

98. Naomi S. Thulien, Denise Gastaldo, Stephen W. Hwang, and Elizabeth McCay, "The Elusive Goal of Social Integration: A Critical Examination of the Socio-economic and Psychosocial Consequences Experienced by Homeless Young People Who Obtain Housing," *Canadian Journal of Public Health* 109, no. 1 (2018): 89.

99. Angela Ly and Eric Latimer, "Housing First Impact on Costs and Associated Cost Offsets: A Review of the Literature," *Canadian Journal of Psychiatry* 60, no. 11 (2015): 475–87.

100. Cameron Parsell, Maree Petersen, and Dennis Culhane, "Cost Offsets of Supportive Housing: Evidence for Social Work," *British Journal of Social Work* 47, no. 5 (2017): 1534–53.

101. Ibid.

102. Dennis P. Culhane, "The Costs of Homelessness: A Perspective from the United States," *European Journal of Homelessness* 2, January (2008): 97–114.

103. Geoffrey DeVerteuil, "The Local State and Homeless Shelters: Beyond Revanchism?," *Cities* 23, no. 2 (2006): 109–20; Gordon MacLeod, "From Urban Entrepreneurialism to a Revanchist City? On the Spatial Injustices of Glasgow's Renaissance," *Antipode* 34 (2002): 602–24.

104. Adam Brinklow, "Oracle Convention Pulls Out of SF over 'Street Conditions,'" *Curbed: San Francisco* (2019), https://sf.curbed.com /2019/12/11/21011250/oracle-open-world-sf-travel-association-moscone -las-vegas; Lyanne Melendez, "Pier 39 Business Owner to San Francisco: Stop Ignoring Issues of Homelessness, Dirty Streets," ABC7-News (2019), https://abc7news.com/business/pier-39-business-blames -homeless-dirty-streets-for-revenue-loss/5750312/; Jennifer Sullivan, "Seattle's Growing Homeless Population Could Impact Tourism as Season Gets Underway," KOMONEWS (2018), https://komonews .com/news/local/seattles-growing-homeless-problem-could-be -impacting-tourism-as-head-tax-vote-looms.

105. Brinklow, "Oracle Convention Pulls out of SF over 'Street Conditions.'"

106. Sullivan, "Seattle's Growing Homeless."

107. Such is the philosophy of the Housing First approach cited above.

108. Binyamin Appelbaum, "America's Cities Could House Everyone If They Chose To," *New York Times*, May 15, 2020, https://www .nytimes.com/2020/05/15/opinion/sunday/homeless-crisis-affordable -housing-cities.html.

109. Daniel Gubits, Marybeth Shinn, Michelle Wood, Scott R. Brown, Samuel R. Dastrup, and Stephen H. Bell, "What Interventions Work Best for Families Who Experience Homelessness? Impact Estimates from the Family Options Study," *Journal of Policy Analysis and Management* 37, no. 4 (2018): 835–66.

110. The vast majority of this research has focused on individuals with disabilities; little research exists on the population without disabilities.

III. Tim Aubry, Sam Tsemberis, Carol E. Adair, Scott Veldhui-zen, David Streiner, Eric Latimer, Jitender Sareen, et al., "One-Year Outcomes of a Randomized Controlled Trial of Housing First with Act in Five Canadian Cities," *Psychiatric Services* 66, no. 5 (2015): 463–69; Kenneth W. Kizer, Barbara Brush, Seiji Hayashi, Stephen Hwang, Mitchell Katz, Mahasin Mujahid, James O'Connell, et al., *Permanent Supportive Housing: Evaluating the Evidence for Improving Health Outcomes among People Experiencing Chronic Homelessness* (Washington, DC: The National Academies Press, 2018); Debra J. Rog, Tina Marshall, Rich-ard H. Dougherty, Preethy George, Allen S. Daniels, Sushmita Shoma Ghose, and Miriam E. Delphin-Rittmon, "Permanent Supportive Housing: Assessing the Evidence," *Psychiatric Services* 65, no. 3 (2014): 287–94; Sam Tsemberis, Leyla Gulcur, and Maria Nakae, "Housing First, Consumer Choice, and Harm Reduction for Homeless Indi-viduals with a Dual Diagnosis," *American Journal of Public Health* 94, no. 4 (2004): 651–56; Sam J. Tsemberis, Linda Moran, Marybeth Shinn, Sara M. Asmussen, and David L. Shern, "Consumer Preference Pro-grams for Individuals Who Are Homeless and Have Psychiatric Dis-abilities: A Drop-in Center and a Supported Housing Program," *American Journal of Community Psychology* 32, no. 3–4 (2003): 305–17.

112. Kizer et al., *Permanent Supportive Housing*; Rog et al., "Perma-nent Supportive Housing: Assessing the Evidence."

113. David S. Lucas, "The Impact of Federal Homelessness Fund-ing on Homelessness," *Southern Economic Journal* 84, no. 2 (2017): 548–76; William Harris Troutman, John D. Jackson, and Robert B. Ekelund, "Public Policy, Perverse Incentives, and the Homeless Problem," *Pub-lic Choice* 98, nos. 1–2 (1999): 195–212.

114. Thomas Byrne, Jamison D. Fargo, Ann Elizabeth Mont-gomery, Ellen Munley, and Dennis P. Culhane, "The Relationship between Community Investment in Permanent Supportive Housing and Chronic Homelessness," *Social Service Review* 88, no. 2 (2014): 234–63; Shawn Moulton, "Does Increased Funding for Homeless Programs Reduce Chronic Homelessness?," *Southern Economic Journal* 79, no. 3 (2013): 600–620.

115. Igor Popov, "Homeless Programs and Social Insurance," work-ing paper, Stanford Institute for Economic Policy Research.

116. Lucas, "The Impact of Federal Homelessness Funding on Homelessness."

117. Osborne Jackson and Laura Kawano, "Do Increases in Subsidized Housing Reduce the Incidence of Homelessness? Evidence from the Low-Income Housing Tax Credit," Working Papers, no 15–11, Federal Reserve Bank of Boston, 2013.

118. Moulton, "Does Increased Funding for Homeless Programs Reduce Chronic Homelessness?"; Quigley and Raphael, "The Economics of Homelessness."

CHAPTER 3. INDIVIDUAL

1. Jack Fowler, "'What If Seattle Is Dying, and We Don't Even Know It?,'" *National Review*, August 2019, https://www.nationalreview.com/corner/what-if-seattle-is-dying-and-we-dont-even-know-it/.

2. Heather Mac Donald, "San Francisco, Hostage to the Homeless," *City Journal* (Autumn 2019), https://www.city-journal.org/san-francisco-homelessness.

3. O'Flaherty, "Homelessness as Bad Luck."

4. The Council of Economic Advisors, *The State of Homelessness in America.*

5. Paul Brewer and Sunil Venaik, "The Ecological Fallacy in National Culture Research," *Organization Studies* 35, no. 7 (2014): 1063–86; Paul Connolly. "Summary Statistics, Educational Achievement Gaps and the Ecological Fallacy," *Oxford Review of Education* 32, no. 2 (2006): 235–52; Steven Piantadosi, David P. Byar, and Sylvan B. Green, "The Ecological Fallacy," *American Journal of Epidemiology* 127, no. 5 (1988): 893–904; Hume Winzar. "The Ecological Fallacy: How to Spot One and Tips on How to Use One to Your Advantage," *Australasian Marketing Journal* 23, no. 1 (2015): 86–92.

6. W. S. Robinson, "Ecological Correlations and the Behavior of Individuals," *American Sociological Review* 15, no. 3 (1950): 351–57.

7. Barrett A. Lee, Kimberly A. Tyler, and James D. Right, "The New Homelessness Revisited," *Annual Review of Sociology* 36 (2010): 501–21.

8. Byrne et al., "Predictors of Homelessness among Families and Single Adults"; Early, "The Determinants for Homelessness"; Early,

"An Empirical Investigation of the Determinants"; Greenberg and Rosenheck, "Mental Health Correlates."

9. In our dataset, we also measure the relationship between median income and per capita rates of homelessness and find a strong, positive relationship. Higher incomes are strongly associated with higher rates of homelessness.

10. Benjamin Maritz and Dilip Wagle, "Why Does Prosperous King County Have a Homelessness Crisis?," McKinsey & Company, January 22, 2020, https://www.mckinsey.com/industries/public-and-social-sector/our-insights/why-does-prosperous-king-county-have-a-homelessness-crisis; Maggie Stringfellow and Dilip Wagle, "The Economics of Homelessness in Seattle and King County," McKinsey & Company, May 18, 2018, https://www.mckinsey.com/featured-insights/future-of-cities/the-economics-of-homelessness-in-seattle-and-king-county.

11. Thomas J. Sugrue, *The Origins of the Urban Crisis: Race and Inequality in Postwar Detroit* (Princeton, NJ: Princeton University Press, 2005), 1.

12. Geoff Lewis, John Avault, and Jim Vrabel, *History of Boston's Economy: Growth and Transition 1970–1998* (Boston, MA: Boston Redevelopment Authority, 1999), 3, http://www.bostonplans.org/getattachment/15ca7a2f-56d1-4770-ba7f-8c1ce73d25b8.

13. Applied Survey Research, *Count Us In*.

14. National Coalition for the Homeless, "Employment and Homelessness," 2009, https://www.nationalhomeless.org/factsheets/employment.html.

15. David Long, John Rio, and Jeremy Rosen, "Employment and Income Supports for Homeless People," in *Toward Understanding Homelessness: The 2007 National Symposium on Homelessness Research* (Washington, DC: Assistant Secretary for Planning and Evaluation, 2007), 1–34, https://aspe.hhs.gov/report/toward-understanding-homelessness-2007-national-symposium-homelessness-research-employment-and-income-supports-homeless-people.

16. Community Solutions, "Analysis on Unemployment Projects 40–45% Increase in Homelessness This Year," *Homelessness Report* (blog), May 11, 2020. https://community.solutions/analysis-on-unemployment-projects-40-45-increase-in-homelessness-this-year/.

17. In the full data set, we also measure the relationship between lagged unemployment (one year) and per capita homelessness under the theory that there may be a delay between the loss of a job and a bout of homelessness. The relationship using lagged unemployment yields results virtually identical to the figure shown in this section. Therefore, lagging this indicator does not change our interpretation of this relationship.

18. Philadelphia Works (2016). "Philadelphia's Economy. https://www.philaworks.org/philadelphias-economy/.

19. Margaret O'Mara, *The Code* (New York: Penguin Press, 2019).

20. Shinn and Khadduri, *In the Midst of Plenty.*

21. Greenberg and Rosenheck, "Mental Health Correlates"; Lee et al., "Determinants of Homelessness in Metropolitan Areas."

22. Mac Donald, "San Francisco, Hostage to the Homeless."

23. Fargo et al., "Community-Level Characteristics."

24. Olivet et al., "SPARC Phase One Study Findings."

25. O'Flaherty, "Homelessness as Bad Luck."

CHAPTER 4. LANDSCAPE

1. Christopher Rufo. "The Politics of Ruinous Compassion: How Seattle's Homelessness Policy Perpetuates the Crisis—And How We Can Fix It," Discovery Institute, 2018, https://www.discovery.org/m/2018/10/The-Politics-of-Ruinous-Compassion.pdf.

2. Ibid., 2.

3. Council of Economic Advisers, *The State of Homelessness in America* (Washington, DC: US Government Printing Office),1.

4. Ibid., 2.

5. Ibid.

6. Byrne et al., "New Perspectives on Community-Level Determinants of Homelessness"; Corinth and Lucas, "When Warm and Cold Don't Mix"; Dirk W. Early and Edgar O. Olsen, "Subsidized Housing, Emergency Shelters, and Homelessness: An Empirical Investigation Using Data from the 1990 Census," *The B.E. Journal of Economic Analysis & Policy* 2, no. 1 (2002): 1–36; Paul W. Grimes, and George A. Chressanthis, "Assessing the Effect of Rent Control on Homelessness," *Journal of Urban Economics* 41, (1997): 23–37.

7. Recall that our indexing function makes relative rates of homelessness in cities and counties more directly comparable by scaling rates in each group (cities and counties) with respect to the maximum rate in that group across all years in the sample.

8. Corinth, "The Impact of Permanent Supportive Housing on Homeless Populations."

9. The weather story is further complicated by the fact that average January *precipitation* broadly bears a positive statistical relationship with rates of homelessness, including unsheltered homelessness and indexed rates. That is, regions with more precipitation see higher rates of homelessness. And while the magnitude of the effect (and percentage of explained variance) is higher in the case of sheltered homelessness—indicating further support for the policy-response hypothesis—it remains positive in the case of unsheltered homelessness. The latter effect would appear to contradict both the argument that favorable weather encourages unsheltered homelessness *and* the argument that unfavorable weather encourages a shelter-supply response. Furthermore, variation in the proportion of the population experiencing homelessness considered sheltered is poorly explained by precipitation levels.

10. Council of Economic Advisers, *The State of Homelessness in America*, 2 (emphasis added).

11. New York City, Washington, D.C., Salt Lake City, Minneapolis, and the State of Massachusetts all have "shelter all" policies that guarantee shelter to families. New York, Washington, D.C., and Salt Lake City have similar right-to-shelter policies for individuals (as listed in Hanratty, Do Local Economic Conditions Affect Homelessness?).

12. DeVerteuil, "The Local State and Homeless Shelters."

13. Cragg and O'Flaherty, "Do Homeless Shelter Conditions Determine Shelter Population?," 379.

14. Ibid., 377.

15. Brendan O'Flaherty and Ting Wu, "Fewer Subsidized Exits and a Recession: How New York City's Family Homeless Shelter Population Became Immense," *Journal of Housing Economics*, 15 (2006): 99–125.

16. William N. Evans, James X. Sullivan, and Melanie Wallskog, "The Impact of Homeless Prevention Programs on Homelessness," *Science* 353, no. 6300 (2016): 694–99.

17. United Nations, "Water and Climate Change," UN Water, 2020, https://www.unwater.org/water-facts/climate-change/.

18. Qin Fan, Karen Fisher-Vanden, and H. Allen Klaiber, "Climate Change, Migration, and Regional Economic Impacts in the United States," *Journal of the Association of Environmental and Resource Economists* 5, no. 3 (2018): 643–71.

19. J. Leopold D. Culhane, and J. Khadduri, *Where Do Homeless People Come From? Movement of Households from Their Prior Residences into Homeless Residential Facilities in Michigan and Iowa* (Rockville, MD: Abt Associates, 2017), 1–25; George R. Carter, III, "From Exclusion to Destitution: Race, Affordable Housing, and Homelessness," *Cityscape: A Journal of Policy Development and Research* 13, no. 1 (2011): 33–70.

20. Evans et al., "The Impact of Homeless Prevention Programs on Homelessness."

21. Ibid.

22. Byrne et al., "The Relationship between Community Investment in Permanent Supportive Housing and Chronic Homelessness"; Corinth, "The Impact of Permanent Supportive Housing"; Moulton, "Does Increased Funding for Homeless Programs Reduce Chronic Homelessness?"

23. Popov, "Homeless Programs and Social Insurance."

24. Heather Hahn, Laudan Aron, Cary Lou, Eleanor Pratt, and Adaeze Okoli, *Why Does Cash Welfare Depend on Where You Live? How and Why State TANF Programs Vary* (Washington, DC: Urban Institute, 2017).

25. In addition, we also analyzed the relationship between TANF generosity and *total* homelessness and, again, found no relationship.

26. Leopold et al., *Where Do Homeless People Come From?*

27. Carter, "From Exclusion to Destitution."

28. Stephen Metraux, Dan Treglia, and Thomas P. O'Toole, "Migration by Veterans Who Received Homeless Services from the Department of Veterans Affairs," *Military Medicine* 181, no. 10 (2016): 1212–17.

29. Popov, "Homeless Programs and Social Insurance."

30. Jon May, "Housing Histories and Homeless Careers: A Biographical Approach," *Housing Studies* 15, no. 4 (2000): 613–38; R. David Parker and Shana Dykema, "The Reality of Homeless Mobility and

Implications for Improving Care," *Journal of Community Health* 38, no. 4 (2013): 685–89; David E. Pollio, "The Relationship between Transience and Current Life Situation in the Homeless Services-Using Population," *Social Work* 42, no. 6 (1997): 541–51.

31. Kevin Fagen, "Bay Area Homelessness: 97 Answers to Your Questions," *San Francisco Chronicle*, July 28, 2019, https://projects .sfchronicle.com/sf-homeless/homeless-questions/.

32. Anna Griffin, "The 'Magnet Myth,'" *The Oregonian*, February 14, 2015, https://www.oregonlive.com/projects/portland-homeless /magnet.html.

33. Kevin Williams, "An Ohio City Known for Helping the Homeless Now Questions Its Limits," *Washington Post*, January 1, 2020, https://www.washingtonpost.com/national/an-ohio-city-known-for -helping-now-questions-its-limits-when-the-homeless-come-from -somewhere-else/2020/01/01/d58a38ac-2b26-11ea-bcd4-24597950008f _story.html.

34. Fessler, "Trump Continues Criticism of Democrats on Homelessness."

35. For the county jurisdictions, we record the political party affiliation of the mayor for the major city in that county (e.g., Chicago for Cook County and Seattle in King County).

36. Diane Jeantet, "A Brief History of Homelessness in New York," City Limits, March 11, 2013. https://citylimits.org/2013/03/11/a-brief -history-of-homelessness-in-new-york/.

37. Williams Cole, "Against the Giuliani Legacy," *The Brooklyn Rail*, May–June 2001, https://brooklynrail.org/2001/05/local/against-the -giuliani-legacy-part-one.

38. Katherine Beckett and Steve Herbert, *Banished* (Oxford: Oxford University Press, 2009), 14–15.

39. Ibid., 17.

40. Council of Economic Advisors, *The State of Homelessness in America*, 18.

41. O'Flaherty, *Making Room*, 279–80.

42. Ibid.

43. National Homelessness Law Center, "Supreme Court Lets Martin v. Boise Stand: Homeless Persons Cannot Be Punished for

Sleeping in Absence of Alternatives," 2019. https://nlchp.org/supreme
-court-martin-v-boise/.

44. Shinn and Khadduri, *In the Midst of Plenty.*

CHAPTER 5. MARKET

1. "Best States Ranking," *U.S. News and World Report*, 2019, https://
www.usnews.com/news/best-states/rankings.

2. Josh Goodman, "'If Only We Could Be Like Mississippi,'"
Governing: The Future of States and Localities, 2007. https://www
.governing.com/blogs/view/If-Only-We-Could.html.

3. Evan Horowitz, "Poverty Drives Homeless Rates? No so Fast,"
Boston Globe, August 24, 2016, https://www.bostonglobe.com/2016/08
/24/poverty-drives-homeless-rates-fast/1fvvSKgNUg4l5TfqbdEGrM
/story.html.

4. Marcia Fernald, ed., *The State of the Nation's Housing 2016* (Cambridge, MA: Joint Center for Housing Policy of Harvard University,
2016), 31, https://www.jchs.harvard.edu/sites/default/files/media/imp
/jchs_2016_state_of_the_nations_housing_lowres_0.pdf.

5. Glynn et al., "Inflection Points in Community-Level Homeless
Rates."

6. Our estimate of housing cost burdens for low-income renters
takes the twenty-fifth percentile of contract rental costs and divides
it by the twenty-fifth percentile of household incomes, as provided by
the U.S. Census's American Community Survey Public Use Microdata Sample (PUMS) files.

7. Glynn et al., "Inflection Points in Community-Level Homeless
Rates."

8. A new paper—not yet published—draws a link between housing
quality regulations and rent levels. In particular, regulations appear
to have disrupted the naturally affordable rental stock and increased
rental costs. This effect helps explain why housing cost burden is so
high in the Rust Belt. We should be able to discuss this paper in subsequent versions of this manuscript.

9. While the focus of this book remains inter-regional variation,
it's worth noting that for many large cities, *intra*-regional variations in

rates of homelessness are also readily explained by absolute rents. We find this relationship in our data, as does other research (e.g., Hanratty, "Do Local Economic Conditions Affect Homelessness?".

10. Sandra Newman and C. Scott Holupka, *The Quality of America's Assisted Housing Stock: Analysis of the 2011 and 2013 American Housing Surveys.* Washington, DC: U.S. Department of Housing and Urban Development, Office of Policy Development and Research, 2017).

11. Alexander von Hoffman. *The Origins of American Housing Reform* (Cambridge, MA: Joint Center for Housing Studies of Harvard University, 1998); John M. Quigley and Steven Raphael, "Is Housing Unaffordable? Why Isn't It More Affordable?," *Journal of Economic Perspectives* 18, no. 1 (2004): 191–214.

12. Quigley and Raphael, "Is Housing Unaffordable?"

13. Jennifer Erb-Downward and Safiya Merchant, "Losing Home: Housing Instability and Availability in Detroit," working paper, Poverty Solutions, University of Michigan, 2020.

14. Robin Runyan, "Real Estate Report: A Surplus of Buyers Calls for a Solution," *Hour Detroit*, August 20, 2019, https://www.hourdetroit.com/community/real-estate-detroit-housing/.

15. David M. Blank and Louis Winnick, "The Structure of the Housing Market," *Quarterly Journal of Economics* 67, no. 2 (1953): 181–208, https://academic.oup.com/qje/article/67/2/181/1826509; Lawrence B. Smith, "A Note on the Price Adjustment Mechanism for Rental Housing," *American Economic Review* 64, no. 3 (1974): 478–81.

16. In the vacancy rate regressions, note that the charts show curved instead of straight lines. That's because we're fitting the curve to a transformed version of the actual vacancy rates, called the natural log. The natural log function is useful for exploring variance in very small positive numbers (like vacancy rates) without excluding larger positive numbers from the analysis. A standard linear regression would do just fine, but a linear regression onto the natural log— which results in a curve when plotted as we do here—captures a bit more of the natural pattern of variation in the scatter plot.

17. Generally, our other statistical analyses (not shown) suggest that while these factors are related to one another—and that their

correlation will hamper efforts to precisely estimate their respective effect sizes—we're confident in the directionality of the effects and of their unique contributions to the model.

18. R. J. Pozdena, *The Modern Economics of Housing* (New York: Quorum Books, 1998).

19. In Figure 25 we exclude the statistical outlier of Detroit in 2010. We've also tested the impact of lagged population growth (one year) and arrive at the same result: no meaningful relationship.

20. Albert Saiz, "The Geographic Determinants of Housing Supply," *Quarterly Journal of Economics* 125, no. 3 (2010): 1253–96.

21. Adam Brinklow, "San Francisco Has Nearly Five Empty Homes per Homeless Resident," *Curbed: San Francisco*, 2019, https://sf.curbed .com/2019/12/3/20993251/san-francisco-bay-area-vacant-homes-per -homeless-count.

22. American Community Survey and Puerto Rico Community Survey, Washington, DC: U.S. Census Bureau, 2018.

23. M. Finkel and L. Buron, *Study on Section 8 Voucher Success Rates: Volume I, Quantitative Study of Success Rates in Metropolitan Areas* (Washington, DC: U.S. Department of Housing and Urban Development, Office of Policy Development and Research, 2001), https://www.huduser.gov /portal/publications/pdf/sec8success_1.pdf; Kirk McClure, "What Should Be the Future of the Low-Income Housing Tax Credit Program?" *Housing Policy Debate* 29, no. 1 (2019): 65–81.

24. Kenneth T. Rosen and Lawrence B Smith, "The Price-Adjustment Process for Rental Housing and the Natural Vacancy Rate," *The American Economic Review* 73, no. 4 (1983): 785.

25. Stuart A. Gabriel and Frank E. Nothaft, "Rental Housing Markets, the Incidence and Duration of Vacancy, and the Natural Vacancy Rate," *Journal of Urban Economics* 49 (2001): 121–49; Masahiro Igarashi, "The Rent-Vacancy Relationship in the Rental Housing Market," *Journal of Housing Economics* 1 (1991): 251–70.

26. Hanratty, "Do Local Economic Conditions Affect Homelessness?"

27. Brendan O'Flaherty, "Homelessness Research: A Guide for Economists (and Friends)," *Journal of Housing Economics* 44 (2019): 1–25.

28. O'Flaherty. *Making Room: The Economics of Homelessness.*

29. Thomas Hugh Byrne, Benjamin F. Harwood, and Anthony W. Orlando. "A Rising Tide Drowns Unstable Boats: How Inequality Creates Homelessness," *Annals of the American Academy of Political and Social Science*, April 2021, https://doi.org/10.1177/0002716220981864.

CHAPTER 6. TYPOLOGY

1. Benjamin Schneider, "CityLab University: Understanding Homelessness in America," *Bloomberg CityLab*, July 6, 2020, https://www.bloomberg.com/news/features/2020-07-06/why-is-homelessness-such-a-problem-in-u-s-cities.

2. Pozdena, *The Modern Economics of Housing*.

3. Federal Reserve Bank of St. Louis, "FRED Economic Data," 2020, https://fred.stlouisfed.org.

4. Employment at nonprofit organizations accounts for approximately 10 percent of private-sector jobs.

5. Benjamin Austin, Edward Glaeser, and Lawrence Summers, "Jobs for the Heartland: Place-Based Policies in 21st-Century America," *Brookings: Papers on Economic Activity*, Spring (2018): 151–255.

6. Cailin Slattery and Owen Zidar, "Evaluating State and Local Business Incentives," *Journal of Economic Perspectives* 34, no. 2 (2020): 90–118.

7. Derek Thompson, "Amazon's HQ2 Spectacle Isn't Just Shameful—It Should Be Illegal." *The Atlantic*, November 12, 2018, https://www.theatlantic.com/ideas/archive/2018/11/amazons-hq2-spectacle-should-be-illegal/575539/.

8. Nicky Woolf, "'The Hunger Games for Cities'—Inside the Amazon HQ2 Bid Process." *New Statesman*, June 19, 2019, https://www.newstatesman.com/science-tech/technology/2019/06/hunger-games-cities-inside-amazon-hq2-bid-process.

9. Louise Matsakis, "Why Amazon's Search for a Second Headquarters Backfired," *Wired*, November 14, 2018, https://www.wired.com/story/amazon-hq2-search-backfired/; Woolf, "The Hunger Games for Cities."

10. In 2018, Taiwanese company, Foxconn, announced intentions to build a state-of-the-art facility to manufacture LCD screens. The

company promised to bring thirteen thousand jobs to Wisconsin, and in return the state and local governments provided $4 billion in aid and incentives to the company. By the end of 2019, the company had only hired 281 people. The contract is currently being renegotiated (source: *Milwaukee Journal Sentinel*).

11. Thompson, "Amazon's HQ2 Spectacle Isn't Just Shameful—It Should Be Illegal."

12. Amelia Pak-Harvey, "What Did City, State Offer for Amazon HQ2? A Judge Is Deciding Whether the Public Should Know," *IndyStar*, February 18, 2020, https://www.indystar.com/story/news/local/marion -county/2020/02/18/amazon-hq-2-proposal-indianapolis-should-public -lawsuit-says/4742217002/.

13. Matsakis, "Why Amazon's Search for a Second Headquarters Backfired."

14. Glenn Fleishman, "How Amazon's Nonstop Growth Is Creating a Brand-New Seattle," *Fast Company*, August 24, 2017, https:// www.fastcompany.com/40451502/how-amazons-nonstop-growth-is -creating-a-brand-new-seattle.

15. Slattery and Zidar, "Evaluating State and Local Business Incentives," 114.

16. *Daily* Editorial Board, "Editorial: Minneapolis Not Being an Amazon HQ2 Finalist Is Good News." *Minnesota Daily*, January 22, 2018, https://mndaily.com/195899/opinion/opeditorial-5a64f9b6ee551/.

17. Saiz, "The Geographic Determinants of Housing Supply."

18. In 2018, the Seattle Planning Commission found that 75 percent of all residential parcels in the city were zoned single-family. That number fell after the city council up-zoned roughly 6 percent of parcels as a part of their Mandatory Housing Affordability (MHA) package in 2019. Seattle Planning Commission, *Neighborhoods for All: Expanding Housing Opportunities in Seattle's Single-Family Zone* (Seattle, WA: Author, 2018), https://www.seattle.gov/Documents /Departments/SeattlePlanningCommission/SPCNeighborhoodsFor AllFINALdigital2.pdf.

19. Emily Badger and Quoctrung Bui, "Cities Start to Question an American Ideal: A House with a Yard on Every Lot." *New York Times*,

June 18, 2019. https://www.nytimes.com/interactive/2019/06/18/upshot /cities-across-america-question-single-family-zoning.html.

20. Joseph Gyourko and Raven Molloy, "Regulation and Housing Supply," in *Handbook of Regional and Urban Economics* (Amsterdam: Elsevier B.V., 2015), 5:1289–337.

21. Alexandra Killewald and Brielle Bryan, "Does Your Home Make You Wealthy?," *RSF: The Russell Sage Foundation Journal of the Social Sciences* 2, no. 6 (2016): 110–28.

22. William A. Fischel, "The Rise of the Homevoters: How the Growth Machine Was Subverted by OPEC and Earth Day," working paper, Dartmouth University, Hanover, NH, 2016, 2.

23. Katherine Levine Einstein, Maxwell Palmer, and David M. Glick, "Who Participates in Local Government? Evidence from Meeting Minutes," *Perspectives on Politics* 17, no. 1 (2018): 28–46; William Marble and Clayton Nall, "Where Interests Trump Ideology: The Persistent Influence of Homeownership in Local Development Politics," paper presented at 11th Annual Experimental Political Science Conference, New York, 2018.

24. Randy Shaw, *Generation Priced Out: Who Gets to Live in the New Urban America* (Oakland: University of California Press, 2018), 4.

25. Conor Dougherty, *Golden Gates: Fighting for Housing in America* (New York: Penguin Press, 2020), 134–35.

26. Early evidence suggests Austin is beginning to lose ground. Data from 2019 and 2020 show that vacancies are starting to fall and homelessness is rising in the Texas capital. The conditions in Austin offer a warning sign to other growing Sun Belt cities: If housing production fails to keep up with persistent population growth, homelessness may rise in kind.

27. Maritz and Wagle, "Why Does Prosperous King County Have a Homelessness Crisis?"

28. Glynn et al., "Inflection Points in Community-Level Homeless Rates."

29. Willaim Fulton, Shelly G. Hazle, Wendie Choudary, and Stephen Sherman, "The Urban Sun Belt: An Overview," working paper, Rice–Kinder Institute for Urban Research, 2020.

30. David Collier, Jody Laporte, and Jason Seawright, "Typologies: Forming Concepts and Creating Categorical Variables," in *Oxford Handbook of Political Methodology*, ed. Janet M. Box-Steffensmeir, Henry E. Brady, and David Collier (Oxford: Oxford University Press, 2008), 152–73.

CHAPTER 7. RESPONSE

1. Jessica Stillman, "Got a Hard Decision to Make? Borrow Obama's Simple 3-Part Strategy for the Toughest Calls," *Inc.*, March 8, 2019, https://www.inc.com/mbvans/contest.html.

2. See Shinn and Khadduri, The Center for Evidence-Based Solutions to Homelessness (https://endhomelessness.org/resource/center -evidence-based-solutions-homelessness/); The U.S. Interagency Council on Homelessness (www.usich.gov/solutions/).

3. Charles E. Lindblom, *Politics and Markets* (New York: Basic Books, 1977), 3.

4. Graham Kendall, "Apollo 11 Anniversary: Could an IPhone Fly Me to the Moon?" *The Independent*, July 9, 2019, https://www .independent.co.uk/news/science/apollo-11-moon-landing-mobile -phones-smartphone-iphone-a8988351.html.

5. *Times* Editorial Board, "Homelessness in New York," *New York Times*, December 27, 2001; *Times* Editorial Board, "Battling Homelessness in New York City," *New York Times*, December 14, 2013.

6. Lasana T. Harris and Susan T. Fiske, "Dehumanizing the Lowest of the Low: Neuroimaging Responses to Extreme Out-Groups," *Psychological Science* 17, no. 10 (2006): 847–53.

7. "Franklin Delano Roosevelt—State of the Union 1935." American History—From Revolution to Reconstruction and Beyond. 1994. http://www.let.rug.nl/usa/presidents/franklin-delano-roosevelt/state -of-the-union-1935.php.

8. Jack Tsai, Crystal Yun See Lee, Thomas Byrne, Robert H. Pietrzak, and Steven M. Southwick, "Changes in Public Attitudes and Perceptions about Homelessness between 1990 and 2016," *American Journal of Community Psychology* 60 (2017): 599–606.

9. Jack Tsai, Crystal Y.S. Lee, Jianxun Shen, Steven M. Southwick, and Robert H. Pietrzak, "Public Exposure and Attitudes about Homelessness," *Journal of Community Psychology* 47 (2019): 76–92.

10. Erick Trickey, "How Minneapolis Freed Itself from the Stranglehold of Single-Family Homes," *Politico*, July 11, 2019, https://www.politico.com/magazine/story/2019/07/11/housing-crisis-single-family-homes-policy-227265.

11. Ly and Latimer, "Housing First Impact on Costs and Associated Cost Offsets."

12. Katie Honan, "New York City Council Speaker Wants More from State on Homelessness: Spending by City's Homeless Department Is More Than $3 Billion per Fiscal Year," *Wall Street Journal*, January 30, 2020.

13. Parsell et al., "Cost Offsets of Supportive Housing."

14. Ly and Latimer, "Housing First Impact on Costs and Associated Cost Offsets."

15. Hannah Wiley and Sophia Bollag, "How Much Does California Really Spend on Homelessness? Democrat Wants a Final Answer," *Sacramento Bee*, February 18, 2020, https://www.sacbee.com/news/politics-government/capitol-alert/article240314016.html.

16. Zach Weissmueller. "Los Angeles Is Spending over $1 Billion to House the Homeless: It's Failing," *Reason*, December 5, 2019, https://reason.com/video/los-angeles-is-spending-over-1-billion-to-house-the-homeless-its-failing/.

17. Nouran Salahieh, "L.A.'s $1.2 Billion Bond Measure to Combat Homelessness Not Keeping Pace with Growing Need for Housing: Audit," *KTLA5*, October 8, 2019, https://ktla.com/news/l-a-s-1-2-billion-bond-measure-to-combat-homelessness-not-keeping-pace-with-growing-need-for-housing-audit/.

18. Maritz and Wagle, "Why Does Prosperous King County Have a Homelessness Crisis?"

19. Meg Wiehe, Aidan Davis, Carl Davis, Matt Gardner, Lisa Christensen Gee, and Dylan Grundman, *Who Pays? A Distributional Analysis of the Tax Systems in All 50 States* (Washington, DC: Institute on Taxation and Economic Policy, 2018).

20. Alana Semuels, "How Amazon Helped Kill a Seattle Tax on Business," *The Atlantic,* June 13, 2018, https://www.theatlantic.com /technology/archive/2018/06/how-amazon-helped-kill-a-seattle-tax -on-business/562736/.

21. Jared Bernstein. "Why the Seattle 'Head Tax' Is Relevant to the Nation," *Washington Post,* May 16, 2018, https://www.washingtonpost .com/news/posteverything/wp/2018/05/16/why-the-seattle-head-tax -is-relevant-to-the-nation/.

22. Roy Shapiro, "National Cranberry Cooperative, 1996," revised 2011, https://hbsp.harvard.edu/product/688122-PDF-ENG.

23. Shinn and Khadduri, *In the Midst of Plenty.*

24. Michelle Wood, Jennifer Turnham, and Gregory Mills, "Housing Affordability and Family Well-Being: Results from the Housing Voucher Evaluation," *Housing Policy Debate* 19, no. 2 (2011): 367–412.

25. Communication with Stephen Norman, executive director of the King County Housing Authority.

26. See Shinn and Khadduri, *In the Midst of Plenty,* for greater detail.

27. Ibid.

28. Note: Gregg served on the Evaluation Committee of this initiative.

29. "A Decade of Innovation: Lessons from the Puget Sound Family Homelessness Initiative," Bill & Melinda Gates Foundation, January 2021. https://local.gatesfoundation.org/wp-content/uploads/2021 /01/Gates-FHI-White-Paper-FINAL.pdf

30. Henry et al., *The 2019 Annual Homeless Assessment Report (AHAR) to Congress: Part I.*

31. Helen A. Ingram, Anne Schneider, and Peter DeLeon, "Social Construction and Policy Design," in *Theories of the Policy Process,* edited by P. A. Sabatier (Boulder, CO: Westview Press, 2007), 93–126.

32. Jack Tsai, Jianxun Shen, Steven M. Southwick, and Robert H. Pietrzak, "Is There More Public Support for US Veterans Who Experience Homelessness and Posttraumatic Stress Disorder Than Other US adults?" *Military Psychology* 33, no. 1 (2021): 15–22.

33. Thomas O'Toole and Vincent Kane, "Return on Investment Analysis and Modeling" (white paper, VA National Center on

Homelessness among Veterans, U.S. Department of Veterans Affairs, Washington, DC, 2014), https://www.va.gov/HOMELESS/nchav/docs/Return_on_Investment_Analysis_and_Modeling_White-Paper.pdf.

34. Henry et al., *The 2019 Annual Homeless Assessment Report (AHAR) to Congress: Part I.*

35. Kaitlyn Ranney, "Abilene, Texas: Functional Zero Case Study," Community Solutions, November 18, 2020, https://community.solutions/case-studies/abilene-texas-functional-zero-case-study/; Kaitlyn Ranney, "Rockford, Illinois: Functional Zero Case Study," Community Solutions, July 13, 2020, https://community.solutions/case-studies/case-study-rockford-illinois-reaches-and-sustains-functional-zero-for-veteran-and-chronic-homelessness/; Claudia D. Solari, Nicole DuBois, Jorge Morales-Burnett, *Community Strategies to Understand and Reduce Veteran Inflow into Homelessness* (Washington, DC: Urban Institute, November 2020), https://www.urban.org/research/publication/community-strategies-understand-and-reduce-veteran-inflow-homelessness.

BIBLIOGRAPHY

Adams, J., R. Rosenheck, L. Gee, C. L. Seibyl, and M. Kushel. (2007). "Hospitalized Younger: A Comparison of a National Sample of Homeless and Housed Inpatient Veterans." *Journal of Health Care for the Poor and Underserved, 18*, 173–84.

Allgood, S., and R. S. Warren. (2003). "The Duration of Homelessness: Evidence from a National Survey." *Journal of Housing Economics, 12*(4), 273–90.

Appelbaum, B. (2020, May 15). "America's Cities Could House Everyone If They Chose To." *New York Times.* https://www.nytimes.com/2020/05/15/opinion/sunday/homeless-crisis-affordable-housing-cities.html.

Applied Survey Research. (2019). *Count Us In: Seattle/King County Point-In-Time Count of Persons Experiencing Homelessness 2019.* Seattle, WA: Applied Survey Research.

Aubry, T., S. Tsemberis, C. E. Adair, S. Veldhuizen, D. Streiner, E. Latimer, J. Sareen, M. Patterson, K. McGarvey, B. Kopp, C. Hume, and P. Goering. (2015). "One-Year Outcomes of a Randomized Controlled Trial of Housing First with Act in Five Canadian Cities." *Psychiatric Services, 66*(5), 463–69.

Aurand, A., D. Emmanuel, E. Errico, D. Pinsky, and D. Yentel. (2020). *The GAP: A Shortage of Affordable Homes.* Washington, DC: National Low Income Housing Coalition.

Austin, B., E. Glaeser, and L. Summers. (2018, Spring). "Jobs for the Heartland: Place-Based Policies in 21st-Century America. *Brookings: Papers on Economic Activity,* 151–255.

Badger, E., and Q. Bui. (2019, June 18). "Cities Start to Question an American Ideal: A House with a Yard on Every Lot." *New York Times.* https://www.nytimes.com/interactive/2019/06/18/upshot /cities-across-america-question-single-family-zoning.html.

Bassuk, E. L., and L. Rosenberg. (1990). "Psychosocial Characteristics of Homeless Children and Children with Homes." *Pediatrics, 85*(3), 257–61.

Bates, D. S., and P. A. Toro. (1999). "Developing Measures to Assess Social Support among Homeless and Poor People." *Journal of Community Psychology, 27*(2), 137–56.

Beckett, K., and S. Herbert. (2009). *Banished.* Oxford: Oxford University Press.

Benfer, E., D. B. Robinson, S. Butler, L. Edmonds, S. Gilman, K. L McKay, L. Owens, N. Steinkamp, and D. Yentel. (2020). *The COVID-19 Eviction Crisis: An Estimated 30–40 Million People Are at Risk.* Washington, DC: National Low Income Housing Coalition. https:// nlihc.org/sites/default/files/The_Eviction_Crisis_080720.pdf.

Bernstein, J. (2018, May 16). Why the Seattle "Head Tax" Is Relevant to the Nation. *Washington Post.* https://www.washingtonpost.com /news/posteverything/wp/2018/05/16/why-the-seattle-head-tax -is-relevant-to-the-nation/.

Blank, D. M., and L. Winnick. (1953). "The Structure of the Housing Market." *Quarterly Journal of Economics, 67*(2), 181–208. https:// academic.oup.com/qje/article/67/2/181/1826509.

Bowen, M., T. Marshall, A. Yahyouche, V. Paudyal, S. Marwick, K. Saunders, S. Burwood, and D. Stewart. (2019). "Multimorbidity and Emergency Department Visits by a Homeless Population: A Database Study in Specialist General Practice." *British Journal of General Practice, 69*(685), E515–25.

Brewer, P., and S. Venaik. (2014). "The Ecological Fallacy in National Culture Research." *Organization Studies, 35*(7), 1063–86.

Brinklow, A. (2019). "Oracle Convention Pulls Out of SF over 'Street Conditions.'" *Curbed: San Francisco.* https://sf.curbed.com/2019/12 /11/21011250/oracle-open-world-sf-travel-association-moscone-las -vegas.

———. (2019). "San Francisco Has Nearly Five Empty Homes per Homeless Resident." *Curbed: San Francisco.* https://sf.curbed.com /2019/12/3/20993251/san-francisco-bay-area-vacant-homes-per -homeless-count.

Burt, M. R. (2001). "Homeless Families, Singles, and Others: Findings from the 1996 National Survey of Homeless Assistance Providers and Clients." *Housing Policy Debate, 12*(4), 737–80.

Byrne, T., J. D. Fargo, A. E. Montgomery, E. Munley, and D. P. Culhane. (2014). "The Relationship between Community Investment in Permanent Supportive Housing and Chronic Homelessness." *Social Service Review, 88*(2), 234–63.

Byrne, T., B. F. Harwood, and A. W. Orlando. (2021, April). "A Rising Tide Drowns Unstable Boats: How Inequality Creates Homelessness." *Annals of the American Academy of Political and Social Science.* https://doi.org/10.1177/0002716220981864

Byrne, T., E. A. Munley, J. D. Fargo, A. E. Montgomery, and D. P. Culhane. (2013). "New Perspectives on Community-Level Determinants of Homelessness." *Journal of Urban Affairs, 35*(5), 607–25.

Byrne, T., D. Treglia, D. P. Culhane, J. Kuhn, and V. Kane. (2015). "Predictors of Homelessness among Families and Single Adults after Exit from Homelessness Prevention and Rapid Re-housing Programs: Evidence from the Department of Veterans Affairs Supportive Services for Veteran Families Program." *Housing Policy Debate, 26*(1), 252–75.

Carter, G. R. III. (2011). "From Exclusion to Destitution: Race, Affordable Housing, and Homelessness." *Cityscape: A Journal of Policy Development and Research, 13*(1), 33–70.

Castellanos, H. D. (2016). "The Role of Institutional Placement, Family Conflict, and Homosexuality in Homelessness Pathways among

Latino LGBT Youth in New York City." *Journal of Homosexuality*, *63*(5), 601–632.

Cobb-Clark, D., N. Herault, R. Scutella, and Y. Tseng (2016). "A Journey Home: What Drives How Long People are Homeless?" *Journal of Urban Economics 91*, 57–72.

Cole, W. (2001, May–June). "Against the Giuliani Legacy." *The Brooklyn Rail.* https://brooklynrail.org/2001/05/local/against-the-giuliani -legacy-part-one.

Collier, D., J. Laporte, and J. Seawright. (2008). "Typologies: Forming Concepts and Creating Categorical Variables." In *Oxford Handbook of Political Methodology*, edited by Janet M. Box-Steffensmeir, Henry E. Brady, and David Collier, 152–73. Oxford: Oxford University Press.

Community Solutions. "Analysis on Unemployment Projects 40–45% Increase in Homelessness This Year." *Homelessness Report* (blog), May 11, 2020. https://community.solutions/analysis-on-unemployment- projects-40-45-increase-in-homelessness-this-year/.

Connolly, P. (2006). "Summary Statistics, Educational Achievement Gaps and the Ecological Fallacy." *Oxford Review of Education*, *32*(2), 235–52.

Corinth, K. (2017). "The Impact of Permanent Supportive Housing on Homeless Populations." *Journal of Housing Economics*, *35*, 69–84.

Corinth, K., and D. S. Lucas. (2018). "When Warm and Cold Don't Mix: The Implications of Climate for the Determinants of Homelessness." *Journal of Housing Economics*, *41*(August 2017), 45–56.

Corinth, K., and C. Rossi-de Vries. (2018). "Social Ties and the Incidence of Homelessness." *Housing Policy Debate*, *28*(4), 592–608.

Council of Economic Advisers. (2019). *The State of Homelessness in America.* Washington, DC: U.S. Government Printing Office.

Cragg, M., and B. O'Flaherty. (1999). "Do Homeless Shelter Conditions Determine Shelter Population? The Case of the Dinkins Deluge." *Journal of Urban Economics*, *46*, 377–415.

Culhane, D. P. (2008). "The Costs of Homelessness: A Perspective from the United States." *European Journal of Homelessness*, *2* (January), 97–114.

Curtis, M. A., H. Corman, K. Noonan, and N. E. Reichman. (2013). "Life Shocks and Homelessness." *Demography*, *50*(6), 2227–53.

Cutuli, J. J., C. D. Desjardins, J. E. Herbers, J. D. Long, D. Heistad, C.-K. Chan, E. Hinz, and A. Masten. (2013). "Academic Achievement Trajectories of Homeless and Highly Mobile Students: Resilience in the Context of Chronic and Acute Risk." *Child Development, 84*(3), 841–57.

Daily Editorial Board. (2018, January 22). "Editorial: Minneapolis Not Being an Amazon HQ2 Finalist Is Good News." *Minnesota Daily.* https://mndaily.com/195899/opinion/opeditorial-5a64f9b6ee551/.

Dear, M. J., and J. R. Wolch. (1987). *Landscapes of Despair: From Deinstitutionalization to Homelessness.* Princeton, NJ: Princeton University Press.

DeVerteuil, G. (2006). "The Local State and Homeless Shelters: Beyond Revanchism?" *Cities, 23*(2), 109–20.

Dougherty, C. (2020). *Golden Gates: Fighting for Housing in America.* New York: Penguin Press.

Draine, J., M. S. Salzer, D. P. Culhane, and T. R. Hadley. (2002). "Role of Social Disadvantage in Crime, Joblessness, and Homelessness among Persons with Serious Mental Illness." *Psychiatric Services, 53*(5), 565–73.

Early, D. W. (1999). "A Microeconomic Analysis of Homelessness: An Empirical Investigation Using Choice-Based Sampling." *Journal of Housing Economics, 8*(4), 312–27.

———. (2004). "The Determinants for Homelessness and the Targeting of Housing Assistance." *Journal of Urban Economics, 55*(1), 195–214.

———. (2005). "An Empirical Investigation of the Determinants of Street Homelessness." *Journal of Housing Economics, 14*(1), 27–47.

Early, D. W., and E. O. Olsen. (2002). "Subsidized Housing, Emergency Shelters, and Homelessness: An Empirical Investigation Using Data from the 1990 Census." *The B.E. Journal of Economic Analysis & Policy, 2*(1), 1–36.

Einstein, K. L., M. Palmer, and D. M. Glick. (2018). "Who Participates in Local Government? Evidence from Meeting Minutes." *Perspectives on Politics, 17*(1), 28–46.

Erb-Downward, J., and S. Merchant. (2020). "Losing Home: Housing Instability and Availability in Detroit." Working paper. Poverty Solutions, University of Michigan.

Evans, W. N., J. X. Sullivan, and M. Wallskog. (2016). "The Impact of Homeless Prevention Programs on Homelessness. *Science, 353*(6300), 694–99.

Faber, J. W. (2019). "On the Street during the Great Recession: Exploring the Relationship between Foreclosures and Homelessness." *Housing Policy Debate, 29*(4), 588–606.

Fagen, K. (2019, July 28). "Bay Area Homelessness: 97 Answers to Your Questions." *San Francisco Chronicle.* https://projects.sfchronicle.com /sf-homeless/homeless-questions/.

Fan, Q., K. Fisher-Vanden, and H. A. Klaiber. (2018). "Climate Change, Migration, and Regional Economic Impacts in the United States." *Journal of the Association of Environmental and Resource Economists, 5*(3), 643–71.

Fantuzzo, J., and S. Perlman. (2007). "The Unique Impact of Out-of-Home Placement and the Mediating Effects of Child Maltreatment and Homelessness on Early School Success." *Children and Youth Services Review, 29*(7), 941–60.

Fargo, J. D., E. A. Munley, T. H. Byrne, A. E. Montgomery, and D. P. Culhane. (2013). "Community-Level Characteristics Associated with Variation in Rates of Homelessness among Families and Single Adults." *American Journal of Public Health, 103*(SUPPL. 2).

Fazel, S., J. R. Geddes, and M. Kushel. (2014). "The Health of Homeless People in High-Income Countries: Descriptive Epidemiology, Health Consequences, and Clinical and Policy Recommendations. *The Lancet, 384*(9953), 1529–40.

Fazel, S., V. Khosla, H. Doll, and J. Geddes. (2008). "The Prevalence of Mental Disorders among the Homeless in Western Countries: Systematic Review and Meta-Regression Analysis." *PLoS Med, 5*(12), 1670–81.

Fernald, M., ed. (2016). *The State of the Nation's Housing 2016.* Cambridge, MA: Joint Center for Housing Policy of Harvard University. https://www.jchs.harvard.edu/sites/default/files/media/imp/jchs _2016_state_of_the_nations_housing_lowres_0.pdf.

Fertig, A. R., and D. A. Reingold. (2008). "Homelessness among At-Risk Families with Children in Twenty American Cities." *Social Service Review, 82*(3), 485–510.

Fessler, P. (2020, January 2). "Trump Continues Criticism of Democrats on Homelessness, but Hasn't Intervened." National Public Radio. https://www.npr.org/2020/01/02/793134351/trump-continues-criticism-of-democrats-on-homelessness-but-hasnt-intervened.

Finkel, M., and L. Buron. (2001). *Study on Section 8 Voucher Success Rates: Volume I, Quantitative Study of Success Rates in Metropolitan Areas.* Washington, DC: U.S. Department of Housing and Urban Development, Office of Policy Development and Research. https://www.huduser.gov/portal/publications/pdf/sec8success_1.pdf.

Fischel, W. A. (2001). *The Homevoter Hypothesis: How Home Values Influence Local Government Taxation, School Finance, and Land-Use Policies.* Cambridge, MA: Harvard University Press.

———. (2016). "The Rise of the Homevoters: How the Growth Machine Was Subverted by OPEC and Earth Day." Working paper. Dartmouth University.

Fitzpatrick, K. M., M. E. LaGory, and F. J. Ritchey. (1999). "Dangerous Places: Exposure to Violence and Its Mental Health Consequences for the Homeless." *American Journal of Orthopsychiatry, 69*(4), 438–47.

Fleishman, G. (2017, August 24). How Amazon's Nonstop Growth Is Creating a Brand-New Seattle. *Fast Company.* https://www.fastcompany.com/40451502/how-amazons-nonstop-growth-is-creating-a-brand-new-seattle.

Fowler, J. (2019, August). "What If Seattle Is Dying, and We Don't Even Know It?" *National Review.* https://www.nationalreview.com/corner/what-if-seattle-is-dying-and-we-dont-even-know-it/.

Freeman, R. B., and B. Hall. (1987). "Permanent Homelessness in America?" *Population Research and Policy Review, 6*(1), 3–27.

Fulton, W., S. G. Hazle, W. Choudary, and S. Sherman. (2020). "The Urban Sun Belt: An Overview." Working paper. Rice–Kinder Institute for Urban Research.

Fusaro, V. A., H. G. Levy, and H. L. Shaefer. (2018). "Racial and Ethnic Disparities in the Lifetime Prevalence of Homelessness in the United States." *Demography, 55*(6), 2119–28.

Gabriel, S. A., and F. E. Nothaft. (2001). "Rental Housing Markets, the Incidence and Duration of Vacancy, and the Natural Vacancy Rate." *Journal of Urban Economics, 49,* 121–49.

Glomm, G., and A. John. (2002). "Homelessness and Labor Markets." *Regional Science and Urban Economics*, *32*(5), 591–606.

Glynn, C., T. H. Byrne, and D. P. Culhane. (2020). "Inflection Points in Community-Level Homeless Rates." Unpublished paper. Available at http://works.bepress.com/dennis_culhane/228/.

Glynn, C., and E. B. Fox. (2019). "Dynamics of Homelessness in Urban America." *Annals of Applied Statistics*, *13*(1), 573–605.

Goodman, J. (2007). "'If Only We Could Be Like Mississippi.' Governing: The Future of States and Localities." https://www.governing.com/blogs/view/If-Only-We-Could.html.

Goodman, S., P. Messeri, and B. O'Flaherty. (2016). "Homelessness Prevention in New York City: On Average, It Works." *Journal of Housing Economics*, *31*, 14–34.

Greenberg, G. A., and R. A. Rosenheck. (2010). Mental Health Correlates of Past Homelessness in the National Comorbidity Study Replication. *Journal of Health Care for the Poor and Underserved*, *21*(4), 1234–49.

Griffin, A. (2015, February 14). "The 'Magnet Myth.'" *The Oregonian*. https://www.oregonlive.com/projects/portland-homeless/magnet.html.

Grimes, P. W., and G. A. Chressanthis. (1997). "Assessing the Effect of Rent Control on Homelessness." *Journal of Urban Economics*, *41*, 23–37.

Gubits, D., M. Shinn, M. Wood, S. R. Brown, S. R. Dastrup, and S. H. Bell. (2018). "What Interventions Work Best for Families Who Experience Homelessness? Impact Estimates from the Family Options Study." *Journal of Policy Analysis and Management*, *37*(4), 835–66.

Gutman, D., and S. Brownstone. (2020, September 22). "Proposed King County Budget Includes New Sales Tax for Housing, 450 Job Losses," *Seattle Times*. https://www.seattletimes.com/seattle-news/politics/proposed-king-county-budget-includes-new-sales-tax-for-housing-450-job-losses/.

Gyourko, J., R. Molloy. (2015). "Regulation and Housing Supply." In *Handbook of Regional and Urban Economics*, *5*:1289–337. Amsterdam: Elsevier B.V.

Hahn, H., L. Aron, C. Lou, E. Pratt, and A. Okoli. (2017). *Why Does Cash Welfare Depend on Where You Live? How and Why State TANF Programs Vary.* Washington, DC: Urban Institute.

Hanratty, M. (2017). "Do Local Economic Conditions Affect Homelessness? Impact of Area Housing Market Factors, Unemployment, and Poverty on Community Homeless Rates." *Housing Policy Debate*, *27*(4), 640–55.

Harris, L. T., and S. T. Fiske. (2006). "Dehumanizing the Lowest of the Low: Neuroimaging Responses to Extreme Out-Groups." *Psychological Science*, *17*(10), 847–53.

Hartwell, S. (2003). "Deviance over the Life Course: The Case of Homeless Substance Abusers." *Substance Use and Misuse*, *38*(3–6), 475–502.

Henry, M., R. Watt, A. Mahathey, J. Ouellette, and A. Sitler. (2020). *The 2019 Annual Homeless Assessment Report (AHAR) to Congress: Part I.* Washington, DC: The U.S. Department of Housing and Urban Development: Office of Community Planning and Development.

Herbers, J. E., J. J. Cutuli, L. M. Supkoff, D. Heistad, C.-K. Chan, E. Hinz, and A. S. Masten. (2012). Early Reading Skills and Academic Achievement of Students Facing Poverty, Homelessness, and High Residential Mobility. *Educational Researcher*, *41*(9), 366–74.

Honan, K. (2020, January 30). "New York City Council Speaker Wants More from State on Homelessness; Spending by City's Homeless Department Is More Than $3 Billion per Fiscal Year." *Wall Street Journal*.

Hopper, K., M. Shinn, E. Laska, M. Meisner, and J. Wanderling. (2008). "Estimating Numbers of Unsheltered Homeless People through Plant-Capture and Postcount Survey Methods." *Innovations in Design and Analysis, 98*(8), 1438–42.

Horowitz, E. (2016, August 24). "Poverty Drives Homeless Rates? No So Fast." *Boston Globe*. https://www.bostonglobe.com/2016/08/24/poverty-drives-homeless-rates-fast/1fvvSKgNUg4l5TfqbdEGrM/story.html.

Hudson, A. L., K. Wright, D. Bhattacharya, K. Sinha, A. Nyamathi, and M. Marfisee. (2010). "Correlates of Adult Assault among Homeless Women." *Journal of Health Care for the Poor and Underserved, 21*(4), 1250–62.

Igarashi, M. (1991). "The Rent-Vacancy Relationship in the Rental Housing Market." *Journal of Housing Economics, 1*, 251–70.

Ingram, H., A. L. Schneider, and P. DeLeon. (2007). "Social Construction and Policy Design." In *Theories of the Policy Process*, edited by P. A. Sabatier, 93–126. Boulder, CO: Westview Press.

Jackson, O., and L. Kawano. (2013). "Do Increases in Subsidized Housing Reduce the Incidence of Homelessness? Evidence from the Low-Income Housing Tax Credit." Working Papers, nos. 15–11. Federal Reserve Bank of Boston.

Jeantet, D. (2013, March 11). "A Brief History of Homelessness in New York." City Limits. https://citylimits.org/2013/03/11/a-brief-history-of-homelessness-in-new-york/.

Johnson, G., and C. Chamberlain. (2008). Homelessness and Substance Abuse: Which Comes First? *Australian Social Work*, *61*(4), 342–56.

Kang, S. (2019). "Beyond Households: Regional Determinants of Housing Instability among Low-Income Renters in the United States." *Housing Studies*, *36*(1), 80–109.

Kendall, G. (2019, July 9). "Apollo 11 Anniversary: Could an iPhone Fly Me to the Moon?" *The Independent*. https://www.independent.co.uk/news/science/apollo-11-moon-landing-mobile-phones-smartphone-iphone-a8988351.html.

Killewald, A., and B. Bryan. (2016). Does Your Home Make You Wealthy? *RSF: The Russell Sage Foundation Journal of the Social Sciences*, *2*(6), 110–28.

Kim, M. M., J. D. Ford, D. L. Howard, and D. W. Bradford. (2010). "Assessing Trauma, Substance Abuse, and Mental Health in a Sample of Homeless Men." *Health And Social Work*, *35*(1), 39–48.

Kizer, K. W., B. Brush, S. Hayashi, S. Hwang, M. Katz, M. Mujahid, J. O'Connell, B. Samuels, M. Shinn, P. Wang, and S. Wenzel. (2018). *Permanent Supportive Housing: Evaluating the Evidence for Improving Health Outcomes among People Experiencing Chronic Homelessness*. Washington, DC: The National Academies Press.

Klein, E. (2020). *Why We're Polarized*. New York: Avid Reader Books.

Kondratas, A. (1991). "Estimates and Public Policy: The Politics of Numbers." *Housing Policy Debate*, *2*(3), 629–47.

Kuhn, R., and D. P. Culhane. (1998). "Applying Cluster Analysis to Test a Typology of Homelessness by Pattern of Shelter Utilization: Results from the Analysis of Administrative Data." *American Journal of Community Psychology*, *26*(2), 207–32.

Kushel, M. B., J. L. Evans, S. Perry, M. J. Robertson, and A. R. Moss. (2003). "No Door to Lock: Victimization among Homeless and

Marginally Housed Persons." *Archives of Internal Medicine, 163*, 2492–99.

Kushel, M. B., S. Perry, D. Bangsberg, R. Clark, and A. R. Moss. (2002). "Emergency Department Use among the Homeless and Marginally Housed: Results from a Community-Based Study." *American Journal of Public Health, 92*(5), 778–84.

LaGory, M., F. Ritchey, and K. Fitzpatrick. (1991). Homelessness and Affiliation." *The Sociological Quarterly, 32*(2), 201–18.

Lee, B. A., T. Price-Spratlen, and J. W. Kanan. (2003). "Determinants of Homelessness in Metropolitan Areas." *Journal of Urban Affairs, 25*(3), 335–56.

Lee, B. A., K. A. Tyler, and J. D. Right. (2010). "The New Homelessness Revisited. *Annual Review of Sociology, 36*, 501–21.

Lehmann, E. R., P. H. Kass, C. M. Drake, and S. B. Nichols. (2007). "Risk Factors for First-Time Homelessness in Low-Income Women." *American Journal of Orthopsychiatry, 77*(1), 20–28.

Leopold, J., D. Culhane, and J. Khadduri. (2017). *Where Do Homeless People Come From? Movement of Households from Their Prior Residences into Homeless Residential Facilities in Michigan in Iowa.* Rockville, MD: Abt Associates.

Lewis, G., J. Avault, and J. Vrabel. (1999). *History of Boston's Economy: Growth and Transition 1970–1998.* Boston: Boston Redevelopment Authority. http://www.bostonplans.org/getattachment/15ca7a2f-56d1-4770-ba7f-8c1ce73d25b8.

Lindblom, C. E. (1977). *Politics and Markets.* New York: Basic Books.

Link, B. G., E. Susser, A. Stueve, J. Phelan, R. E. Moore, and E. Struening. (1994). "Lifetime and Five-Year Prevalence of Homelessness in the United States." *American Journal of Public Health, 84*(12), 1907–12.

Lippert, A. M., and B. A. Lee. (2015). "Stress, Coping, and Mental Health Differences among Homeless People." *Sociological Inquiry, 85*(3), 343–74.

Long, D., J. Rio, and J. Rosen. (2007). "Employment and Income Supports for Homeless People." In *Toward Understanding Homelessness: The 2007 National Symposium on Homelessness Research*, 1–34. Washington, DC: Assistant Secretary for Planning and Evaluation. https://aspe.hhs.gov/report/toward-understanding-homelessness-2007

-national-symposium-homelessness-research-employment-and
-income-supports-homeless-people.

Lucas, D. S. (2017). "The Impact of Federal Homelessness Funding on Homelessness." *Southern Economic Journal*, *84*(2), 548–76.

Ly, A., and E. Latimer. (2015). Housing First Impact on Costs and Associated Cost Offsets: A Review of the Literature. *Canadian Journal of Psychiatry*, *60*(11), 475–87.

Mac Donald, H. (2019, Autumn). "San Francisco, Hostage to the Homeless." *City Journal*. https://www.city-journal.org/san-francisco -homelessness.

MacLeod, G. (2002). "From Urban Entrepreneurialism to a Revanchist City? On the Spatial Injustices of Glasgow's Renaissance." *Antipode*, *34*, 602–24.

Marble, W., and C. Nall. (2018). "Where Interests Trump Ideology: The Persistent Influence of Homeownership in Local Development Politics." Paper presented at 11th Annual Experimental Political Science Conference, New York.

Maritz, B., D. Wagle. (2020). "Why Does Prosperous King County Have a Homelessness Crisis?" McKinsey & Company, January 22, https://www.mckinsey.com/industries/public-and-social -sector/our-insights/why-does-prosperous-king-county-have-a -homelessness-crisis.

Matsakis, L. (2018, November 14). "Why Amazon's Search for a Second Headquarters Backfired." *Wired*. https://www.wired.com/story /amazon-hq2-search-backfired/.

May, J. (2000). "Housing Histories and Homeless Careers: A Biographical Approach." *Housing Studies*, *15*(4), 613–38.

McClure, K. (2019). "What Should Be the Future of the Low-Income Housing Tax Credit Program?" *Housing Policy Debate*, *29*(1), 65–81.

Merrill, R. M., R. Richards, and A. Sloan. (2011). "Prenatal Maternal Stress and Physical Abuse among Homeless Women and Infant Health Outcomes in the United States." *Epidemiology Research International*, *2011*, 1–10.

Metraux, S., D. Treglia, and T. P. O'Toole. (2016). "Migration by Veterans Who Received Homeless Services from the Department of Veterans Affairs." *Military Medicine*, *181*(10), 1212–17.

Miller, D. S., and E. H. B. Lin. (1988). "Children in Sheltered Homeless Families: Reported Health Status and Use of Health Services." *Pediatrics, 81*(5), 668–73.

Moulton, S. (2013). "Does Increased Funding for Homeless Programs Reduce Chronic Homelessness?" *Southern Economic Journal, 79*(3), 600–620.

National Coalition for the Homeless. (2009). "Employment and Homelessness." https://www.nationalhomeless.org/factsheets /employment.html.

National Homelessness Law Center. (2019). "Supreme Court Lets *Martin v. Boise* Stand: Homeless Persons Cannot Be Punished for Sleeping in Absence of Alternatives." https://nlchp.org/supreme -court-martin-v-boise/.

National Law Center on Homelessness and Poverty. (2017). *Don't Count on It: How the HUD Point-in-Time Count Underestimates the Homelessness Crisis in America.* Washington, DC: National Law Center on Homelessness & Poverty.

Neale, J. (1997). Housing and Illicit Drug Use. *Housing Review, 46*(5), 104–6.

———. (2001). "Homelessness amongst Drug Users: A Double Jeopardy Explored." *International Journal of Drug Policy, 12*(4), 353–69.

Newman, S., and C. S. Holupka. (2017). *The Quality of America's Assisted Housing Stock: Analysis of the 2011 and 2013 American Housing Surveys.* Washington, DC: U.S. Department of Housing and Urban Development, Office of Policy Development and Research.

Nooe, R. M., and D. Patterson. (2010). "The Ecology of Homelessness." *Journal of Human Behavior in the Social Environment, 20*(2), 105–52.

O'Flaherty, B. (1996). *Making Room: The Economics of Homelessness.* Cambridge, MA: Harvard University Press.

———. (2004). "Wrong Person and Wrong Place: For Homelessness, the Conjunction Is What Matters." *Journal of Housing Economics, 13*, 1–15.

———. (2010). "Homelessness as Bad Luck: Implications for Research and Policy." In *How to House the Homeless*, edited by I. G. Ellen and B. O'Flaherty, 143–82. New York: Russell Sage Foundation.

———. (2019). "Homelessness Research: A Guide for Economists (and Friends)." *Journal of Housing Economics, 44*, 1–25.

O'Flaherty, B., and T. Wu. (2006). "Fewer Subsidized Exits and a Recession: How New York City's Family Homeless Shelter Population Became Immense." *Journal of Housing Economics* 15, 99–125.

———. (2008). "Homeless Shelters for Single Adults: Why Does Their Population Change?" *Social Service Review*, 82(3), 511–50.

Olivet, J., M. Dones, M. Richard, C. Wilkey, S. Yampolskaya, M. Beit-Arie, and L. Joseph. (2018). "SPARC Phase One Study Findings." Needham, MA: Center for Social Innovation. Retrieved from https://center4si.com/wp-content/uploads/2018/03/SPARC-Phase-1-Findings-March-2018i.pdf.

O'Mara, M. (2019). *The Code.* New York: Penguin.

O'Toole, T., and V. Kane, V. (2014). "Return on Investment Analysis and Modeling." White paper, VA National Center on Homelessness among Veterans, U.S. Department of Veterans Affairs. https://www.va.gov/HOMELESS/nchav/docs/Return_on_Investment_Analysis_and_Modeling_White-Paper.pdf.

Pak-Harvey, A. (2020, February 18). "What Did City, State Offer for Amazon HQ2? A Judge Is Deciding Whether the Public Should Know." *IndyStar*. https://www.indystar.com/story/news/local/marion-county/2020/02/18/amazon-hq-2-proposal-indianapolis-should-public-lawsuit-says/4742217002/.

Parker, R. D., and S. Dykema. (2013). "The Reality of Homeless Mobility and Implications for Improving Care." *Journal of Community Health*, 38(4), 685–89.

Parsell, C., M. Petersen, and D. Culhane. (2017). Cost Offsets of Supportive Housing: Evidence for Social Work. *British Journal of Social Work*, 47(5), 1534–53.

Piantadosi, S., D. P. Byar, and S. B. Green. (1988). "The Ecological Fallacy." *American Journal of Epidemiology*, 127(5), 893–904.

Pollio, D. E. (1997). "The Relationship between Transience and Current Life Situation in the Homeless Services-Using Population." *Social Work*, 42(6), 541–51.

Popov, I. (2016). "Homeless Programs and Social Insurance." Working paper. Stanford Institute for Economic Policy Research.

Pozdena, R. J. (1998). *The Modern Economics of Housing.* New York: Quorum Books.

Quigley, J. M., and S. Raphael. (2001). "The Economics of Homelessness: The Evidence from North America." *International Journal of
Housing Policy*, *1*(3), 323–36.

———. (2004). "Is Housing Unaffordable? Why Isn't It More Affordable?" *Journal of Economic Perspectives*, *18*(1), 191–214.

Rafferty, Y., and M. Shinn. (1991). "The Impact of Homelessness on
Children." *American Psychologist*, *46*(11), 1170–79.

Ranney, Kaitlyn. (2020, July 13). "Rockford, Illinois: Functional Zero
Case Study." Community Solutions. https://community.solutions
/case-studies/case-study-rockford-illinois-reaches-and-sustains
-functional-zero-for-veteran-and-chronic-homelessness/.

———. (2020, November 18). "Abilene, Texas: Functional Zero Case
Study." Community Solutions. https://community.solutions/case
-studies/abilene-texas-functional-zero-case-study/.

Raphael, S. (2010). Housing Market Regulation and Homelessness." In
How to House the Homeless, edited by I. G. Ellen and B. O'Flaherty,
110–140. New York: Russell Sage Foundation.

Reitzel, L. R., N. A. Short, N. B. Schmidt, L. Garey, M. J. Zvolensky,
A. Moisiuc, C. Reddick, D. E. Kendzor, and M. S. Businelle. (2017).
"Distress Tolerance Links Sleep Problems with Stress and Health
in Homeless." *American Journal of Health Behavior*, *41*(6), 760–75.

Rescoria, L., R. Parker, and P. Stolley. (1991). "Ability, Achievement, and
Adjustment in Homeless Children." *American Journal of Orthopsychiatry*, *61*(April), 210–20.

Robinson, W. S. (1950). "Ecological Correlations and the Behavior of
Individuals." *American Sociological Review*, *15*(3), 351–57.

Rog, D. J., T. Marshall, R. H. Dougherty, P. George, A. S. Daniels,
S. S. Ghose, and M. E. Delphin-Rittmon. (2014). "Permanent Supportive Housing: Assessing the Evidence." *Psychiatric Services*, *65*(3),
287–294.

Rokach, A. (2004). "The Lonely and Homeless: Causes and Consequences." *Social Indicators Research*, *69*, 37–50.

Roncarati, J. S., T. P. Baggett, J. J. O'Connell, S. W. Hwang, E. Francis Cook, N. Krieger, and G. Sorensen. (2018). "Mortality among
Unsheltered Homeless Adults in Boston, Massachusetts, 2000–
2009." *JAMA Internal Medicine*, *178*(9), 1242–48.

Rosen, B. K. T., and L. B. Smith. (1983). "The Price-Adjustment Process for Rental Housing and the Natural Vacancy Rate." *The American Economic Review*, 73(4), 779–86.

Rufo, C. (2018). "The Politics of Ruinous Compassion: How Seattle's Homelessness Policy Perpetuates the Crisis—and How We Can Fix It." Discovery Institute. https://www.discovery.org/m/2018/10/The-Politics-of-Ruinous-Compassion.pdf.

Rukmana, D. (2020). "The Causes of Homelessness and the Characteristics Associated with High Risk of Homelessness: A Review of Intercity and Intracity Homelessness Data." *Housing Policy Debate*, 30(2), 291–308.

Runyan, R. (2019, August 20). "Real Estate Report: A Surplus of Buyers Calls for a Solution." *Hour Detroit*. https://www.hourdetroit.com/community/real-estate-detroit-housing/.

Saiz, A. (2010). "The Geographic Determinants of Housing Supply." *Quarterly Journal of Economics*, 125(3), 1253–96.

Salahieh, N. (2019, October 8). "L.A.'s $1.2 Billion Bond Measure to Combat Homelessness Not Keeping Pace with Growing Need for Housing: Audit." KTLA5. https://ktla.com/news/l-a-s-1-2-billion-bond-measure-to-combat-homelessness-not-keeping-pace-with-growing-need-for-housing-audit/.

Santos, M. (2020, January 9). "Across the Entire State, WA Voters Rank Homelessness as the No. 1 Issue Lawmakers Must Address." *Crosscut*. https://crosscut.com/2020/01/across-entire-state-wa-voters-rank-homelessness-no-1-issue-lawmakers-must-address.

Schneider, B. (2020, July 6). "CityLab University: Understanding Homelessness in America. *Bloomberg CityLab*." https://www.bloomberg.com/news/features/2020-07-06/why-is-homelessness-such-a-problem-in-u-s-cities.

Seattle Planning Commission. (2018). *Neighborhoods for All: Expanding Housing Opportunities in Seattle's Single-Family Zone*. Seattle, WA: Seattle Planning Commission. https://www.seattle.gov/Documents/Departments/SeattlePlanningCommission/SPCNeighborhoodsForAllFINALdigital2.pdf.

Semuels, A. (2018, June 13). "How Amazon Helped Kill a Seattle Tax on Business" *The Atlantic*. https://www.theatlantic.com/technology

/archive/2018/06/how-amazon-helped-kill-a-seattle-tax-on-business/562736/.

Shaw, R. (2018). *Generation Priced Out: Who Gets to Live in the New Urban America*. Oakland: University of California Press.

Shelton, K. H., P. J. Taylor, A. Bonner, and M. van den Bree. (2009). "Risk Factors for Homelessness: Evidence from a Population-Based Study." *Psychiatric Services*, *60*(4), 465–72.

Shinn, M., D. Gubits, and L. Dunton. (2018). *Behavioral Health Improvements over Time among Adults in Families Experiencing Homelessness*. Washington, DC: U.S. Department of Health and Human Services, Office of Planning, Research, and Evaluation.

Shinn, M., and J. Khadduri. (2020). *In the Midst of Plenty: How to Prevent and End Homelessness*. Hoboken, NJ: Wiley.

Slattery, C., and O. Zidar. (2020). Evaluating state and local business incentives. *Journal of Economic Perspectives*, *34*(2), 90–118.

Smith, L. B. (1974). A Note on the Price Adjustment Mechanism for Rental Housing. *The American Economic Review*, *64*(3), 478–81.

Smolen, A. G. (2003). "Children Born into Loss: Some Developmental Consequences of Homelessness." *Journal for the Psychoanalysis of Culture and Society*, *8*(2), 250–57.

Solari, C. D., N. DuBois, and J. Morales-Burnett. (2020, November). *Community Strategies to Understand and Reduce Veteran Inflow into Homelessness*. Washington, DC: Urban Institute. https://www.urban.org/research/publication/community-strategies-understand-and-reduce-veteran-inflow-homelessness.

Stillman, J. (2019, March 8). "Got a Hard Decision to Make? Borrow Obama's Simple 3-Part Strategy for the Toughest Calls." *Inc.* https://www.inc.com/mbvans/contest.html.

Stringfellow, M., and D. Wagle. (2018, May 18). "The Economics of Homelessness in Seattle and King County." McKinsey & Company. https://www.mckinsey.com/featured-insights/future-of-cities/the-economics-of-homelessness-in-seattle-and-king-county.

Sugrue, T. J. (2005). *The Origins of the Urban Crisis: Race and Inequality in Postwar Detroit*. Princeton, NJ: Princeton University Press.

Thompson, D. (2018, November 12). "Amazon's HQ2 Spectacle Isn't Just Shameful—It Should Be Illegal." *The Atlantic*. https://www

.theatlantic.com/ideas/archive/2018/11/amazons-hq2-spectacle -should-be-illegal/575539/.

Thulien, N. S., D. Gastaldo, S. W. Hwang, and E. McCay. (2018). "The Elusive Goal of Social Integration: A Critical Examination of the Socio-economic and Psychosocial Consequences Experienced by Homeless Young People Who Obtain Housing." *Canadian Journal of Public Health*, *109*(1), 89–98.

Trickey, E. (2019, July 11). "How Minneapolis Freed Itself from the Stranglehold of Single-Family Homes." *Politico*. https://www .politico.com/magazine/story/2019/07/11/housing-crisis-single -family-homes-policy-227265.

Troutman, W. H., J. D. Jackson, and R. B. Ekelund. (1999). "Public Policy, Perverse Incentives, and the Homeless Problem." *Public Choice*, *98*(1–2), 195–212.

Tsai, J. (2018). "Lifetime and 1-Year Prevalence of Homelessness in the US Population: Results from the National Epidemiologic Survey on Alcohol and Related Conditions-III." *Journal of Public Health (United Kingdom)*, *40*(1), 65–74.

Tsai, J., C. Y. S. Lee, T. Byrne, R. H. Pietrzak, and S. M. Southwick. (2017). "Changes in Public Attitudes and Perceptions about Homelessness between 1990 and 2016." *American Journal of Community Psychology* 60 (2017): 599–606.

Tsai, J., C. Y. S. Lee, J. Shen, S. M. Southwick, and R. H. Pietrzak. (2019). "Public Exposure and Attitudes about Homelessness." *Journal of Community Psychology*, *47*, 76–92.

Tsai, J., J. Shen, S. M. Southwick, and R. H. Pietrzak. (2021). "Is There More Public Support for US Veterans Who Experience Homelessness and Posttraumatic Stress Disorder Than Other US Adults?" *Military Psychology* 33, no. 1, 15–22.

Tsemberis, S., L. Gulcur, and M. Nakae. (2004). "Housing First, Consumer Choice, and Harm Reduction for Homeless Individuals with a Dual Diagnosis." *American Journal of Public Health*, *94*(4), 651–56.

Tsemberis, S. J., L. Moran, M. Shinn, S. M. Asmussen, and D. L. Shern. (2003). "Consumer Preference Programs for Individuals Who Are Homeless and Have Psychiatric Disabilities: A Drop-In Center and a Supported Housing Program." *American Journal of Community Psychology, 32*(3–4), 305–17.

Tyler, K. A., and R. M. Schmitz. (2018). A Comparison of Risk Factors for Various Forms of Trauma in the Lives of Lesbian, Gay, Bisexual and Heterosexual Homeless Youth." *Journal of Trauma & Dissociation, 19*(4), 431–43.

———. (2018). "Child Abuse, Mental Health and Sleeping Arrangements among Homeless Youth: Links to Physical and Sexual Street Victimization." *Children and Youth Services Review, 95*(April), 327–33.

U.S. Department of Housing and Urban Development. (2007). *The Annual Homeless Assessment Report to Congress.* Washington, DC: U.S. Department of Housing and Urban Development, Office of Policy Development and Research.

U.S. Government Accountability Office. (1985). *Homelessness: A Complex Problem and the Federal Response.* Washington, DC: United States General Accounting Office.

———. (2020). *Homelessness: Better HUD Oversight of Data Collection Could Improve Estimates of the Homeless Population.* https://www.gao.gov/assets/710/708090.pdf.

von Hoffman, A. (1998). *The Origins of American Housing Reform.* Cambridge, MA: Joint Center for Housing Studies of Harvard University.

Weissmueller, Z. (2019, December 5). "Los Angeles Is Spending Over $1 Billion to House the Homeless: It's Failing." *Reason.* https://reason.com/video/los-angeles-is-spending-over-1-billion-to-house-the-homeless-its-failing/.

Wiehe, M., A. Davis, C. Davis, M. Gardner, L. C. Gee, and D. Grundman. (2018). *Who Pays? A Distributional Analysis of the Tax Systems in All 50 States.* Washington, DC: Institute on Taxation and Economic Policy.

Wiley, H., and S. Bollag. (2020, February 18). "How Much Does California Really Spend on Homelessness? Democrat Wants a Final Answer." *The Sacramento Bee.* https://www.sacbee.com/news/politics-government/capitol-alert/article240314016.html.

Williams, K. (2020, January 1). "An Ohio City Known for Helping the Homeless Now Questions Its Limits." *Washington Post.*

https://www.washingtonpost.com/national/an-ohio-city-known
-for-helping-now-questions-its-limits-when-the-homeless-come
-from-somewhere-else/2020/01/01/d58a38ac-2b26-11ea-bcd4-245979
50008f_story.html.

Winzar, H. (2015). "The Ecological Fallacy: How to Spot One and Tips on How to Use One to Your Advantage." *Australasian Marketing Journal, 23*(1), 86–92.

Wogan, J. B. (2016, January 29). "While Homeless Veterans Get Housing, Rest Are Left in the Cold." Governing: The Future of States and Localities. https://www.governing.com/topics/health-human -services/gov-veteran-homelessness-obama-washington.html.

Wood, M., J. Turnham, and G. Mills. (2008). "Housing Affordability and Family Well-Being: Results from the Housing Voucher Evaluation." *Housing Policy Debate, 19*(2), 367–412.

Woolf, N. (2019, June 19). "'The Hunger Games for Cities'—Inside the Amazon HQ2 Bid Process." *New Statesman*. https://www.new statesman.com/science-tech/technology/2019/06/hunger-games -cities-inside-amazon-hq2-bid-process.

Zima, B. T., K. B. Wells, and H. E. Freeman. (1994). "Emotional and Behavioral Problems and Severe Academic Delays among Sheltered Homeless Children in Los Angeles County." *American Journal of Public Health, 84*(2), 260–64.

INDEX

Alabama, 87; rates of homelessness in, 9

Amazon, search of for a second corporate headquarters (HQ), 150–54; approaches of cities to try and lure Amazon, 150–51; effect of on housing, 153–54; selection process of, 151–52; what Amazon wanted from prospective cities, 150

American Community Survey (ACS), 36, 139

Annual Homeless Assessment Report to Congress (HUD report), 48

Appelbaum, Benyamin, 64

Atlanta: poverty rates in, 79; rental market vacancy rates in, 131

Austin, Benjamin, 150

Austin, Texas, 138, 162, 165, 232n26

Auxier, Richard, 189

Baltimore, 84, 91, 94; unemployment rate in (2009), 82

Bernstein, Jared, 189

Bezos, Jeff, 152, 188

Bill and Melinda Gates Foundation, investment of in improving the crisis response system in the Puget Sound area, 197–98

Black Lives Matter movement, 28

Black people, disproportionate number that are homeless, 27, 42–43

Bloomberg, Michael, 175

Boston, 19, 91, 127; constrained availability of rental housing in, 131; elite educational institutions and professional industry leadership in, 80–81; homelessness in, 10, 11, 81, 84; loss of its core population to the suburbs, 80; poverty rates in, 79, 80, 81

Boston Redevelopment Authority, 80

Byrne, Thomas, 66

California, 183; challenges of new housing construction in, 158–59;

California (*continued*)
rates of homelessness in, 9;
unsheltered homelessness in, 119
Callahan v. Carey (1979), 114, 118
capitalism, 173
Carter, George, 110
Center for Social Innovation, 91
Centers for Disease Control and
Prevention (CDC), 26–27
Charlotte, 10; elastic housing
supply in, 138–39; substantial
number of new housing units
built in response to population
growth, 138
Chicago, 79, 84, 114, 160, 161;
Continuums of Care (CoCs) in,
18–19; rates of homelessness
in, 7, 10
Chui, David, 183
City Journal (Manhattan Institute),
71–72, 88
Clark County, Nevada, rental
market vacancy rates in, 131
Cleveland, 18, 84, 94, 114, 160, 161,
164; housing values in, 148; low
rates of homelessness in, 10, 11;
poverty rates in, 79
climate change, relationship with
migration, 106
Cobb-Clark, Deborah, 210n30
cognitive dissonance, 15
Cole, Williams, 115
Collier, David, 165
Colorado, 87
Commins, Glen, 63
Community Development Block
Grants, 181
computers, processing power of,
172–73
Connecticut, 87
Continuums of Care (CoCs), 40,
45, 98, 100–101, 164, 197, 199;

construction and distribution
of, 16; main administrative
duties of, 16; studies concerning,
56–57. *See also* Cook County,
Illinois, Continuums of Care
(CoCs) in; Ohio, Continuums
of Care (CoCs) in; Texas,
Continuums of Care (CoCs)
Cook County, Illinois, Continuums
of Care (CoCs) in, 18–19
Corinth, Kevin, 52
cost analysis, benefits of, 61
Council of Economic Advisors
(Trump Administration), report
on homelessness, 73, 77, 95–96,
98, 102–3
COVID-19 pandemic, 200, 201;
economic consequences of, 26–27,
82; steps to protect the homeless
population from the virus, 25–26
Cragg, Michael, 105
crisis response/crisis response
systems, 30, 105, 168, 170–71, 185,
191, 192, 195–98, 199–200, 203
Culhane, Dennis P., 43, 61
Curtis, Marah, 58
Cuyahoga County, Ohio, 17, 18, 127;
unemployment rate in (2009), 82

Dallas County, Texas: poverty
rates in, 77; rental market
vacancy rates in, 131
de Blasio, Bill, 151, 175
Delaware, 87
Detroit, 84, 91, 94, 114, 127, 160, 161,
164, 207n16; effects of the decline
of manufacturing in, 78–80;
households below the federal
poverty rate in, 113; housing cost
burdens in, 124–25; low rates of
homelessness in, 10, 80, 81;
percentage of unemployment in

homelessness, systems approach to
(*continued*)
homelessness system, 191–92;
operationalization and
management of homelessness as
a function of systems thinking,
191; Stage 1: Inflow, 193–95;
Stage 2: Crisis Response, 195–98;
Stage 3: Outflow, 198–201
homelessness, typology/
classifications of, 43–44; chronic
homelessness, 43–45, 209n14;
episodic homelessness, 43;
importance of the classifications, 44–45; transitionally
homeless, 43
homelessness, variations in, 9, 15,
16; in cities with Democratic
leadership and policies, 6–7;
city-to-city variation, 11;
decrease in the overall national
levels of homelessness even as
variations in different cities'
rates of have risen, 24, 25*fig.*;
four factors explaining variation
(high housing costs, conditions
more amenable to sleeping
outside, shelter capacity,
overrepresentation of people at
risk for homelessness), 96; by
geography, 7; and housing
market variations, 142–43;
potential causes of, 7–8;
systemic variation, 9. *See also*
homelessness, variations in,
analysis of; homelessness,
variations in, regional
homelessness, variations in,
analysis of: evaluation of
through the median (midpoint
in a distribution of values),
variance, and standard

deviation, 21–23; and intra-
regional variations in rates of
homelessness, 227–28n9; use of
the coefficient of determination
(R^2) in, 23–24
homelessness, variations in,
regional, 9, 14, 15, 28–29, 51, 68, 81,
99, 135–44; factors that do not
explain regional variations, 83,
87, 90, 91, 93, 96; underlying
causes, 72; understanding
housing market dynamics and
regional variation in homelessness, 135–44; use of regression to
explain, 56–57. *See also* homelessness, analysis of variations in
homelessness, and the weather, 55,
97–103, 224n9; relationship
between temperature and
homelessness, 98, 99–100, 99*fig.*;
relationship between temperature and unsheltered homelessness, 101–3, 102*fig.*
homeownership: as a hallmark of
American society, 157; homeowners opposed to new
residential development, 158; and
the "Homevoter Hypothesis,"
157–58
Hopper, Kim, 46
Horowitz, Evan, 122
Hour Detroit (Runyan), 132
housing: access to, 30, 36, 130, 168,
193, 200; allocation of housing
services, 35; challenges of new
housing construction, 158–59;
de-commodified housing, 194;
expansion and investment in
permanent housing, 169; high
housing costs and family
homelessness, 58; homelessness
and the housing cost burden,

Founded in 1893,
UNIVERSITY OF CALIFORNIA PRESS
publishes bold, progressive books and journals
on topics in the arts, humanities, social sciences,
and natural sciences—with a focus on social
justice issues—that inspire thought and action
among readers worldwide.

The UC PRESS FOUNDATION
raises funds to uphold the press's vital role
as an independent, nonprofit publisher, and
receives philanthropic support from a wide
range of individuals and institutions—and from
committed readers like you. To learn more, visit
ucpress.edu/supportus.